The Management School
Imperial College of Science, Technology and Medicine

Managing in the NHS
A Study of Senior Executives

Sandra Dawson

Diana Winstanley

Veronica Mole

Jim Sherval

London: HMSO

ISBN 0 11 321878 8

The Authors

Sandra Dawson was Professor of Organisational Behaviour at The Management School, Imperial College of Science, Technology and Medicine, University of London. In October 1995 she moved to the University of Cambridge as KPMG Professor of Management and Director of the Judge Institute of Management Studies.

Dianna Winstanley is a Lecturer in Human Resource Management at The Management School, Imperial College of Science, Technology and Medicine, University of London.

Veronica Mole is a Research Associate at The Management School, Imperial College of Science, Technology and Medicine, University of London.

Jim Sherval, was a Research Assistant at The Management School, Imperial College of Science, Technology and Medicine, University of London, and is now a Researcher at The Centre of HIV/AIDS/Drug Dependency, Lothian Health, Scotland.

Addresses for Correspondence

Professor Sandra Dawson
The Judge Institute of Management Studies
University of Cambridge
Trumpington Street
Cambridge CB2 1AG
Tel 01223 339700
Fax 01223 339701

Dr Diana Winstanley
The Management School
Imperial College
53 Prince's Gate
London SW7 2PG
Tel 0171 594 9114
Fax 0171 823 7685

Acknowledgements

The research team would like to acknowledge and thank the Department of Health for funding this research and the participating organisations and senior managers for their helpful cooperation. They are also grateful to the members of the project advisory committee and to colleagues in the Research and Development Division of the Department of Health, for their helpful advice.

Published by HMSO and available from:

HMSO Publications Centre
(Mail, fax and telephone orders only)
PO Box 276, London SW8 5DT
Telephone orders 0171-873 9090
General enquiries 0171-873 0011
(queuing system in operation for both numbers)
Fax orders 0171-873 8200

HMSO Bookshops
49 High Holborn, London WC1V 6HB
0171-873 0011 Fax 0171-831 1326 (counter service only)
68-69 Bull Street, Birmingham B4 6AD
0121-236 9696 Fax 0121-236 9699
33 Wine Street, Bristol BS1 2BQ
0117-926 4306 Fax 0117 9294515
9-21 Princess Street, Manchester M60 8AS
0161-834 7201 Fax 0161-833 0634
16 Arthur Street, Belfast BT1 4GD
01232 238451 Fax 01232 235401
71 Lothian Road, Edinburgh EH3 9AZ
0131-228 4181 Fax 0131-229 2734
The HMSO Oriel Bookshop,
The Friary, Cardiff CF1 4AA
0122 395548 Fax 01222 384347

HMSO's Accredited Agents
(see Yellow Pages)

and through good booksellers

Contents

List of Tables

Appendix 2

List of Figures

Glossary

Abbreviations and Definition of Terms

BAMM British Association of Medical Managers

BMA British Medical Association

CD Clinical Director

CEO Chief Executive Officer

CHC Community Health Council

CM Clinical Managers
(Those who in addition to, or instead of, their clinical or health responsibilities have significant managerial executive responsibilities for the delivery or commissioning of healthcare)

CSM Clinical Service Manager

Dr Doctor

DoH Department of Health

DHA District Health Authority

DMS Diploma in Management Studies

DMU Directly Managed Unit

ECR Extra Contractual Referral

FCE Finished Consultant Episode

FHSA Family Health Services Authority

FPE Funded Patient Episode

FM Functional Manager
(Professionally qualified or experienced in a non-clinical, non-health functional area)

GM General Manager

GMC General Medical Council

GP General Practitioner

GPFH General Practitioner Fund Holder

HA Health Authority

HC Health Commission

HR Human Resources

HRM Human Resource Manager/ment

HISS Hospital Information Support Systems

IHSM	Institute of Health Services Management
IIP	Investors in People
IPM/IPD	Institute of Personnel Management – (IPD Institute of Personnel Development from 1994)
IPR	Individual Performance Review
IT	Information Technology
LA	Local Authority
MAP	Management Development Action Planning
MBA	Masters Degree in Business Administration
MCI	Management Charter Initiative
MD	Management Development
MESOL	Management Education Scheme by Open Learning
MTS	Management Training Scheme
n	Number of cases on which percentages are based
NHS	National Health Service
NHSTD	National Health Service Training Directorate / Division (Up to 1994 was Directorate, from 1994 it is a division within the Human Resource Directorate of the NHSE)
NHSME/ NHSE	National Health Service Management Executive (from April 1994 NHSE)
Nr	Nurse
NVQ	National Vocational Qualification
OHP/ohp	Other Health Professionals (Professionally qualified in health/as a clinician but not in medicine or nursing)
OD	Organisation Development
OU	Open University
PAS	Patient Administration System
PMS	Performance Management Systems
PRP	Performance Related Pay
Qu	Question Number (refers to Interview Schedule)
RCN	Royal College of Nursing
RHA	Regional Health Authority
RMI	Resource Management Initiative

sig	Level of Significance using the Pearson Chi-square Test of Independence between variables in a crosstabulation
SSD	Social Services Departments in Local Authority
VFM	Value for Money
UKCC	United Kingdom Central Council for Nursing, Midwifery and Health Visitors

*	Where * appears in a cross tabulation, indicates statistically significant differences at $p < 0.05$

Foreword

I am pleased to introduce to you this research study which raises many of the key issues relevant to personal and organisational development in the NHS. The report provides useful data which can inform national and local policy and action in the context of organisational change.

I welcome the emphasis on developing appropriate structures for effective management development and succession planning. The work indicates that there is a continuing need to spread good practice in relation to career management and development opportunities. There is also a need to ensure that those professional staff who aspire to senior management posts are recognised and equipped with the skills to realise their full potential as senior managers.

In the context of flatter organisational structures, and changing organisational needs, there is a clear need to develop more explicit links between the short and long term objectives of the organisation and the career aspirations and personal development of individuals. Managers and others engaged in personal and organisational development will find much in the report which stimulates action and good practice.

Ken Jarrold
Director of Human Resources
NHS Executive

Executive Summary: Key Issues and Recommendations

1 The Research Project

- This is a report of a research project which was funded by the Department of Health and began in January 1992. The project was concerned with present practices and future requirements for senior management development and organisation development at local level in the NHS.

- The focus is on senior executives who are directly involved in the local purchase or provision of health care. The study extended beyond those engaged in general and functional management to doctors, nurses and the other health professionals who in addition to, or instead of, their clinical or health responsibilities, had significant managerial responsibilities for the commissioning or delivering of health care. The aim was to establish what they did, what problems they faced, their thoughts on ccreer development and their views on learning needs, given their present and anticipated roles and responsibilities.

- The issues of management development and organisation development are approached through an examination of the strategic requirements of the new organisations on the one hand and the aspirations and abilities of people from clinical and managerial backgrounds in senior executive positions on the other.

- The study involved personal interviews with 271 respondents employed within the 21 participating organisations; 167 respondents in 11 provider organisations and 104 respondents in 10 purchasing organisations.

- The sample was composed of 118 general managers, 45 functional managers and 108 clinical managers (of whom 88, including 62 doctors, were clinicians in provider management and 20 clinically qualified public health staff in purchasing organisations). They were located within the top 3 levels of their organisations with 93 being executive directors.

- In analysing the data from individual respondents 6 demographic variables are used in order to explore patterns of response:
    - purchaser/provider: type of employing organisation
    - Roots: background of respondent
    - Present job of respondent
    - Present level of respondent
    - Age of respondent
    - Gender of respondent

- Considering the 271 senior executives and 21 organisations as a whole, the study has captured a cross section of senior management in the NHS in terms of geography, organisational level, professional background, roles and responsibilities.

- Field work for the project began in June 1992, and ended in October 1993. At that time senior executives in both purchasing and providing organisations were experiencing high rates of change and were attempting to secure far-reaching changes in culture. It is acknowledged that there has been considerable change since the fieldwork was completed.

2 The Organisational Context

- Purchasers were creating new organisations to tackle new tasks. The following issues emerged as important in creating the context for management development and organisation development in purchasing organisations:
    - Strong expectations of diverse groups of stakeholders.
    - The need for partnership and alliances with other agencies and organisations.
    - The need to generate and share reliable information on the effectiveness of clinical and organisational interventions.
    - Uncertainty and anxiety about joint working between DHAs and FHSAs.
    - Movement from preoccupation with short term to longer term goals.
    - The creation of effective, smaller, flatter, organisations.
    - The creation of flexible organisations which will secure cost effective disbursement of public money.
    - The development of staff who are excellent in their own discipline and who will work cross functionally; particular importance being attached to securing effective involvement of clinically qualified public health physicians in purchasing.
    - The development of capacity for innovation.

- Providing organisations were also engaged in major programmes of organisational change in what was seen to be a highly turbulent environment. In particular the following issues emerged as important in creating the context for management development and organisation development:
  - The creation of viable corporate organisations which support professional excellence so that there is a balance between professional and organisational commitment.
  - The creation of effective multi-disciplinary and cross-functional teams.
  - The development of effective systems for leadership, communication and devolution, so that key professional workers feel empowered and involved.
  - The development of different ways of working including changes in job design and skill mix.
  - The need to secure changes in the timing and substance of the contracting process, to facilitate longer term investments.
  - The development of capacity for innovation.
  - Adaptation to the contradictions of being independent, and yet subject to central controls.

Presentation of results

- The results of the study of individual senior executives are presented in terms of six areas:
  - Career: Past, Present and Future
  - Managerial Activity: Competence, Roles and Responsibilities
  - Individual Performance Management and Review
  - Contributions to Teams: Sources of Conflict and Consensus
  - Contacts, Networks and Information
  - Management Development

- A section outlining the key issues which arose in each area now follows, together with a summary of the recommendations which we consider follow from the analysis.

3 Careers: Past, Present and Future

Key Issues

- Many respondents felt an uncertainty about their future careers. Arbitrary career boundaries are seen to exist between DHAs, NHS Trusts and the NHS Executive at regional and headquarters levels. The emergence of a dual career structure between DHAs and NHS Trusts was a subject for considerable comment and regret.

- It was felt that collaboration between DHAs and Trusts was important to create a workable internal market but that collaboration was not always encouraged on a local level.

- Staff with qualifications in nursing (or PAMs) do not feature significantly in senior positions in DHAs and they are fairly poorly represented in NHS Trusts.

- A significant minority of respondents with a nursing background felt they would like to move out of the NHS; feeling that their advancement was blocked.

- A significant minority of respondents with a medical background felt they would like to move out of management, and return to full-time clinical work, as they felt their 'doctors in management' positions were inadequately supported or defined.

- A career climbing frame illustrated in Figure 1 was constructed on the basis of the three dimensions of professional identity, organisational location and demonstrable competences. It can be used to facilitate discussion in DHAs and NHS Trusts of the competences, and professional and organisational experience, which are sufficient for filling medium and top level jobs. It can also be used as a basis for considering individual career development and organisational recruitment and promotion.

- Investment in career counselling as part of the establishment of an organisational infrastructure to support self development is necessary.

Recommendations

- Efforts must be made at local, regional and national level to identify the benefits which would accrue to the NHS (and to its constituent parts) if greater movement between DHAs and NHS Trusts and other parts of the NHS, can be facilitated.

- Efforts must be made at all levels to change the mind set, so that, rather than presuming that there are now separate labour markets for DHAs and Trusts, the presumption should be that cross-recruitment is feasible, until, in particular circumstances, it is shown to be inappropriate.

- Efforts must be made at local level to develop a mind set which emphasises that career development is an important individual responsibility.

Figure 1 *A Career Climbing Frame for the NHS*

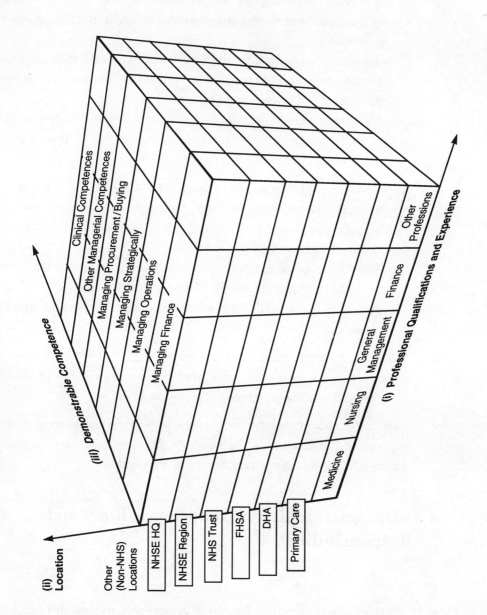

- DHAs and Trusts must develop an infrastructure which supports self development. This will include
    - making career opportunities more visible to people from a variety of professional backgrounds and organisational experience.
    - fostering ways to help people develop their careers, to provide bridges between individuals and organisations.
    - identifying the types of posts which are particularly suitable as 'sideways' moves between organisational locations.
    - identifying opportunities for secondments and exchanges between organisations and within organisations, between functions and service divisions.
    - supporting secondments, exchanges and cross-recruitment through Human Resource Management practices, particularly appraisal, supervision and reward practices.
    - establishing workshops at local and regional level in which specialists in career development and organisational change will facilitate discussion of the issues identified in this report.

- Appropriate recognition should be given at local level to the nature and level of managerial competences already demonstrated by many nurses and PAMs, and ways should be sought to enable nurses and PAMs to expand their competence base. This will include.
    - identifying courses and development programmes through which nurses and PAMs can improve their professional qualifications.
    - identifying managerial jobs to which nurses and PAMs could expect to be recruited.

- The issue of whether nurses and PAMs can combine clinical with managerial responsibility (as doctors do) rather than being expected to forgo all clinical work, should be addressed both nationally and locally.

- NHS Trusts should consider how to cope with the fast turnover of doctors in management, and address the issues of the appropriateness of a clinical directorship being a temporary rotational responsibility.

4   Managerial Activity: Competence, Roles and Responsibilities

Key Issues

- Management competence has three complementary but distinct aspects: inputs (e.g. qualifications, psychometric test results), processes (managerial practices) and outcomes (e.g. performance on financial or service criteria).

- An emphasis on the outcomes of managerial activity is very important to secure a performance oriented culture, but good management development programmes also pay attention to inputs and processes.

- The determination of essential and desirable managerial competences for any position can only be successfully accomplished within a context set by the organisation's strategic objectives and key tasks, which in turn require consideration of the organisation's environment.

- Specific and generic competences which are required of any post holder can be identified. At the same time, it is important to have a clear view of what particular jobs offer in terms of capacity for competence development and enhancement.

- The language used by managers in this study suggests they place more emphasis on formal approaches to strategic planning and to reacting to change, than on actively and pragmatically managing change.

- Many respondents were found to be limiting their managerial horizons to problems of internal management and attaching comparatively less importance to external aspects of management. This was particularly marked for clinical professionals newly come to management.

- It is important to have a framework in which essential and desirable management competencies are mapped if people are to be able to manage their own careers, and organisations, to retain and recruit effective managers. This is especially important in identifying which competences are transferable between purchasing and providing organisations.

- Whilst the possession of specialist functional skills is important it is not sufficient for senior executives in the NHS. They must develop the capacity to manage across functions and professions and, particularly within purchasing, across organisations. This requires management development and organisation development.

- The link between managerial effectiveness and organisational performance is especially pertinent when organisations are undergoing rapid change. The identification of the core competencies of an organisation is an essential base for effective management. Discussion around such issues was relatively underdeveloped in local NHS organisations at the time of field work.

Recommendations

- The assessment and development of managerial competence must be approached in terms of the inputs, processes and outcomes of managerial activity. Assessment should indicate the areas which are amenable to further development.

- Essential and desirable managerial competences for any position must be determined in the light of an organisation's overall strategy and core competences.

- Employing organisations should undertake job analysis of key middle level positions in order to identify routes for individual development.

- Profiles of different job categories (showing which aspects of managerial work are regarded as important) should be examined within local organisations as a basis for questioning whether some activities are regarded as less important by some groups because they feel ill-equipped to tackle them.

- If cross-functional and more outward looking ways of working are to be encouraged, consideration must be given to developing sources of support for managers in addition to that which flows from their own functional or departmental group.

- Support must be given to management development programmes which encourage senior managers to give,
  - less emphasis to formal planning and strategic management and more emphasis to managing strategically in a flexible way, so as to take advantage of opportunities and changes as they occur within a framework of well defined strategic obJectives.
  - less emphasis on passively trying to cope with changes as they occur and more on helping them to understand and develop the capacity actively to thrive on change,
  - more emphasis on managing outwards and appreciating managerial responsibilities in a wider context than just dealing with (the nonetheless important) internal management issues.
  - more emphasis on the skills involved in working in cross-functional and cross-organisational task forces and project teams.

- DHAs and Trusts must carefully identify their particular core competences (what they are really good at, what they know well and the range of ways in which they can use their knowledge and expertise) as a benchmark for strategic decision making and management development.

5   Individual Performance Management and Review

Key Issues

- Although all participating organisations operated some variant of an Individual Performance Review system at the time of study, considerable reservations were expressed in some sites about system effectiveness. In particular,
    - poor management commitment to the system, and inadequate implementation,
    - insufficient attention to identifying corporate objectives, priorities and performance and linking these to individual objectives,
    - too much emphasis on formal review and not enough opportunity for informal evaluation and constructive feedback,
    - too much emphasis on judgement and not enough on development,
    - insufficient attention to team performance, encouraging unnecessary individual competition and fragmentation,
    - inflexible systems poorly adapted to reviewing managers who were participating in high levels of change.

- There was a fairly widespread feeling that managers at all levels did not attach high priority in their role to developing others notwithstanding their wishes to have some one take a positive interest in their own performance and career.

- The coverage of Individual Performance Review systems was incomplete. It was particularly patchy with regard to doctors in provider management.

- The issue of performance evaluation and appraisal for clinical managerial staff, particularly doctors in provider management, is highly charged and its practice is undeveloped. Respondents spoke of difficulties of shortage of time, cultural and status differences and lack of trust between doctors and managers, as blocking developments in this area. Nonetheless, many clinical directors said they would welcome the opportunity to discuss and develop appropriate objectives.

- There was very little support expressed for the existing performance related pay system for those on senior management pay. The dissatisfaction was particularly acute over its inability to reward good team performance and corporate success. The current PRP system was not felt to improve motivation and performance.

- In summarising their own view of the attributes which lead to their being effective, respondents drew attention to the human side of management rather than its technical or knowledge base and emphasised in particular,
    - the ability to work through and with others, within and beyond departments, professional groupings and organisations,
    - skill in communication, persuasion and negotiation, to secure agreement and commitment from others.

- Comparatively little importance was attached to willingness to take risks or creativity as a basis for effective management in the NHS.

- The main barriers to effective working were identified as internal management problems, financial constraints and operational overload which encourage too much 'firefighting' .

- Doctors in provider management identified seven areas which presented problems for them in their managerial work,
    - conflicting and unmet demands on their time
    - issues of succession when their term of office finished
    - managing independent, autonomous colleagues with divergent views
    - ill-defined or unsupported budgetary responsibilities
    - meeting increasing demands for human resource management
    - securing appropriate support and terms of reference
    - finding the time and developing the skills to act in the marketplace.

Recommendations

- Action should be taken at local level (with help and support from the NHS Executive) to develop an approach to performance review which,
    - relates individual objectives to organisational priorities,
    - provides constructive feedback and helps individuals to identify the positive steps they can take to improve their performance and develop their competences,
    - facilitates individual objective setting within a fast changing context and links this to corporate priorities.

- Mechanisms for performance review should be adjusted where appropriate to reflect the need for strong team working, e.g. through team based reviews. Where teams are cross-functional, dual appraisals should be undertaken, one relating to specialist or professional performance and development, the other relating to team performance.

- The introduction of systems of upward and sideways appraisal and feedback is recommended, but to be effective it needs wholehearted support from the top.

- Consideration should be given to enhancing individual developmental opportunities, for example, through access to coaching, mentoring and 'away days', as a basis for individuals and teams to decide, develop and review corporate and team objectives and priorities and to clarify individual roles, responsibilities and objectives for achieving these aims.

- Managers' roles in providing feedback and support to others should become a more valued activity which features in their own performance appraisal.

- If rewards are to be linked to performance, careful consideration should be given to the evaluation of team or group as well as individual performance.

- Programmes of management development should normally
  - provide opportunities to develop the human side of management to facilitate the development of skills in working with others, communication, persuasion and negotiation
  - be multidisciplinary (in subject content and audience) although there are occasions when particular groups may sometimes need a unidisciplinary input,
  - include guidance on time management and prioritising.

- Programmes of management development for doctors should address the issues identified as particularly problematic for them in their roles of 'doctors as managers'.

6 Contributions to Teams: Sources of Conflict and Consensus

Key Issues

- Membership of the top teams in DHAs and Trusts was most commonly identified in terms of the Executive Directors. Proportionately more providing than purchasing respondents included Non Executive Directors as members of the top team. DHAs were seen to be 'flatter' with a broader group of people at the top, compared to providers which were still seen as pyramids with a clear central apex.

- The strengths of top teams were seen to lie predominantly in their ability to work as a team, their capacity to act as a forum in which different groups and interests were represented and the personal strengths of individuals. There was proportionately little mention of the top team providing leadership or vision, or of communicating with the rest of the organisation.

- The weaknesses of the top teams were seen to lie in their own poor organisation, in their lack of a team or integrative approach and their poor communications with the rest of the organisation. These weaknesses were mentioned by significantly more of those who saw themselves as outside rather than inside the top team.

- A large majority of respondents said they detected recurring sources of conflict and disagreement between members of the team. In providing organisations recurring conflicts were mainly seen to arise from differences between a clinical professional perspective and a managerial perspective. In purchasing, disagreements were also seen to arise largely from differences of function and discipline. Institutional differences between DHAs and FHSAs in areas where joint commissioning was developed were also notable.

- Respondents referred to the rapid pace of change and experience of recurrent restructuring, as creating a climate of fear and insecurity, which encouraged people to be defensive about their own functional interests, and to inhibit the development of strong, cohesive teams with diverse membership.

- There was a commonly held view that people with a clinical background do and should make a different contribution to managerial work when compared with those of a general or functional management background.

- The majority of respondents believed there was mutual trust and respect between managers and clinicians even though they were frequently in disagreement. However, a minority of managers criticised clinicians as unable to take a corporate managerial view and a minority of clinically qualified respondents were disdainful about managers being narrowly focused on achieving their own deadlines and objectives which were not always seen to contribute to patient care or health status.

Recommendations

- Top management teams need to consider how,
    - to develop or sustain visionary forms of leadership within their organisations,

- to ensure good communication both upwards and downwards, and in particular between clinicians and managers,
- to question whether the membership and functioning of the top team facilitates sufficient access to the views of others.

- Careful thought should be given to nurturing the diversity of perspectives which is essential for effective management of complex health care organisations. This requires organisation development, management development and self development.

- Common value frameworks need to be developed so that diversities can flourish without tearing organisations apart. At local level the following may be considered,
  - conducting a communications audit,
  - 'away days' and other discussions in order to bring diverse groups together to generate stronger mutual understanding and common values,
  - ensuring that the signals the top team gives to the rest of the organisation in its literature, its functions and its human resource practices are consistent with the values position it espouses.

7 Contacts, Networks and Information

Key Issues

- Internal contacts and communication are more lateral in purchasing organisations and more hierarchical in providing organisations. Clinical managers in provider organisations in particular have comparatively little contact and communication outside their departments.

- For purchasers and providers alike there were concerns about the lack of shared information between and within purchasers and providers.

- There is a tendency to see all information as 'commercial' in the marketplace. Some information is commercially sensitive but good communication between purchasers and providers is seen as essential for the development of cost effective services. Determination of the content of provider performance indicators, as a requirement of the internal market, is seen as essential but problematic.

- Whilst there are complaints of information overload, purchasing and providing managers complained their work was hindered by lack of appropriate, accessible and timely information. Information systems and information management were relatively underdeveloped in most of the participating sites.

- Expectations for information among many clinicians are higher than present systems are able to deliver. Ironically, many clinicians do not ensure accurate and comprehensive data input. Lack of integration of financial, activity, payroll and personnel information was a problem for many providers.

Recommendations

- If clinical managers are to develop skills and competence necessary to function at a more strategic level, a focus of their management development should be to help them to work collaboratively with and through other departments and functions.

- All senior managers must become more outwardly focused, and pay more attention to external communication, if their organisations are to achieve benefits from collaboration and competition.

- Internal communication needs to be improved to ensure that the users of information systems appreciate their purpose and requirements, and their relationship to the achievement of organisational objectives.

- Clear leadership and formal commitment to information strategy and systems must be reflected in the senior management structure.

- Decisions on investment in information systems should be subject to rigorous investment appraisal to ensure they are managerially 'fit for purpose'.

- The effective development and use of information systems must be supported by job design to reflect new ways of working and training in both the technical and interpersonal skills required.

- Ongoing work at local, regional and national level to determine and refine appropriate measures of provider and purchaser performance needs to be sustained.

- Information capture, analysis and use must be given high priority as aspects of management and organisation development.

8   Management Development

Key Issues

- Management development in the NHS continues to be conducted largely in an ad hoc way at the instigation of individual managers. This presents problems where there is no culture for self-development and where there are no routes to help managers identify opportunities.

- Management development results from a combination of individual initiative and commitment and organisational initiative and support. Unless there is energy from both it will not be fully effective.

- The restructured NHS has created new learning needs for managers. Problems arise where changes in demand for management development have not been matched in changes to its supply.

- There is an increased requirement in both purchasing and providing organisations for management development in,
  - the evaluation of organisational performance,
  - business planning,
  - evaluating new services for development,
  - marketing services,
  - strategic planning,
  - computing and IT.

  Within purchasing, there is a particular need for,
  - health economics.

- Respondents with a medical background identified additional learning needs in,
  - managing across organisational boundaries,
  - individual performance review,
  - time management.

- Formal programmes are important in creating a climate for greater understanding of managerial roles, awareness of issues and processes of management but are only cited by a minority as being influential in their development as managers.

- Where formal management courses and programmes were said to be successful, this was seen to result from,
  - their being "contextualised" within the NHS,

- structured opportunities for managers to reflect on their own context and careers,
- associated help for self-development,
- opportunities to network and learn from other participants,
- their being structured to fit in with other demands.

- Self-development, where managers believe they engage in it, is perceived as "learning by experience", general reading, and reference to role models. Self development is not on the whole supported by mechanisms to provide managers with the skills to develop themselves in a more pro-active way, such as with personal development plans and access to information about available opportunities.

- Informal mentoring, coaching, protégé relationships and role models are seen as central to the development of managers, and these were believed by respondents to have been highly influential in their own development and progression.

- Observation in action and, to a lesser extent, emulation, was the main mode of learning from role models, whereas learning from informal mentors was more through advice, support, encouragement, and being given opportunities.

- Although the majority of respondents identified the importance of informal mentoring and guidance in their own careers, considerably fewer placed importance on their role in this area for the development of others.

Recommendations

- Diversity in content and style of management development is to be expected in the reformed structure of the NHS: nonetheless variety must be supported by evaluation, review and bench marking to ensure value for money.

- Management development for doctors, nurses and PAMs should be a theme throughout their training and undergraduate and postgraduate studies.

- Courses for clinical managers need to be designed so that they allow for their clinical schedules, for example through short immersion courses tailored to their context, supplemented with work which can be done at times to suit individuals.

- Formal programmes of management development need to demonstrate ways in which the learning "off the job" will be taken back and reinforced in the organisational context. This requires management development providers and users to work closely together.

- Each organisation should produce its own management development strategy, action plan and budget and should make efforts to have a co-ordinated approach which can be evaluated.

- Each organisation should have a senior executive as the champion of management development to lead and support the strategy as it is put in place.

- The content of training courses and development programmes should be linked to the priorities identified in terms of learning needs and where possible, information should be contextualised and useable within the NHS framework.

- Some programmes of management development should be specifically constructed to bring together people from different disciplines, backgrounds and parts of the health care sector.

- The NHS Executive Headquarters and regional offices should,
    - provide information and advice on the content and form of development programmes appropriate for different organisations, different levels and functions,
    - disseminate good practice,
    - ensure that appropriate weight is given to the provision and funding of management development within the newly emerging arrangements for the commissioning of education and training.

- Managerial work as role models, coaches and informal mentors should be recognised, rewarded and encouraged through training, formal and informal feedback and performance review mechanisms.

- Cross-organisation secondments, joint projects, learning sets, networking as well as national and regional databases for use in management selection, should all be encouraged as key parts of any management development strategy.

- Policies and cultures need to be developed at the organisational level to underpin self-development, for example, to help individuals to identify and follow personal development plans. Managers need support, funding and advice on good practice, if they are to secure these developments.

Introduction

The research project began in January 1992 and was funded through the R&D Division of the Department of Health. Chapter I describes the research context, identifies the research aims, describes the research method and provides a definition of the key terms of organisation development, management development and self-development. It also describes the characteristics of the senior executives who were the individual respondents in the study. Chapter 2 provides an outline description of the organisations selected for study and a discussion of key issues of management and organisation which emerged for a majority of the sites. Subsequent chapters rely heavily on the results of the personal interviews conducted with senior executives. They deal sequentially with careers, managerial activity, individual performance management and review, contributions to teams, networks and information, and, lastly management development. The final chapter summarises general issues and themes which emerged from the project as a whole. The Executive Summary at the start of the report focuses on the key issues to emerge from the study and presents a set of associated recommendations.

Chapter 1 The Research Project

1.1 The Research Aims

In the light of the 1991 NHS Reforms the project was designed to fulfil four aims :

i) To increase knowledge about present practices and future requirements for senior management development in the NHS. The intention was to concentrate on all types of senior executives who were directly involved in the local purchase or provision of healthcare; to establish what they did, what problems they faced and the extent to which they felt they were equipped to fulfil the roles and responsibilities which the structure of the NHS in the 1990s demanded. In addition to senior executives who were general or functional (e.g. finance, human resources) managers, the study also embraced doctors, nurses and other clinically trained health professionals who combined significant clinical or health professional work with senior managerial responsibilities as clinical directors, clinical service managers and senior nurse managers in providing organisations and public health physicians in DHAs.

ii) To examine past careers and present roles of senior executives and to investigate the extent to which there is scope for career planning within the NHS.

iii) To understand the nature of managerial work and careers in the context of the restructured NHS, through identifying the key organisational and managerial issues which senior executives were facing at local level. Originally the study was focused on the acute sector, however once the research was underway, it was modestly expanded to include two providing organisations concerned solely with secondary care provision in the community.

iv) To provide input into policy making at national, regional and local levels on senior management development and, where appropriate, on matters of organisation development and career and succession planning.

In order to achieve these aims the project was designed to study both the senior executives and their organisational context. The requirements for management development and organisation development were approached through an examination of the strategic requirements of the new organisations on the one hand and the aspirations and abilities of the senior managerial, functional, clinical and health professionals on the other.

1.2 Definition of Terms

'Purchaser' and 'provider'

At the time of fieldwork, much health care provision was still in the control of directly managed units, rather than Trusts. Accordingly the now somewhat dated terminology of 'purchaser' and 'provider' is used to describe organisations which would now be known as DHAs and NHS Trusts.

Organisation development, management development and self-development

The terms 'organisation development', 'management development' and 'self-development' are used throughout this report in the ways indicated in the following definitions. Each definition is amplified with some examples of the activities included in the generic term and a statement of what each set of activities presupposes about organisations and the people within them.

Organisation development refers to all the processes which

- identify, develop, review and sustain or change the sense of corporate purpose,
- identify, develop, review and sustain or change organisational objectives and the organisational structures, culture and management systems which it is hoped will enhance the achievement of organisational objectives.

Organisation development includes making changes in:

- job descriptions
- decision making processes and arenas
- shape, size and nature of groups and departments
- managerial style
- work organisation
- quality programmes

- mechanisms for reporting and exercising accountability

- human resource management practices, including supervision and appraisal, management development, performance management.

Effective Organisation development presupposes senior executives with a will to:

- establish and review a sense of corporate purpose

- establish and review corporate objectives

- manage change and seek to develop what is done and how it is done.

Management development refers to interventions primarily oriented towards developing individuals in ways which are complementary with the organisation and its objectives, although it may be initiated from a number of sources.

Management development includes formal and informal activities and processes which provide focused opportunities for individuals to develop cognitively in their understanding of management, and behaviourally in their managerial skills and competences, for example

- induction and mid-job training

- in-house and external courses

- secondments and mentoring

- learning sets

- targeting under-represented groups for development.

Effective Management development presupposes:

- a positive attitude towards learning in the individuals

- organisational commitment to enhance organisational performance through the development of senior and middle ranging employees.

Self-development refers to interventions primarily concerned to further the setting and achievement of an individual's own personal development plans and future career aspirations, usually instigated by the individual, albeit within a supportive organisational framework.

Self-development includes individual initiative:

- to establish personal development plans and to develop a strong sense of personal responsibility for career

- to identify the content and form of personal programmes of developmental activities which may include

  - management development activities
  - career planning exercises
  - observing role models
  - identifying in-house and external courses
  - establishing networks
  - volunteering for special project work.

Effective Self-development presupposes:

- self-motivation to develop on the part of the individual

- individual ability to take initiatives

- external support from the employing organisation to encourage self motivation, possibly through facilitating mentorships and to respond appropriately to initiatives as they are suggested.

Other terms and abbreviations

Other terms and abbreviations used in this report are defined in the glossary at the beginning.

1.3   Research Method

Data Collection

Relevant information and documentary evidence at an organisational level were collected from purchasing and providing organisations using a **check list of selected dimensions of organisation context and structure**, including age and history, strategy and objectives, service profile, budget, management structure and performance issues. In the first instance, data was collected via an interview with the Chief Executive of each organisation. This was supplemented by other interviews and the collection of secondary material, such as Trust application documents and Annual Reports. The researchers also spent time in and around each site talking informally to managers and clinicians.

The study of individual Senior Executives engaged in general, functional and clinical management was the main focus of the work at the individual level. Data collection took the form of a personal interview. The **interview schedule** was based on a survey of the relevant management literature and preliminary discussions with NHS staff at national, regional and local levels. The interview probed managerial activity with 'what' and 'how' questions. It was designed to be administered to every individual respondent taking into account different professional backgrounds and work locations.

The **interview schedule** combined both closed and open-ended questions. The closed (or pre-coded) sections consisted of **self-administered questionnaire** sheets which respondents completed at appropriate times during the interview. Participants scored the degree of importance of specific managerial activities in their job, the time spent on specific managerial activities, personal attributes they considered important to bring to the job and finally, a list of learning needs they considered relevant to their development in their job. The use of the survey technique, combining precoded self-completion items with open-ended questions administered by committed and sensitive researchers, was chosen to ensure systematic coverage, whilst at the same time allowing individual and group differences and nuances to shine through.

A copy of the interview schedule is given in Appendix 1. The interviews took approximately one hour although there was great variation between individuals with extremes of 20 minutes and over two hours. In some cases a respondent's shortage of time meant that some questions were omitted.

A final phase of data collection, or at least data validation, took place in the form of **participant feedback** after the completion of the first draft of the research report. Each of the participating sites was given the opportunity to discuss the findings of the study both in general terms, as reported here, and in terms of their own particular organisation. Furthermore, representatives of all participating sites, together with other interested parties at national and regional level, were invited to a project conference in October 1994. These discussions have provided further input into this report.

The overwhelming response to the release of preliminary findings was endorsement. As one conference participant put it

"reading the (draft) report was like holding up a mirror to me and to my Trust".

The Choice of Organisations

The choice of organisations for the pilot was on the basis of links between The Management School, Imperial College and NHS Organisations in its own region. Data collected from the pilot sites are included in this report, although given changes in the research instruments, not all the pilot data were usable.

The choice of organisations for the main study was tackled initially by identifying four regions (three out of London and one of the Thames regions) in which to undertake the fieldwork. Attention was given to the geographic and demographic nature of each region, particularly the urban/rural balance. Contact was then made with the relevant regional headquarters and a discussion took place concerning the selection of organisations to approach. The next stage was to approach the chief executives of the identified organisations about the possibility of conducting the study. This process took some while, but, of the 22 organisations approached, only one organisation felt it was unable to take part. 21 organisations therefore form the basis of this project; 3 of these were pilot sites.

The Choice of Respondents

The population of senior executives who are the subject of this study was identified by virtue of their employment in the 21 organisations which were selected for study. A list of participants within each organisation was agreed with the chief executive or their representative. The researchers then made contact with potential participants by an explanatory letter and a follow up phone call seeking a date and time for an interview. The CEO was asked to give the names of all the Executive and non-Board Directors and those who reported directly to them. In providing organisations the CEO was also asked for a list of those clinicians whom s/he considered had senior executive or managerial responsibilities beyond those normally expected of a clinician. Such people usually combined managerial with clinical professional duties.

Given the interest of the project in examining the careers, responsibilities and learning needs of clinical and other health professionals who were significantly involved in management, we sought to include such people even if, on a strict application of the above criteria of reporting to a director, they would not have been included. In this way the list of potential participants, particularly in providing organisations, was increased. This accounts for why, in terms of reporting level, the sample of respondents includes some people who are two levels below Director.

The lists which were forthcoming from CEOs sometimes included everyone who fell into the desired categories but sometimes they were more restricted, depending on how much executive time the CEO felt their organisation could contribute to the project.

In the main cooperation from those we approached was very positive. In purchasing organisations letters were written to 111 people and 104 interviews secured, a **response rate** of 94%. In providing organisations letters were written to 224 people and 167 interviews secured, a **response rate** of 75%. Overall for the whole study, the response rate was 81% with a total number of respondents of 271. The majority of refusals in provider organisations came from clinical directors or equivalent, who felt they could not spare the time for the interview.

No pretence is made that our group of respondents for this study is a scientifically established random sample of the national population of senior executives in purchasing and providing organisations in the NHS. However, we feel that those whom we interviewed are sufficiently varied in terms of geography, organisational level, and professional background to provide a sound base from which generalisable conclusions can be drawn. Discussions of the results with a wide cross section of NHS employees has provided further support that the findings presented here are generalisable within the NHS.

Pilot Work and Fieldwork Timetable

Fieldwork for the project began in June 1992 with pilot studies of two providing and one purchasing organisations. As a result of the pilot work the interview schedule was substantially redrafted and fieldwork for the main study in the remaining 18 sites conducted between January and October 1993. Where appropriate, the results of the pilot studies have been combined with those of the main study and are included in this report.

Data Analysis and Presentation of Results

Responses to the precoded questionnaire sheets were easily handled, since they were ready for immediate input into a data set for analysis. In order to capture general trends and widely held views, and to identify differences in response between people of different occupational groups, organisational levels, gender and age, the open-ended data was post coded into a form that could be analysed with basic statistics. The process was lengthy. Initially all the qualitative data were transcribed from hand written notes to the word processor. Whilst doing this, the researchers were developing implicit categories which they felt captured the essential differences between the responses. These implicit categories were discussed within the team; used as a basis for a trial coding exercise for the data from two sites, refined, discussed again and then finalised. Each interview was then post coded and entered, along with its precoded sections, onto a PC based statistical package to form a large data set.

The basic statistical format used for the analysis of individual responses is the crosstabulation or contingency table, showing a combination of the values of two variables that provides information on their relationship. The Pearson chi-square test of independence is used as a test of goodness of fit for the contingency tables. This works on the hypothesis that the two variables of a crosstabulation are independent of each other. Pearson calculates the probability that this is true. If the probability (p) is less than 0.05 then the independence hypothesis is rejected and the existence of a relationship is accepted. Taking a significance level of 0.05 means that the chance of the two variables being independently associated is 5%. The smaller the level of significance, the greater the chance of the two variables being dependent. However the test on its own gives little information on the form of the relationship. Its interpretation relies upon an understanding of the qualitative data from the interview and the researchers' understanding of the organisational context for purchasing and providing organisations in the NHS.

In analysing individual responses, relationships were explored between the variables which describe managerial career, responsibilities, performance review, communication, team work and management development and the independent variables of type of organisation, present job, organisational level, professional background, gender and age. In order to avoid an over- production of tables, one or two particular cross tabulations have usually been selected for each variable. Where cross tabulation with variables other than those shown in the tables, revealed interesting statistically significant relationships they are noted in the text, but the tables are not always reproduced. The crosstabulations are normally in the form of column percentages, with the total number of respondents being given at the top of each column.

Shortage of time within some interviews and some differences between the pilot study and the main study mean that some questions were not answered by all respondents. In cases where the responses to the questions are less than 271, the analysis is conducted on the basis of the numbers replying, excluding missing values.

In addition to their representation in numerical analysis as a result of post coding, the qualitative data are also used in this report in the form of direct illustrative quotations from respondents.

1.4 Characteristics of the sample of senior executives

This section describes the group of 271 senior executives who were interviewed for this study. It also introduces the following six demographic variables which provide the basis for most of the analysis:

- **Purchaser/Provider** : type of employing organisation

- Roots : **Background** of respondent

- **Present Job** of respondent

- Present **level** of respondent

- **Age** of respondent

- **Gender** of respondent

As much of the analysis is concerned to explore variations in the experience of management between purchasing and providing organisations, each of the other 5 key variables is now described to show its distribution in purchaser and provider organisations as well as for the whole sample.

1. **Purchaser/Provider :** This describes the type of organisation in which the respondent is working. There are just two categories: Purchaser and Provider. The sample of respondents was distributed as follows:

	N	%
Purchaser	104	38
Provider	167	62
	271	**100**

2. **Background or "Roots" :** This describes the subject area in which the respondent initially qualified, and/ or the area in which they had their training and early work experiences. The following five categories are used for this variable.

General Manager : General management qualifications or training or experience (not restricted to Griffiths (1983) interpretations), without any of the following as prior qualifications.

Functional Manager : Professionally qualified or experienced in a non-clinical, non-health functional area, eg Finance, Personnel, Estates.

Medical : Medical qualifications and training.

Nursing : Nursing qualifications and training.

Other Health Professional : Inter alia, includes qualifications and training in professions Professional allied to medicine, pharmacy, radiography. Given the relatively small number of Other Health Professionals, this category has occasionally been excluded from crosstabulation analysis in order to improve the basis of the test of significance.

The sample of respondents was distributed by Background/ "Roots" as follows:

	Purchaser		Provider		All	
	N	%	N	%	N	%
general manager	43	41	27	16	70	26
functional manager	21	20	30	18	51	19
medical	22	21	62	37	84	31
nursing	11	11	34	20	45	17
other health professional	7	7	14	8	21	8
	104	100	167	100	271	100

3. **Present Job :** This describes the type of work in which our respondents were engaged at the time of interviewing. Three categories were used for this variable.

General Manager : Respondents who are not specified as functional or clinical managers as defined below and who have general management posts; these cover inter alia, operations, corporate development and business management in providing organisations, and commissioning and contracting in purchasing organisations.

| Functional Manager : | Respondents who are responsible for managing a non-clinical, non-health, specialist function, notably Finance, Personnel, Information, Estates and Facilities |
| Clinical manager : | Respondents who are directly responsible for the management of clinical services or public health. Alternative titles would have been public health/ clinical manager or, given their qualifications, "clinically qualified manager". However, for ease of reference we have settled with 'clinical manager'. |

The sample of respondents was distributed by 'Present Job' as follows:

	Purchaser		Provider		All	
	N	%	N	%	N	%
general manager	64	62	54	32	118	44
functional manager	20	19	25	15	45	17
clinical manager	20	19	88	53	108	40
	104	**100**	**167**	**100**	**271**	**100**

| 4 **Present Level:** | This describes the level in the executive hierarchy for each respondent. It will be recalled that all our respondents are senior executives but the following four levels can be discerned in terms of reporting arrangements: |

| Level 1 Executive Board Member : | an executive director of a DHA, NHS Trust or shadow NHS Trust. |
| Level 2 Non-Board Director : | a director who reports to a Board member (often the CEO) and who is not formally a member of the board. Frequently they had specific responsibility for a significant area of work which is not directly the responsibility of any of the board members apart from the CEO. |

Level 3   Reporting to Director : a senior executive who reports to a Director (level 1 or 2). This category included the largest proportion of clinical managers since it covered all the clinical directors. It is the most professionally mixed level.

Level 4   Reporting to Level 3 :   a relatively small group explained below.

Whereas we sought to interview as many people as possible at levels 1 and 2 and a significant proportion of level 3, we only interviewed people at level 4 if there was some particular organisational or individual reason why they were of interest to the study. This usually meant they were a nurse or other health professional in a strong managerial position, and therefore, as has already been explained, they were of particular interest to the study. This group of respondents is the least representative of any of our groups.

The distinction between levels 2 and 3 is fairly arbitrary. Therefore in addition to using all four levels together, there is also analysis using the following divisions:

(i)   Executive Board Member (level 1)/ Others (levels 2, 3 and 4)

(ii)   Director (levels 1 and 2)/ Others (levels 3 and 4)

The sample of respondents was distributed by 'Level' as follows:

	Purchaser		Provider		All	
	N	%	N	%	N	%
executive board director	44	42	49	29	93	34
non-board director	15	14	20	12	35	13
reporting to director	45	43	73	44	118	44
reporting to level 3	0	0	25	15	25	9
	104	99	167	100	271	100

5 **Age :**

Occasionally analysis is sometimes done on the basis of 'younger' (44 and under) and 'older' (45 and above). The sample of respondents was distributed by 'Age', as follows:

Age	Purchaser N	%	Provider N	%	All N	%
25–34	15	14	22	13	37	14
35–44	50	48	62	37	112	41
45–54	31	30	60	36	91	34
55–64	8	8	23	14	31	11
	104	**100**	**167**	**100**	**271**	**100**

6 **Gender :**

The issue of gender and equal opportunities is important in the NHS. We were therefore interested in seeing some of the relationships between gender and managerial activity. However, because of the bias in terms of present job, level and background it is not always easy to tease out the effects of gender from those of other variables.

The sample of respondents was distributed by 'Gender' as follows:

	Purchaser N	%	Provider N	%	All N	%
male	62	60	107	64	169	62
female	42	40	60	36	102	38
	104	100	167	100	271	100

Appendix 2 gives fuller information on the relationships between the six demographic variables (type of organisation, background, present job, present level, age and gender) which are used to describe the sample of senior executives who participated in the study. It shows that some of these variables, for example present job, present level and gender are as one might expect, interdependent rather than independent variables. Account needs to be taken of these interdependencies in interpreting the results. Where appropriate this is indicated in the discussion.

Chapter 2 The Organisational Context

A time of change

Ten purchaser and eleven provider organisations constituted the base for this research project. The interviews took place over a 17 month period, in which there was much change. When the pilot work began in June 1992, the reforms were only 14 months old. Trusts were just beginning to consider how they were going to use their new found freedoms. They were apprehensive about what the internal market would mean for them. Was their contract base secure? Would they be able to influence purchasers? Were they really viable as the separate entities that had crystallised out of the old command and control model? Would they be able to acquire or develop the skills and knowledge that were needed amongst their senior managers and their senior clinicians, if they were successfully to operate in the post-reforms new world? Furthermore, it was by no means certain that all providing organisations would become NHS Trusts. It looked at that time as if substantial numbers might remain as D.M.Us. (Directly Managed Units).

Equally purchasers were experiencing enormous change. Not only were they placed in a new organisational context with a new agenda of tasks to be undertaken, but they had been given a raison d'etre which had not previously existed in the NHS. Thus they too were concerned with their ability to acquire or develop appropriate skills and knowledge in their senior executives.

This context of change means that there have been considerable developments in the lapse of time between the fieldwork and this publication. Nonetheless, feedback discussions of the results suggest that the key organisational and managerial issues identified in this report are still highly relevant to DHAs and NHS Trusts in 1995.

2.1. Provider Organisations : Descriptions of Sites

The key characteristics of the 11 participating providing organisations are summarised in Tables 2.1 – 2.6. Table 2.1 shows that each 'Trust wave' was represented.

Table 2.1 *Providing Organisations: Key characteristics at time of interviewing*

Region	Region A (Pilot)		Region B				Region C		Region D		Region E
Site	A	B	C	D	E	F	G	H	I	J	K
Period of Interviewing: Month/Year	June 1992	Sept 1992	Jan-March 1993	Jan-March 1993	Sep-Oct 1993	Sep-Oct 1993	July-Aug 1993	July-Aug 1993	July-Aug 1993	July-Sep 1993	Sep-Oct 1993
Trust wave	1	2	2	2	4	3	2	3	4	4	3
Acute (A)/community (C)	A	A	A	A	C	C	A	A	A	A	A
Teaching Hospital	N	N	N	N	N	N	N	Y	N	Y	Y
Number of Beds	600	450	350	850	648	430	881	1496	717	@	940
Budget 92/3 £	50m	32m	26m	50m	39m	36.9m	52m	140m	49m	80m	128m
No. of Employees	1443	1500	1300	2000	3300	1570	2300	5000	1724	4000	5137

Notes:
Site C merged with the Community Unit and became a whole district Trust in 1993.
@: Site J is in the process of closing two hospitals and moving into a new building on the hospital site.

Pilot work was undertaken in a first and a second wave Trust. In the main study there were three second wave Trusts, three third wave Trusts and three DMUs which had applied for fourth wave entry. They ranged in size from an annual budget (1992–3) of £26M to £140M and a total workforce of 1300 to 5137. They included three teaching hospitals, and two community trusts. Geographically they spanned England from the South to the North and from East to West.

They had all made significant changes to their internal management structure since 1990 and were engaged in major programmes designed to secure changes in culture and the development of a more corporate identity. They all had policies and practices which sought significantly to involve clinicians in management. Although similar aims were apparent in each of their endeavours to manage change, there was considerable variation between sites in how their plans were operationalised.

Table 2.2 summarises comparative information on their clinical management structures. There is considerable variation in the language of titles. In some sites clinical or service groups were called directorates, with doctors as clinical directors, in others, doctors were clinical managers or clinical coordinators, and in one case, Chairs of Service Centres. Whereas in the acute sector, the models of clinical management were largely hierarchical with doctors in the most senior positions, the two community units had matrix structures with senior positions held by doctors, nurses or PAMs and with an emphasis on securing representation in the management structure from service areas or care groups (defined in terms of service users e.g. elderly people or adult mentally ill), functional clinical specialities (e.g. physiotherapy, nursing, psychology, psychiatry) and geographical localities.

In the acute units, the doctors who headed up the clinical units all worked part-time, notionally devoting between 1 and 6 sessions per week to their managerial work. The rest of their time was taken up with normal clinical work as consultants. In the community units some of the service directors and clinical coordinators were in full-time managerial positions.

The degree and nature of involvement of nurses was much more variable than that of doctors. It was usual to have a nurse manager attached to each of the clinical groups; often providing support as a service manager and taking overall responsibility for aspects of patient care. Typically in the acute sector nurses were in positions subordinate to the doctors who had overall managerial responsibility. Business managers were always associated with each grouping and in some sites there were arrangements to secure dedicated access to finance and personnel staff.

Table 2.2 *Providing Organisations: Clinical Management Structures*

Site	Numbers & Names	Involvement of Medical Staff	Involvement of Nursing Staff	Support Provided	Budget Arrangement
A	9 Clinical Directorates	Doctor Directors	Ward managers	Shared service managers Business managers	Devolved Budgets
B	10 Clinical Directorates	Doctor Directors	Part-time nurse managers	Shared business managers	Devolved Budgets (paper exercise at time of interviewing)
C	9 Clinical Managers	Doctor Managers	Patient care managers Senior nurse managers	Patient care managers Business manager: Pathology	Devolved Budgets
D	8 Clinical Managers	Doctor Managers	Clinical nurse managers	Service managers (Shared) Business managers (Shared) Info & finance dept help	Devolved Budgets
E	A Matrix of 8 Service Directorates 5 Clinical Services 8 localities	Some Service Directors	Locality managers Senior Clinical Nurse	Business managers	Devolved Budgets
F	A Matrix of 10 Clinical coordinators 9 Functional Managers	Some Clinical coordinators	Some Clinical coordinators	Business managers	Budgets held by Functional managers Clinical coordinators ensure contracts fulfilled
G	9 Clinical Directorates 2 Further Clinical Areas	Doctor Directors reporting to Medical Director reporting to Nurse Director	Nurse managers	Business managers Shared accountants	Devolved Budgets
H	15 Clinical Service Directorates	Doctor Directors	Senior Clinical Nurse – Also many CSMs	Clinical Service managers (CSM) Business manager: Radiology	Devolved Budgets
I	7 Clinical Directorates	Doctor Directors	Nurse managers	Business managers liaise with Business Planning dept.	Devolved Budgets
J	10 Clinical Directorates	Doctor Directors	Nurse managers	General managers Junior finance dept. help	Devolved Budgets
K	8 Chairs of Service Centres	Doctor Chairs Coordinating 2-3 Service development units	Shared DNS (Directors of Nursing) Nurse manager	4 General Managers covering 1/2/3 service centres	Devolved Budgets

Each clinical group was allocated a budget and also had some responsibility for managing its clinical activity. However, the inclusivity of the budgets and the degree of local discretion about activity varied considerably.

Table 2.3 shows that the division of responsibilities between members of the Senior Executive team was subject to some variation. All Trusts are required to have a chief executive and financial director. The latter is sometimes given additional specific responsibilities, for example in Site E for information as well as finance. In addition they must have a medically qualified doctor and a qualified nurse on their Trust Executive Team. The doctor is normally called the Medical Director.

The nurse may be called the Director of Nursing or may be given a different title and a wider brief, for example, as Director of Operational Services in Site E or Director of Quality Assurance and Nursing in Site G. National studies have found that the role and function of the Nurse Executive Director is subject to considerable variability, and that there is considerable scope for development (NHSME 1992d).

The designation and remit of the fifth Executive director varies considerably between sites. In our 11 provider organisations, there were broadly three different areas of responsibility which were represented on the Board:
– Human Resources/Personnel
– Commercial/Corporate Development/Strategy, and
– Operations.

Typically one of these finds a seat on the Board and the other two may become non-Board Directors or Senior Managers. Other non-Board Directors were typically responsible for Estates, Planning and Information.

Had it been possible, we would have liked to examine the role and function of senior executives with a professional background, and possibly continuing practice, in professions allied to medicine. In the event, as will be shown, there were very few such people employed in the organisations which we studied.

Table 2.4 shows the clinical departments of the clinical managers who participated as respondents in this study.

Table 2.3 *Providing Organisations: Analysis of All Respondents*

	Sites A	B	C	D	E
Level 1 Executive Directors					
Chief Executive	1	1	1	1	1
Finance Director	1	1	–	1	Finance & Information
Medical Director	1	1	1	1	–
Nursing Director	–	1	1	1	Operational Services
5th Executive Director	–	Commercial	Human Resources	Operations	Corporate Development
Level 2 Non Board Directors	3 Operations, Personnel, Estates.	1 Human Resources	2 Operations, Contracts & Information.	–	3 Service Director (Learning Disabilities), Human Resources, Estates & Facilities.
Level 3 Reporting to Directors					
3A General & Functional Managers	–	–	–	–	2
3B Clinical/Professional Directors/Managers shown in Table 2.4	9	9	9	5	–
Level 4					
Reporting to 3A or 3B as above	–	1	3	1	–
Total	**15**	**16**	**18**	**11**	**9**

Notes:
Level 1,2,3 & 4 refer to 'level' as coded for each respondent

F	G	H	I	J	K	TOTAL
1	1	1	1	1	1	11
1	1	1	1	1	1	10
1	1	1	1	1	–	9
1	Nursing & Patient Services	Quality Assurance & Nursing	1	1	–	9
Human Resources	Personnel	Personnel	Corporate Strategy	General Services	Service Development	10
2 Performance Management, Business Development.	–	3 Planning, Hospital Services, Hospital (Site) Manager.	–	2 Estates & Facilities, Planning & Administration.	4 Human Resources, Information & computing, Quality, Estates.	20
1	–	–	1	4	3	11
4	2	10	5	4	5	62
–	–	16	1	–	3	25
12	**7**	**34**	**12**	**15**	**18**	**167**

Table 2.4 *Providing Organisations: Analysis of Respondents: Departments of Clinical Directors and Service Heads*

Sites	A	B	C	D	E	F	G	H	I	J	K	Total
Respondents												
Clinical Directors/Managers/Chairs:												
A&E/Trauma/Orthopaedics	1	–	1	–	–	–	–	1	–	–	–	3
Anaesthetics/Theatres	1	1	1	1	–	–	–	–	1	1	–	6
Cardiothoracic	–	–	–	–	–	–	–	–	–	–	1	1
Learning Disabilities	–	–	–	–	1	1	–	–	–	–	–	2
Medicine	1	1	–	1	–	–	–	1	1	–	1	6
Medicine/Elderly	1	1	1	–	–	–	1	–	–	–	1	5
Mental Health/Psychiatry	–	–	1	–	–	1	–	1	–	–	–	3
Neurosciences	–	–	–	–	–	–	–	–	–	–	1	1
Obstetrics & Gynaecology	1	1	1	–	–	–	–	–	–	–	–	3
Paediatrics/Child Health	1	1	1	–	–	–	–	1	–	–	–	4
Pathology	1	1	1	1	–	–	–	1	1	1	–	7
Professional & Scientific Services	–	–	–	–	–	–	–	–	–	–	1	1
Radiology	1	–	1	1	–	–	–	1	–	–	–	4
Specialist Surgery/Oral, M-F	–	1	–	–	–	–	–	1	–	–	–	2
Surgery	–	1	1	1	–	–	1	1	1	–	–	6
Clinical Service Heads												
Clinical Psychology	–	–	–	–	–	–	–	–	–	1	–	1
Communication Therapy	–	–	–	–	–	1	–	–	–	–	–	1
Midwifery/Nursing	–	1	–	–	–	–	–	–	–	–	–	1
Occupational Therapy	–	–	–	–	–	1	–	–	–	1	–	2
Pharmacy	1	–	–	–	–	–	–	1	1	–	–	3
Physiotherapy Services	–	–	–	–	–	–	–	1	–	–	–	1
Total	9	9	9	5	1	4	2	10	5	4	5	62

2.2   Purchasing Organisations : Description of Sites

The genesis of all purchasing organisations was Autumn 1990 when the new District Health Authorities were established with a Chair appointed by the Secretary of State and up to 5 executive and 5 non-executive directors. They not only had the enormous task of building purchasing organisations, with capacity to commission for health gain and contract for service provision, but unless and until their provider units attained Trust status, they had responsibility for directing managed units as well.

The key characteristics of the 10 purchasing organisations are summarised in Table 2.5. By the time fieldwork was conducted in each site, there was de facto operational separation of the purchasing and providing roles even if, as in Sites L, O and T, there were still directly managed units.

Two aspects of boundary configuration have created far reaching demands for change management in purchasing: the merging of DHAs and the relationship between DHAs and the FHSAs (Family Health Service Authorities).

Even though only reconstituted in 1990, DHAs have been subject to merger in order to secure increased purchasing power and decreased management overheads as a fraction of purchasing budgets. As Table 2.5 shows, 6 of the study sites had experience of merger since 1990. The relationship between DHAs and FHSAs is not so easily formally resolved as each authority is established by law and its constitution can only be changed by primary legislation. Such legislation is now a formal recommendation of the Functions and Manpower Review Report 1993, but until such time as it becomes legally possible, the two authorities must continue as separate entities. The reasons for the suggested merger, which was first mooted in the 1989 White Paper 'Working for Patients', are that in order to commission healthcare one needs a strategic vision which embraces both primary and secondary care. In anticipation of the change some authorities have already sought some kind of joint working arrangements. These range from fully merged operations, as in Sites Q and R, where the only separation was at formal authority meetings, through various forms of shared appointments for CEOs or other Executive Directors, to arrangements where there was little or no contact between the staff or the Boards.

The experience of merging DHAs or joint working with FHSAs added considerably to feelings of insecurity and defensiveness in purchasing authorities. Even where

Table 2.5 *Purchasing Organisations: Key characteristics at time of interviewing*

	L (Pilot)	Region A		Region B		Region C		Region D		Region F
		M	N	O	P	Q	R	S	T	U
Period of Interviewing (Month/Year)	July 1992	Jan/Feb 1993	Jan/Feb 1993	Mar 1993	Mar 1993	May 1993	June/July 1993	July-Sept 1993	July-Sept 1993	Aug/Oct 1993
Population (000's) OPCS 1990	230	650	330	406	279	423	658	290	504	571
No. of DHA's merged since 1990	0	2.5	1.5	2	0	0	2	0	2	3
FHSA Arrangements++	N	SC	SC	N	SC	FM	FM	SC	SD	SD
No. of DMUs	2	0	0	2	0	0	0	0	2	0
No. of Sites	1	2	2	1	3	1	1	2	2	3

Notes:
++ FHSA Arrangements: refers to relation between DHA & FHSA
FM: Fully Merged
SC: Shared CEO
SD: Shared Directors (not CEO)
N: No formal arrangements

there is general agreement that institutional change is important, individuals nonetheless may feel threatened. Whilst trying to develop a commissioning agenda which requires an outward focus on the local community and on working collaboratively with other agencies to secure health gain, senior executives in purchasing authorities are facing considerable challenges in internal management.

The involvement of health professionals in purchasing is arguably just as important as, but different to, their involvement in providing. Purchasing is dependent on having access to sources of clinical judgement. Hence the appointment of Public Health Physicians to fulfil this role, as well as to develop needs assessment as a basis for a district's health strategy. Public health physicians do not normally have responsibility for the care of individual patients, but they are medically qualified and hence they fall into the research category of health professionals who are also managers. Somewhat inappropriately that means that they are known in this study as 'clinical managers' to distinguish them from 'general' or 'functional' managers.

There is a government commitment that there should be more nurses involved at a senior level in purchasing (NHSE 1994). However as yet this is more of a statement of desire than of reality. There is little we can say about senior managers with nursing qualifications in purchasing as we found comparatively few of them in this study.

The structure of executive teams in purchasing organisations shows some variation between sites. An illustration of the variation is given in Table 2.6 which provides an analysis of the respondents from purchasing organisations in this study. All authorities have a Chief Executive, a Finance Director and a Director of Public Health, although the titles and scope of responsibilities for the last two may vary. For example Site U had a Director of Resources and Site R, a Director of Finance, Information and Contracting rather than the direct designation of a Finance Director. Similarly Site M had a Director of Health Gain and Strategy and Site N a Director of Health rather than a Director of Public Health. The fourth and fifth Executive Directors are usually some combination of Directors of Purchasing, Planning, Acute and Community Commissioning, Contracting, Quality and Primary Care.

As in providing, there is some juggling of titles around the boundaries of the Board between Executive and non-Board Directors. Some authorities have effectively expanded their Board membership by making shared appointments to the Board whereby 2, 3 or even 4 directors may sit on the Board, but have 1 or 2 votes between them. There are also quite a number of joint appointments between DHAs and FHSAs whereby one director may be appointed to work for both authorities.

Table 2.6 *Purchasing Organisations: Analysis of Respondents*

Site	L	M	N	O	P
Level 1 Executive Directors					
CEO/DGM	1	1*	1*	1	1*
Finance Director	1	1	1	1	1
Director of Public Health	1	Health Gain & Strategy 1	Health 1	1	1
4th Executive Director	–	Primary Care 1*	–	Purchasing & Corporate Strategy 1	Information 1
5th Executive Director	–	Acute Commissioning 1+ Performance Management & Business Affairs 1+	–	Contracting 1	Corporate Planning* 1
Level 2 Non Board Directors	–	–	Primary Care ++1	–	Administration 1
Level 3 Staff Reporting to Directors	3	–	–	3	9(3*)
Total	**6**	**6**	**4**	**8**	**15**

Notes:
Level 1,2 & 3 refer to 'level' as coded for each respondent
* Joint Appointments with FHSA
+ These 2 people shared voting rights of one Executive on the Authority
++ Non Board Director Acting up as Executive Board Member
+++ These posts are technically held by Non Board Directors to accommodate merged working relations with FHSA
Titles of posts shown for directors except where they exactly correspond to title in 1st column
Numbers indicate numbers of posts
 – indicates no interview at this level

Q	R	S	T	U	Total
1*	1*	1*	1	1	10
1	Finance Information Contracting 1	1	1	Resources 1	10
1	(1)+++	1	1	1	9
Health Care Purchasing 1	(Consumer & Corporate Affairs)+++	Strategy 1	Planning & Contracting 1	Purchasing & Planning 1	7
Primary Care Development 1+	(Planning)+++	–	Quality Assurance 1	Quality & Community Relations 1	8
Policy & Business Manager 1+					
–	Public Health 1	Information Adminstration 1	Divisional Director FHSA *1	Organisation & Employee Development 1	15
	Consumer & Corporate Affairs 1			Locality Directors 3	
	Planning 1			Primary Care *1 DDGM 1 Public Health 1	
11	4	5	1	9	45
17	**9**	**11**	**7**	**21**	**104**

2.3 Key Issues of Management and Organisation

Each of the purchasing and providing sites was in some ways unique. The research team has conducted some site specific analysis which has been used as a basis for feedback to individual organisations; a process which, in turn, yielded additional contextual information. However, given the scale and primary purpose of this study the discussion of organisational and management issues in this report is kept at a general level. What follows is a summary of the trends and issues which emerged as important in setting the context for management development and organisational development in the majority of organisations which were studied. An outline of issues for purchasing is followed by a similar discussion for providing organisations. The findings briefly summarised here, have considerable resonance with those which were reported more fully by the Audit Commission in 1993 for DHAs and in 1994 for Trusts.

Purchasing Organisations

Issues of general concern to purchasers which emerged in this study all related to their task of **creating new organisations** for new tasks in a newly created, yet turbulent, environment.

The creation of the internal market created a **new environment** for health management. Never before in the UK have health managers had to negotiate contracts for mainstream clinical work, although since 1983 they have had some experience of contracting out catering and other aspects of facilities. The raison d'etre for DHAs is to secure a strategy for health gain for their local population. Rather than managing a 'sickness service' they are seeking to commission a range of services and interventions which will address the health needs which they identify in their local populations.

Within this strategy they need to establish means to secure an internal organisation, sets of contractual arrangements and sets of collaborating relationships which will enable them to deliver services which are concerned to try to meet expectations from **diverse groups of interested parties or stakeholders** which include:

* patients and carers whose expectations have been raised by discussions of Patients' Charters, the publication of hospital league tables and greater emphasis upon responsive, timely and appropriate service provision and interventions,

* health professionals and managers in secondary care with whom purchasers may place contracts,

* GPs and the large number of nurses, midwives, health visitors and therapists who are employed in primary care provision,

* GPs in their own purchasing and commissioning role, either as fundholders or as non-fundholding members of consultative bodies,

* officials in the Department of Health and NHS Executive, who, under Ministerial guidance, require purchasers to meet specified financial and service requirements,

* local authority agencies in social services and housing with which DHAs are engaged in joint planning and joint commissioning, particularly at the interface between health and social care, but also in respect of a wide range of environmental conditions which have a bearing on health needs and health status.

The purchaser's task is to create an organisation which can engage **in partnership** with each of these groups, notwithstanding that each group has autonomy and embodies considerable heterogeneity amongst diverse interests. As the centre of a network of stakeholders, DHA staff need to find ways to relate to each group, consult with them and where appropriate, engage them in decision making, planning and implementation.

With an underlying concern to address the health needs of their resident population, DHAs are desperately in need of **valid and reliable information** on the effectiveness of different forms of clinical and organisational interventions. This requires the generation of shareable information and the development of analytical and evaluative skills to use information appropriately. We found an awareness within some, but not all, DHAs of the intention of the NHS R&D strategy (Department of Health 1993) to facilitate the evaluation and dissemination of effectiveness information, but as yet little evidence to show whether this promise will be realised at local level.

The achievement of the purchasing agenda has to be accomplished within a **highly politicised context** and in the spotlight of intense media interest. The challenge for purchasing, which executive directors all acknowledge, is to be innovative, open and creative and committed to partnership with a variety of other organisations. This in itself is a daunting task for any organisation, but particularly so for DHAs in 1992 and 1993 since the legislative and managerial changes which created this new context, had already created a great deal of **uncertainty, turbulence and hence defensiveness** within the organisations themselves.

The large task of **internal organisation development** and the degree of effort and energy required to develop new ways of working which were signalled by the creation of the internal market, were felt to be difficult to achieve. Senior managers in DHAs were themselves pre-occupied with day to day operational issues and by personal concerns about their own careers and those of their staff. Not surprisingly, therefore, many senior executives were focusing on organisational design (who does what now) rather than development (what new ways of working can we develop), and with meeting short term, rather than longer term, targets.

The feeling of being trapped in solving immediate problems, was exacerbated by the uncertainty surrounding relationships between **DHAs and FHSAs.** The responses to this uncertainty varied and in any case could not be bilaterally determined by the DHA or FHSA, since they are subject to national and regional policy. Within this context, some DHAs became part of a de-facto merged Health Commission, others were involved in an intermediate ad-hoc series of joint appointments as vacancies arose, or set up ad-hoc joint working groups on particular issues at the interface between primary and secondary care. Others continued to work as entirely separate organisations. Whatever the response, on a continuum from full merger to complete separation, it presented uncertainty, anxiety and defensiveness within and between various groups of purchasing staff. Beyond the variety of joint working arrangements with FHSAs, many DHAs were also participating in the reconfiguration and enlargement of DHA boundaries.

Against this background of change it is not surprising to note that there was agreement amongst the senior purchasing executives in this study that their organisations needed to tackle a **major agenda of organisation development.** The key issues may be summarised as follows:

*   adjusting to working in a small organisation which continued to bear the name but was otherwise very different from its large bureaucratic predecessor,

*   seeking to secure a fundamental change in strategic orientation, through combining a set of very familiar, with a set of very new, tasks, whilst jettisoning other long established tasks, of which the direct management of secondary care providers was the most notable,

*   developing ways of working with flatter structures,

*   relying less internally on command and control hierarchies and more on delegated powers, with all staff feeling empowered to act within their own spheres of responsibility,

* establishing and maintaining tight and systematic procedures to secure cost effective disbursement of large amounts of public money, albeit within small, more flexible organisations,

* recruiting and developing groups of staff, who are excellent in their original discipline or function, eg finance, information, public health, contracting, and who are prepared to work and to develop cross functionally, often in multi-functional project teams.

* where matrix organisations, with crossing elements of functional, geographical and care group responsibilities, exist, to seek to make them 'lighter' rather than 'heavier' structures,

* externally developing staff and organisational structures which facilitate collaborative work with other agencies and organisations,

* developing ways of working which encourage innovation and experimentation to tackle the 'new' commissioning agenda,

* developing an understanding and a practice which acknowledges that if one is going to put high value on flexibility, experimentation and innovation, one needs to be 'naturally' less risk averse.

The last point is central to the **management of change.** It requires an investment in at least two directions. First, in developing a framework for evaluating whether innovations (be they in medical practice, service delivery or organisational arrangements) are contributing to the achievement of established objectives. Secondly, to develop a mind set which is prepared to acknowledge and learn from failures without necessarily jumping to the conclusion that they are due to the incompetence of individuals. This requires major cultural as well as structural change.

Providing Organisations

Issues of general concern to providers which emerged from this study also focused on the **scale and rate of organisational change** even though in comparison to purchasing, organising and managing health care provision has greater continuity with the past. Thus the managerial challenges in providing organisations in 1992 and 1993 in some ways appeared as less dramatic and more familiar than those in purchasing. However, the appearance of continuity was seen to be dangerous as it meant that senior executives faced significant difficulties in persuading their colleagues of the need for change. In fact the need for change in the ways of working and organising in provider organisations was profound.

The internal market required providers to demonstrate the cost effectiveness of their services in order to secure contracts for work and thereby their continued viability. Taking the eleven provider sites included in this study, there was a range of between 50% and 98% dependence on contracts with a main purchaser. However, even where geography and history suggested they had a captured market, there was great awareness that changes on the margins, as indicated by the preferences of one or two GP FHs, could significantly alter a provider's viability. Other noted triggers for change included developments in medical and nursing education and training, changes in junior doctors hours, the cost and service implications of developments in pharmaceuticals, technology and medical equipment and the established policy of shifting resources from secondary to primary care.

There was an awareness that within this **turbulent context** few provider organisations would have the same shape and size in 5 years time as they had at the time of fieldwork. It was expected that some providers would grow in size and complexity, others would shrink. Some would become more specialised over fewer activities; some would gain, and others loose 'independent' existence, as services were reconfigured as a result of the decisions and actions of local purchasers and other providers, as well as being influenced by regional and national considerations. Whilst it was felt that the shape, nature and size of any provider would, to some extent, be determined by forces beyond their immediate control, it was also acknowledged that a great deal hinges on local abilities in strategic and operational management.

Providing organisations all faced issues derived from the need to create viable corporate organisations which support professional excellence. It was felt that effective management in the internal market required everyone in the organisation to feel part of a single corporate organisation. This requirement is particularly challenging given the importance which was attached to recruiting and developing health professionals who are committed to the highest standards of professional care. Each participating provider site was grappling with trying to find appropriate ways to involve clinicians within the organisation so that they could flourish professionally with an organisation which was flourishing corporately in the market. The two endeavours should be complementary but creating that complementarity requires that an appropriate balance is struck between professional and organisational identity and loyalty.

Indicative of difficulties at the organisational/professional boundaries was the ambiguity which was found to surround the role of the Doctor or Nurse on the

Board. From the views expressed three extremes can be distilled. One view was that they were professional representatives and therefore deemed to have failed when they do not stand up to represent the many diverse and individual viewpoints held by their colleagues. A second view was that they were a conduit for communication in a rather neutral way between the Board and professional groups; merely passing information to and from each group and standing aside from decisions. Thirdly, they were seen primarily as a Board member, sharing collective responsibility with their director colleagues and bringing to the Board the benefit of their professional experience, but not necessarily guaranteeing the support of their professional colleagues. Interestingly amongst those who held each view as an accurate reflection of reality, there were those who thought it absolutely right and others who thought it absolutely wrong. In reality, most medical and nurse directors were found to reflect bits of each view, but the three extremes demonstrate something of the difficult balances which have to be struck.

The need for effective involvement of health professionals reflected three dominant concerns in provider organisations: **leadership, communication and devolution.** In all our provider sites, from all groups of respondents, there was consensus that leadership was important, but that it needed to be developed on the basis of credibility from, and sensitivity to, the diverse groups involved. Many below Board level felt disenfranchised as if their place was 'merely' to ensure that cost and activity targets were achieved. Many felt the lacked effective means of making their voices heard on important strategic or operational issues. Ironically, the feeling of distance and disenfranchisement was not dissipated by considerable devolution of financial and operational management. Indeed financial devolution can make clinicians who are involved in monitoring and managing services, feel that they are merely the agents of senior management, rather than having any influence on senior management plans.

A further unanticipated outcome of greater devolution is that the created 'business units' or 'clinical directorates' can become very insular, concentrating on achieving their objectives, irrespective of what is happening elsewhere. Less cross fertilisation of ideas, less learning and less capacity to innovate and collaborate, can result.

Another major issue for provider organisations concerned developments in **job design, skill mix and job reprofiling.** All providers were looking at the ways in which members of different managerial and professional groups worked together and at the scope for multi-disciplinary team working. There was also considerable activity being devoted to the development and utilisation of patient management protocols, clinical guidelines, and project team working.

There was considerable anxiety expressed about **contracting timescales.** Given the size of the change agenda, providers were concerned that contracting with purchasers on an annual basis was leading to an over investment of time and energy in the present, to the detriment of investment in longer term planning. Many of the major changes required in the provision of health care need longer than a few month's timescale to bring to fruition. Just as purchasers felt that they were over-concentrating scarce resources on the 'here and now' when they would rather be investing in the future, providers echoed this sentiment.

The annual nature of the contracting cycle makes major shifts of patterns of investment more difficult to manage. This issue was often raised in respect of changes in investment between acute and community provision. Where they are managed within one trust, the issues revolve around securing increasing investment in community provision; where they are separate there are concerns about how best to manage across organisational boundaries. If each party is only working to an annual timescale, those seeking to manage the associated changes are considerably hampered in their approach.

A final general issue which arose in providing organisations concerned **relationships between local organisations and the centre.** Senior managers experienced contradictions over the extent to which their organisations were expected to be independent, autonomous units in which they were to be encouraged to embark upon a more entrepreneurial and less risk averse approach to strategic and operational management. They had all heard the messages of encouragement that they should take any independent and creative actions which careful evaluation suggested would lead to cost beneficial improvements in patient care, yet they were extremely nervous about their real powers in this respect as well as about the possibility of failure. The comments made at the end of the previous section on purchasing issues, about the need for cultural as well as structural change to support the development of innovatory practices and ways of working which acknowledge and learn from failures as well as successes, are equally applicable to providers. It was acknowledged in the more far-sighted Trusts that significant organisation development as well as individual management development was required if Trusts were to become better equipped to thrive in a dynamic environment through the delivery of more cost effective healthcare.

The issues raised about autonomy and regulation beg the question of the role of regions and the centre in managing the internal market, and in exercising control over individual purchasing and providing organisations. Senior managers in all the sites who participated in this study were aware that the centre – regional – local relationship was still evolving and would always form a variable and politicised backdrop which set the context for their own managerial activities.

Chapter 3 **Career: Past, Present and Future**

During the last decade, the organisational and societal context of careers has changed radically. Layers of middle management have disappeared out of many publicly and privately owned organisations as business and service practices are restructured in response to rapidly changing external and internal circumstances (Dopson and Stewart 1990, Nicolson 1993, Mayo 1994). Devolved management, task-oriented work processes, flexible working practices designed to avoid rigid, bureaucratic hierarchies, decrease the probability of promotion through grades (Kanter 1989). Nowadays, few managers are likely to enjoy 'orderly', predictable career paths within bureaucratically structured organisations (Scase & Goffee 1989, 1992). However, while hierarchical promotion opportunities may be less well-defined, more informal work settings can increase opportunities for internal job development and self-development (Morgan 1986, Arthur 1994).

Individuals depend on organisations to provide them with opportunities to utilize their skills and competences, and organisations need to match skills and competences to job or task responsibilities (Schein 1978). Individual careers are carved out within the context of sectors of economic activity and organisations within them (Collin 1986, Evetts 1992 Gunz 1989). For the NHS this context has been one of rapid change, reducing hierarchies and organisational fragmentation. This chapter presents findings concerning the careers of our respondents and illustrates relationships between individual careers and organisational change.

The study focuses on managerial careers and the managerial component of clinical managers' jobs. It does not address clinical careers as such. Complementary but more detailed studies, under the general title of 'Creative Career Paths in the NHS' were being undertaken by IHSM consultants at the same time as this study (1994). There is broad consensus between the findings of the two studies.

The chapter is divided into the following sections:

- Paths to Executive Positions in Purchasing and Providing.

- Reasons for Choices Made in Careers

- The Impact of the NHS Restructuring on Careers

- Career Aspirations

- Career Discontinuities and Career Management

- Summary

3.1 Paths to Executive Positions in Purchasing and Providing

Education and Qualifications

Table 3.1 shows the level of qualifications achieved by respondents who are currently in general, functional or clinical management. Sixty nine per cent of respondents had at least graduate level qualifications. This figure included 82% of clinical managers, reflecting the predominance of medically qualified staff in this group. Other studies support the finding that significant proportions of managers in the UK are increasingly well-qualified (Scase & Goffee 1989). In their survey of 374 managers, of whom 323 are men and 51 women, Scase and Goffee found that 37% of the women had university degrees, whereas this was the case for only 22% of the men. The higher qualifications of the women reported in the Scase and Goffee study fits with the findings of this study and other studies of the NHS (IHSM Consultants 1994).

Table 3.2 shows the subject matter of qualifications obtained. Almost 50% of both graduate and postgraduate qualifications are in medicine, with the next largest group of each being in the social sciences and humanities. Seventeen per cent of those with post graduate qualifications held them in management. This group was disproportionately drawn from functional rather than general managers. It reflects functional managers' increasing involvement in management as they reach higher levels within their functional area and suggests that formal management qualifications are seen as an important route out of functional into general management top positions. One respondent commented:

"Professional training was very useful... may do an MBA as a stepping stone" (functional manager, provider, board level)

Table 3.1   *Levels of Educational Qualifications (Qu.A9)*

Present Job Present Job Level of qualifications obtained	GM (n=16) %	FM (n=44) %	CM (n=108) %	All (n=168) %
a) Below Graduate level	34	33	18	31
b) Graduate Level	66	67	82	69
c) Postgraduate Masters or Professional qualifications	22	20	43	28
d) Postgraduate Doctorate	3	2	13	7

Notes:

Respondents are only counted once in either row (a) or (b). Respondents with appropriate qualifications are counted in rows (c) and (d) as appropriate.

Key:

GM = General Manager: FM = Functional Manager: CM = Clinical Manager

Table 3.2   *Subject of Educational Qualifications (Qu.A9)*

	Graduate (n = 172) %	Taught Postgraduate (n = 77) %
Medical	48	49
Nursing	3	1
Management	2	17
Social Science/Humanities	29	18
Natural Science/Engineering	10	4
Other	8	11
	100	**100**

Experience of Work Prior to Present Position

Forty per cent of respondents said that they had experience of work outside the NHS. Of this 40%, 78% had acquired this experience prior to joining the NHS, and 50% (54) had gained it in other public sector organisations. 20% of the sample had had experience of the 'private' sector, largely in the provision of services rather than in manufacturing or process industries. Table 3.3 summarises respondents' outside work experience and shows that significantly more functional than general or clinical managers have worked outside the NHS.

Table 3.3   *Work Experience Outside the NHS (Qu.A13)*

Outside Work Experience?	GM (n=117) %	FM (n=46) %	CM (n=108) %	All (n=271) %
*Yes	41	74	24	40
*No	59	26	76	60
	100	100	100	100

* statistically significant differences were identified between GM (general manager), FM (functional manager) and CM (clinical manager) respondents at p < 0.05

The following quote shows the relative ease with which functional managers have in the past been able to move across public service organisations:

"Joined [local authority] as graduate trainee accountant, qualified in '74 and moved to another LA as principal accountant. 1979 became Assistant Borough Treasurer and Treasurer in 1981. Joined NHS at Region-level in 1983. 1984 became Deputy Regional Treasurer, 1985 District Treasurer, 1988 Director of Finance at HA" (functional manager, purchaser, board level)

Outside experience was much less likely amongst clinical managers (largely those with 'roots' as doctors, nurses and other health professionals). Where the clinicians had outside work experience it was usually in other health care systems overseas, with a small minority having full time experience of private health care in the UK.

The relative advantages and disadvantages of career experience outside the NHS is a moot point. In our sample, over a third had experience of working in other organisations. This finding is supported by the Creative Career Path Study wherein:

"Thirty per cent of respondents had spent at least 80% of their careers outside the NHS. The 'incoming' managers had predominantly financial and technical/support qualifications" (IHSM Consultants, 1994).

Willcocks and Harrow (1992) argue that one of the noticeable features of the British public services is that public service managers have little experience of managing other types of organisations. Certainly among the general managers within our study, most of the outside experience was not in the private sector so that skills, now pertinent to the NHS, like strategic planning and marketing were having to be developed 'on the job' or bought in via 'incoming' managers.

An examination of experience within the NHS shows that 88% of respondents had gained their previous experience in the provision of health care at local hospital and community level. 14% had regional experience and 4% experience at a national level (Department of Health or NHSME) (Table 3.4).

Table 3.4   *NHS Experience prior to present position (Qu. A7, A. 21-23)*

	All (n=271) %
District level	88
Regional level	14
National level	4

Note:
Respondents were classified in as many levels as they have had experience.

Characteristics of people in executive positions and their consequences for career paths

It was of particular interest to examine the characteristics of the executive directors who had been appointed to the new purchasing and providing organisations, and those who had been appointed to fill positions which reported directly to board members. Thirty five per cent of respondents held executive director positions on the boards of their organisations. Table 3.5 summarises the differences found between levels on the basis of gender and background.

It must be remembered that the middle level in Table 3.5 includes all clinical directors (or equivalent) who, whilst reporting to executive directors in terms of the management and operations of their services, nonetheless may be consultants who, with or without merit awards, may be receiving comparable or higher salaries than the executive directors.

The gender profile of the executive population at levels 1, 2 and 3, shown in Table 3.5, broadly reflects the position found elsewhere in the NHS as a whole. Although women form the majority of the workforce, they are significantly under-represented at the top (Goss and Brown 1991, Brown and Goss 1993, NHSME 1993). Below executive level the difference is less stark. This snapshot tends to confirm the existence of a 'glass ceiling' regarding the advancement of women to executive positions. It also reflects differences between occupational groups, with nurses, and other health professionals, being significantly underrepresented in the higher managerial levels in comparison to doctors.

Table 3.5 *Characteristics of people at different levels*

	Level 1 (n=93) %	Level 2/3 (n=153) %	Level 4+ (n=25) %	All (n=271) %
*Gender				
Female	26	38	80	38
Male	74	62	20	62
	100	100	100	100
*Background				
General Management	34	23	12	26
Functional Management	28	15	8	19
Medical Doctor	24	41	0	31
Nurse	13	12	60	17
Other Health Professional	1	10	20	8
	100	100	100	100

Notes:

* statistically significant differences were identified between respondents by gender and by background at p < 0.05

+ this group of people were all in providing organisations. It will be recalled they were especially sought out in order to increase the numbers of nurses and OHP with managerial responsibilities. It is therefore unlikely to be representative of this level generally and may overstate gender differences.

Key:
Level 1 = Executive Board Members
Level 2/3 = Directors & Managers Reporting to Board
Level 4 = Managers Reporting to Level 2/3

The challenge to 'increase the quality and quantity of women's participation in the workforce' has been taken up by the NHS with the Opportunity 2000 initiative (NHSME 1992, 1992a, 1993, 1994). Support for women in senior management in the NHS includes initiatives such as the NHS Career Development Register jointly run by the NHS and Ashridge Management College. While attempts are being made to support women developing their professional and managerial careers within the NHS, the organisational implications of changing structures in favour of clinical directorates led by a clinical director may prove to be an additional barrier to their career progression (Mark 1991). For general managers, opportunities to develop within the middle management tiers of provider organisations, in particular, have decreased in the restructured NHS.

Following discussions with the Project Advisory Committee our study made a particular effort to access health professionals, other than doctors, who were in senior managerial positions. However, only 1% of the executive directors whom we interviewed came from an 'other health professional' background. Twelve executive directors came from a nursing background of whom 10 were nurse directors on Trust boards, and only 2 were executive directors in DHAs. There is no requirement for a nursing presence on the board of DHAs although there is a wish in the NHSE to see more nursing participation at that level (NHSE 1994a) The proportion of doctors found at executive director level is largely accounted for by the requirements for Trust boards to include a doctor and the fact that the majority of DHAs have elected to include a Director of Public Health or equivalent on their Boards (Cairncross, Ashburner and Pettigrew 1991). Only one chief executive whom we interviewed had a medical background. She was a CEO of a District Health Authority.

The age profile of the executive director respondents shows 11% to be under 35, 44% to be 35–44, 37% to be 45–54 and 9% to be 55 or over. This suggests that the trend toward early retirement at 55 in the wider economy is being reflected within the health service.

In looking at previous work experience there was little to distinguish people currently occupying different levels in the management hierarchy, except slightly more executive directors had some outside work experience, usually before joining the NHS. However, there was a marked difference in their pattern of experience within the NHS. Twenty five per cent of executive board directors had some work experience at regional level, compared with only 8% of non board executives. This reflects the previous importance of Region in the career hierarchy of general and functional management; an importance that is probably less significant now with the creation of the internal market. With RHAs being replaced by a considerably smaller number of Regional Offices of the NHS Executive, it is likely that the percentage with regional experience will decline. The extent to which working experience at regional level will be necessary or important in the leap up to board membership is uncertain.

3.2 Reasons for Choices Made in Careers

All respondents were asked why they decided to become a doctor/nurse/other health professional/manager in the NHS. Respondents were asked to think about their initial choice of career, rather than any subsequent switches within the NHS. The responses are shown in Table 3.6.

Family influences were cited as important by significantly more doctors and nurses than other groups. Often one or other of the parents of doctors and nurses were, or had been, health professionals of some kind. For example,

"I come from a nursing family. We lived where there are a lot of elderly people, and I used to visit them, just wanted to do it" (clinical manager, provider)

"My father was a surgeon and it just happened I followed him. I literally don't remember thinking about it." (clinical director, provider)

Table 3.6 *Influences in Initial Career Choice*

Why did you decide to become a Doctor / Nurse / NHS Manager? (Qu. A8)

	Purchaser Respondents (n=83) %	Provider Respondents (n=139) %	Total (n=222) %
Family	19	18	19
*Nature of the Work	13	28	23
Ambition/Status Opportunity	15	29	23
*Public Service Values	30	17	22
Attractive environment/Conditions	19	17	18
Reorganisation	6	1	3
Chance	29	20	23

* statistically significant differences were identified between purchaser and provider respondents at $p < 0.05$

Note:
1. Respondents could identify more than one influence.

The nature of the work itself emerged as a more significant influence for doctors than for other groups. A number of respondents mentioned wanting to be a doctor from quite a young age:

"Wanted to be a doctor since age 17" (clinical manager, provider)

"Wanted to be a doctor since little" (clinical manager, provider)

Public service values were cited as significant for more general than functional and clinical managers and for more of those who had gone to work in purchasing rather than providing organisations. For example,

"I decided on management after graduating and set up a number of interviews - public service values were important to me and health seemed to be a rewarding career" (general manager, purchaser, level below board)

"I was interested in public services management, I'd done holiday jobs in industry and I wasn't impressed." (executive director, purchaser)

"I really do care about trying to make the health service as good as possible." (clinical manager, purchaser, below board)

Significantly more respondents with a functional management than other backgrounds mentioned the importance of an attractive environment and working conditions:

"I was attracted by the variety of the work and a vocational thing too, as an engineer I have a wide scope in the NHS" (functional manager, provider, board level)

'Chance' or 'luck' was significant for more general and functional managers than other backgrounds. For example, one respondent commented:

"It was not a conscious decision to join NHS - thinking of banking or teaching, youth club leader was a member of HA so put me in touch with group secretary who had a job at the time, loved it and never wanted to do anything else" (general manager, purchaser, board level)

Why clinicians entered management

Given the interest of this project in the involvement of clinical staff in managerial activities, all clinicians were asked when and why they first took on managerial responsibility. The term 'management responsibility' is broad, and for some nurses, for example, it was interpreted to refer to their becoming a staff nurse. Similarly for some doctors it was seen as an inevitable part of being a consultant. However, in discussion the interviewer emphasised that respondents should consider the reasons for accepting particular or designated management responsibility, even though this may only be a fairly small component of their total job. Our sample was selected on the basis that everyone interviewed had a particular managerial role or set of responsibilities and it was to these that we directed respondents' attention.

The results are summarised in Tables 3.7 and 3.8. The total number of respondents for some cells in Table 3.7 is relatively small and therefore it should be treated with caution. The majority of respondents who had medical or nursing qualifications are located in providing rather than purchasing organisations. Nurses and other health professionals take on managerial responsibility earlier and at a lower level than doctors. Reflecting this finding, we also find that proportionately more women than men took on managerial responsibility earlier and at a lower level.

Table 3.7 *Age of Clinicians when first taking Managerial Responsibility (Qu.B.1)*

Background

Age	Doctor (N = 68) %	Nurse (N = 26) %	OHP (N = 11) %	Total (N = 94) %
25 – 34	28	65	82	43
35 – 44	47	23	18	38
45 – 54	25	12	0	19
	100	100	100	100

When asked for the reasons for taking on managerial responsibility, 36% said it was because of promotion. Twenty eight per cent said it was because they were interested in management and/or wanted to be involved in decision making. Twenty five per cent said it was because they were 'next in line' in terms of seniority or they had held a previous position of responsibility (eg Chair of the medical staff committee). Finally, 16% said that there was an element of either default (there was no one else to do it or the role just evolved) often with encouragement from others prompted by concerns to prevent someone else from taking the position. Table 3.8 summarises the responses, divided by the purchaser and provider organisations.

Statistically significant different responses to Qu.B2 were identified as follows. More respondents with a background in nursing rather than medicine cited their interest in management and their wish to move away from clinical work as reasons for taking on managerial responsibility. Proportionately more women expressed this view also.

"I always wanted to be a nurse, had career planned out but had not banked on Griffiths [general management] - if you can't beat them, then join them" (general manager, provider, board level)

The unavoidable managerial demands associated with clinical positions was, not surprisingly only cited by provider respondents, with more doctors than nurses and health professionals, and more men than women, identifying this as a reason for taking on managerial responsibility.

"Began four years ago, as Chair of Division inherited title and consent of colleagues.... just been re-appointed, no-one else came forward" (clinical manager, provider)

Proportionately more purchaser than provider respondents, and more responses from those with an other health professional background than nurses and doctors cited promotion as their reason for involvement in management. Proportionately more doctors cited the 'no-one else to do it' reason for their involvement in managerial activity.

Table 3.8 *Clinicians: Reasons for Undertaking Managerial Responsibility*

Qu.B.2 Why did you take on this managerial responsibility?

	Purchaser Respondents (n=15) %	Provider Respondents (n=84) %	All Respondents (n=99) %
Dominant Responses			
interest in management	27	29	28
*position demanded it	0	30	25
*promotion	73	30	36
no-one to do it	0	19	16

statistically significant differences were identified between purchaser and provider respondents at p < 0.05

Notes:
1. Respondents could mention more than one reason.
2. Mentions with frequencies lower than 3% excluded.

The findings shown in Table 3.8 reflect the different organisational forms and hierarchical structures between purchaser and provider organisations. The dominant health professional involvement in purchasing is through public health appointments and positions which are straightforwardly managerial. Purchaser respondents and other health professionals are more likely to have taken on managerial responsibilities through promotion to a more senior position within their field or specialty or to other managerial jobs. For clinical specialties in provider organisations, position within the specialty group and/or being next in line in terms of seniority are reasons for doctors becoming more involved in managerial activity, albeit reluctantly in some cases.

3.3   The Impact of NHS Restructuring on Careers

Interviewees were asked whether the recent restructuring in the NHS had effected the way in which they thought about their careers. They were also asked to comment on the nature of any effect. Table 3.9 summarises their responses.

Thirty eight per cent of respondents interviewed felt that the recent restructuring in the NHS had had a positive effect on the way they thought about their career. Twenty four percent felt that there had been no effect and twenty percent were unsure of the effect. Only sixteen percent felt the effect had been negative on their career. More purchasers (47%) thought the effects were positive and less (19%) that they were negative, compared to providers.

"I came into purchasing as a deliberate career move, saw unique opportunity to make changes and not go on responding to demand" (general manager, purchaser, board level).

More respondents in providing were uncertain about the effect than those in purchasing. More interviewees below the age of 45 felt positive (41%) and more felt uncertain (24%) than those aged 45 and above, more of whom were negative (23%).

Examples of feelings of uncertainty came from a variety of respondents,

"In the present climate it's difficult to know what a sensible career development path is because traditional assumptions and aspirations have disappeared and there's so much uncertainty. Now we don't know how things are going to work out with the DHA, FHSA and GPFHs." (general manager, purchaser, below board level).

"Yes, the internal market has shot a hole across traditional career paths and has made me think again, there is not a clear next step." (executive director, provider).

"Current job market makes it difficult to move between the two (Purchasing/Providing) and its difficult to move up the ladder. Even if I could get into purchasing, it looks very difficult to get back the other way." (general manager, provider, below board).

"(restructuring has) meant a restriction in the number and type of jobs available and the potential for promotion." (executive director, purchaser).

"The purchaser/provider split means there's less flexibility between roles." (general manager, purchaser below 'board level').

"...... It's created a split and forced people down one of two roads." (executive director, provider).

"The whole nature of the internal market makes career paths more volatile, we can no longer think of it as a steady progression. Now we're at the whim of others, GPs, purchasers .... I don't really have any ambitions, I'm interested in survival, not progression." (clinical manager, provider, 2 levels below board).

In contrast, a general manager in purchasing agency saw change as, on balance, positive,

"Now there's less security and rather brutal redundancies and sackings and I don't like that, and they would have been unthinkable 5 or 10 years ago. But with less security things are more fluid. Far greater acceptance that it is not necessarily just up a ladder; people can now look to do things which interest them. I'm not thinking now what is my next career move, more what can I contribute and where can I contribute it. How you'll get to the top may be changing. I hope it is ...."

This sort of ambivalence, verging to positive, was also found in providing:

"I feel much less secure but I'm excited, its not totally damaging but its definitely more of a gamble than 20 years ago." (general manager, provider, below board).

Others were more clear cut in their positive views,

"There's more scope now in my career and for my personal development ... its less bureaucratic, less outside interference and I feel its up to me to make a success of my job and I feel I can." (general manager, provider, below board).

"Yes, its created opportunities in health care and health provision, its enriched career opportunities quite significantly. The thought of moving into health commissioning has a lot of attraction, its intellectually challenging, and different to the operational challenges here." (CEO, provider).

Table 3.9 *The Impact of NHS restructuring on Career (Qu.J.1)*

	Purchaser respondents (n=98) %	Provider respondents (n=134) %	Total (n=232) %
No effect	20	29	24
positive effect	47	31	38
negative effect	19	14	16
unsure, both positive and negative	13	25	20
	99	**99**	**98**

Significantly more general and functional managers felt the effects were positive than did clinical managers.

"Yes, it's given us a new dimension, we need to develop new skills to do it effectively – til then there's a danger we aspire to be providers. Now looking at being CEO in purchaser or provider, or in social services/FHSA – DoH is not as insular as it was and given new breadth to options". (general manager, purchaser, board level)

"Yes, 6 years ago would have thought I was aiming to be hospital general manager. But next move will be Director of Purchasing in DHA/ Director of Contracting in hospital unit. I will stay on the contracting side". (general manager, purchaser, level below board)

Twenty-three percent of clinical managers considered the effects as negative, 36% that they had no effect and 29% that the effects were positive. It is the presence of a significant proportion of clinical managers in providing organisations which accounts for differences between purchasers and provider organisations in this respect.

"Yes, job has changed substantially - do not believe in the market, commercial model does not fit easily with the NHS. It's not in tune with centrally-driven, political priorities which actually dictate what we do". (director of public health, purchaser)

Proportionately more of those at director level were positive (46%) about the effect of the reforms than those at other levels (30%) in the organisations involved in the study. Proportionately more of those below director level (22%) were negative than were the directors.

One respondent in purchasing described his negative view of change,

"In all this change we're seeing a lot of skill, competence, ability and energy wasted; sidetracked into fruitless power debates and jostling for position throughout the country."

3.4   Career Aspirations

Table 3.10 summarises the responses to the open ended question 'how would you like your career to develop in the future?' Given this was an open ended question it is interesting to note the range of responses. 40% were content either to have no advancement or to develop their existing role with out changing jobs; 25% had their sights set on a top level position; 21% would like to move out of the NHS and 11% to move to another NHS organisation.

Whereas 45% of those with a background in general management feel they will 'aim for the top', 38% of those with a nursing background felt they would like to move out of the NHS.

Significantly more respondents with nursing or OHP background, more women (28%) than men (16%) and more of those from older (55-64) than younger (54 and under) age groups wanted to move out of the NHS. This finding highlights points made earlier about trends toward retiring at 55 or earlier and how the restructuring in the NHS has affected the position of women, and especially nurses. The perceived lack of career opportunities within the NHS has meant that a substantial proportion of nurses, even those now in managerial positions, are thinking about their career in terms broader than the NHS.

Table 3.10   *Career Aspirations*

How would you like your career to develop? (Qu.J2)

Background: Career Aspiration	GM n=67 %	FM n=51 %	Dr. n=78 %	Nr n=42 %	OHP n=20 %	All n=258 %
(a) *No advancement	12	24	26	10	20	19
(b) *Develop existing role	18	33	13	24	20	21
(c) *Aim for the Top	45	22	17	19	15	25
(d) Move into General Management	0	12	6	5	30	7
(e) *Move out of Management	2	0	34	0	5	11
(f) Move to other NHS Organisations	15	20	6	19	10	14
(g) *Move out of NHS	15	16	17	38	30	21
(h) Unsure	13	10	5	26	25	13

* statistically significant differences were identified between respondents from different backgrounds at $p < 0.05$

Notes:
1. Respondents could identify more than one career aspiration.

Key
GM : General Manager
FM : Functional Manager
Dr. : Doctor
Nr. : Nurse
OHP: Other health professional

Clinically qualified staff and their career aspirations in management

This study found evidence that the traditional professional status differentials that have existed between doctors and nurses are being reproduced in the new management structures, with doctors taking on the higher positions in management, and nurses fitting into support roles. This and other concerns raised by nurses in management are presented here.

In the interviews, nurses expressed considerable concerns that they found it difficult to see how they could develop their careers; hence the 38% with a nursing background who said they would like to move out of the NHS. Comments from a nurse manager and a nurse who has moved into general management are indicative:

"... the structure I wanted to progress in is not there any more" (nurse manager)

"Have moved from nursing into education and education management, not really got plans from here, difficult to know where to go" (general manager, provider, level below board)

Fears were expressed by nurses that they were losing out in both the professional and managerial career paths. Some felt that in the old world it was not difficult for them to become relatively senior in unit management teams, but now they were more likely to be in a career cul de sac. At the national centre of the NHS they saw that the nursing role was to ensure professional standards and provide professional advice. However they felt that their role at senior levels in regions, Trusts and DHAs was more difficult to define and enhance. Many Trusts are now seeking to combine the nurse presence on the board with other executive positions, for example, human resources where the executive director may have a nursing background. This, it is feared by nurses, may leave a gap in professional leadership. For example, comments from two different Directors of Nursing address this point,

".... [it is the problem of the] professional management and general management divide. The Sister or nurse manager role at directorate level is very different from the Director of Nursing role, so there is a big gap there. We need different types of nurse role to move from nurse manager to Director of Nursing [for nurses to gain] the progression of behaviours required and experience of issues to be dealt with"

"I wanted to develop professionally and not managerially, but now I find elements of the job which I think are important are being eroded ....sometimes the job seems almost untenable .... and maybe I should be thinking of doing something different."

At the same time, nurses moving into business manager posts require adequate management development and training. One clinical manager with a nursing background noted:

"nursing officers are becoming business managers but do not have adequate training – I am deeply worried about the intermediate level."

A Director of Nursing made a similar point,

"There's a big gap between where nurses are and board level positions. I'm worried that able nurses don't get the experience to function at board level and I can't see how we can give them that experience."

Comparatively few respondents (11%) want to move out of management and yet stay in the NHS but, such as it is, this group is disproportionately found in providing organisations, and amongst those with a medical background. Thirty four per cent of those with a medical background want to move out of management. Proportionately more of those with a medical rather than a nursing or general management background, felt there was no further advancement for them in management. Some doctors wanted to return to being a full-time clinician, seeing their managerial role as a temporary part of their career.

"I have no aspirations to develop further as a manager, I do it as a clinician because someone has to"

"People climb trees in their careers and I have no desire to climb a managerial tree.'

"I need to get used to the role, its probably two years before you know what the role really is, so I will carry on past three year term but I also need to see logical end point, not do it for ever"

"I want my management career to come to an end ... everything is hassle and frustration.'

"I've enjoyed doing what I've done but I would not want to develop a managerial role as a permanent feature of my work"

"Now I look at jobs elsewhere, which I never thought I'd do as a consultant. Its all very destructive and demotivating. Its changed my aspirations. I'm now looking forward to retirement.'

"I want to go back to my clinical job full-time and retire as soon as possible.'

Given the concerns to attract and involve more clinically qualified staff in management, these findings suggest that there are considerable problems in seeking to achieve this aim. We have here a group of clinically qualified staff who are involved in management; 34% of those with medical qualifications want to move out of management and 38% of those with nursing qualifications want to move out of the NHS. The clinical directors in our sample were almost all on three year contracts, and our finding suggests that a third of those will be glad when their term of office is over and they can return to being full-time clinicians. This immediately raises the question of whether there will be people equipped and eager to take their place. This probably depends on whether sufficient doctors come into contact with enthusiastic clinical directors whom we found to be just as positive about the experience as some of their colleagues were negative,

"It's great, we're doing well, I want all clinicians in the directorate to have some exposure to management, so they can contribute managerially."

"I don't want to stop being a doctor – I'm well paid and secure and wouldn't want to give that up ... but I want to get the management system working well – it is a total change of culture and a new game and interest, and we're seeing the benefits of it for patients."

Functional and General Managers and their Career Aspirations

Functional managers in common with those in medical management were proportionately more likely to feel there was no further advancement for them, compared to those in general management. This reflects the relative proportions in each group who felt they had got to the top as well as those lower down who felt there was no further advancement. However some were positive about not wanting further advancement currently, for example feeling there was enough challenge and excitement just keeping pace with the speed at which jobs are evolving, especially in purchasing.

"I have no career aspirations above the level of the job, no desire to be general manager. Not looking at other finance jobs in providers or at Region, see the potential evolving in purchasing but will take a number of years" (functional manager, purchaser, board level)

"Job has changed around me so I have not got bored. One thing begin to ask oneself is how much longer I can go on at these pace and stress levels and that takes over from career aspirations" (general manager, purchaser, board level)

Significantly more of those with a functional management than other backgrounds were concerned to develop their existing role. Again the speed of change and restructuring within the NHS has meant that jobs in functional areas like finance and information have expanded enormously. Respondents commented:

"[Restructuring] made it less clear-cut than it used to be – we're forced to go down more specialist avenues. [Restructuring] has broadened and raised the profile of the role of finance director, so boosted career prospects and pay but made it less secure also – difficult to be too prescriptive about my career but I'm aiming to be Director of Finance" (functional manager, purchaser, below board level)

"Within providers, information is a smaller cog in the wheel and more specialised so not a chance to dip into what others do – within purchasing my job is quite relevant to lots of other areas so able to learn about everything. This job was ahead of me. I am content with this for the time being, there is a steep enough learning curve" (functional manager, purchaser, level below board)

Significantly more of those with a general management background said they were aiming for the top. Generally, this was described in terms of CEO position rather than a move to Region, the Department of Health or NHS Executive. Attention was drawn to the uncertainty of career routes to the top. For example:

"I am looking for CEO role now, move to a smaller unit - would like to be No.1 shortly" (general manager, provider, board level)

"Aspire to be CEO of purchasing organisation but prior to that need time out to gain robust record of operational management and there is the dilemma because at this level it is not easy to jump across the purchaser/provider divide" (general manager, purchaser, board level)

Respondents were asked about the sorts of experiences and qualifications required to achieve their career aspirations (Qu.J.3). Many felt that qualifications were an important route to the top. Specifically formal qualifications were mentioned at senior management level:

"I'm about to launch into an MBA, you need formal qualifications if you want to rise higher. Looking around for a good personal development course but not many of those around." (general manager, purchaser, board level)

"I lack general management experience in the health service. I need qualifications to compete with NHS managers and have done a two year Diploma accredited to the IHSM. I am looking at an MSc in Social Policy which gives a broad background in health studies including the NHS, epidemiology and management skills - it offers the sort of grounding senior people in purchasing need". (general manager, purchaser, level below board)

For those aware of their learning needs and content to stay within purchasing or providing, the moves required to secure their career aspirations were relatively clear:

"It is difficult to plan ahead, you do not know what the world will be like, I hope I am moving towards CEO of commissioning organisation. Need to strengthen understanding of financial management issues, strategic management, be able to do experimental stuff ie. exercise role in a safe environment" (general manager, purchaser, board level)

3.5   Career Discontinuities and Career Management

Career Discontinuities: Breaking Down the Barriers

The NHS is no longer one large bureaucracy. However in some senses it displays features which arguably suggest a large conglomerate, for example, one national CEO, one national policy group and executive, one source of public funds and a common and occasionally highly directed and interventionist, regulatory framework. Yet in other senses the NHS is more accurately described as the overlaying, controlling regulator in a sector of the economy rather than one organisation. It is, after all, a federation of different types of organisations which variously compete, collaborate and cooperate within a regulated market.

From the point of view of careers, however, whether it is a vast conglomerate organisation or a collection of key players in various parts of a service sector, one would expect people to be able to make sense of their careers within the NHS by movement between the parts. Indeed one can argue that it is vitally important for both managers' careers and the effective performance of the NHS that cross fertilisation of ideas and skills, through movement of personnel between the various constituent parts of the NHS, is secured. However we have seen that barriers are felt to exist in the restructured NHS. In particular two dominant career barriers are identified by the respondents in this study:

(i)   professional qualifications, background and experience,

(ii)   organisational boundaries which exist primarily between purchasers and providers, but also between purchasers, between providers, and between local, regional and national organisations.

In terms of the first barrier the critical incidents of effective management identified by respondents and discussed further in Chapter 5, picked up a number of examples of attempts to improve performance through the re-examination of the professional qualifications needed to do various tasks, for example where nurses were undertaking tasks previously the preserve of the medical profession. Despite such innovations many clinical professional barriers will probably continue to be seen as desirable; with team working as the way forward, rather than too much emphasis on multi-skilling. There was also some evidence of people being able to cross functional boundaries between managerial departments. There was, however, also concern amongst some that within certain managerial domains, e.g. finance or contracting it was difficult to gain exposure to a broad range of managerial skills with gradually increasing amounts of responsibility.

The second type of barrier, created by the internal market, regional restructuring and decentralisation was of more immediate importance to many of our managers. For example:

"Up until three years ago I had the belief that I would always keep going as long as I was happy. Now region is out and at provider management level there are only two jobs – CEO or same post

in bigger unit. Will stay here for next few years then think more broadly about areas to move into – not career plan as such, maybe teaching, maybe something completely different" (executive director, provider)

It was clear that amongst our managers gaining a breadth of experience across purchasing and providing was problematic:

"I aspire to be the CEO of a purchasing organisation but prior to that I need time out to gain a robust record of operational management and there is the dilemma because at this level it is not easy to jump across the purchaser provider divide. My weakness as a senior planning manager is that unless I set my feet in the soil of delivering services, as a purchaser my work is not as relevant as it should be..." (general manager, purchaser)

"In the current job market it is difficult to move between the two [purchasing and providing]. It's difficult to move up the ladder at the moment. I would like to get to a senior position in providing (run a unit) then move to purchasing, but if I made the shift now I would not get back. It's possible to move from providing to purchasing but not back again." (general manager, provider, level below board)

"Purchaser/provider split means there is less flexibility between roles. From a personal point of view, I am committed to purchasing but would not mind experience in provider." (general manager, purchaser, level below board)

"I previously worked for provider and now work for a purchaser. I want flexibility to swap between them and think it important because it is easy to forget pragmatic difficulties of managing change in a large organisation full of professionals. People in provider organisation would gain enormously from experience in a purchaser. I have things I want to do, for example – become CEO of a Community organisation, I want to be involved in healthcare in the third-world, but I'm not sure how yet." (general manager, purchaser, board level).

"I'd like to go back to a provider but I'm not sure whether they'd have me now. Would my profile fit? even though they have contracting of course. There is a mismatch because of hierarchy and organisational level. The DHA is small and flat, Trusts are large and hierarchical." (general manager, purchaser, below board level)

Some functional managers were reassessing their future as a result of the restructuring and were considering whether to develop in purchaser or provider organisations.

"My career assumption was to become Director of Finance but don't know yet how I would like to develop within the new regime... do I want to become a general manager, in a purchaser or in a provider? I think longer term future rests with a NHS Trust. Development needs: more

experience at board level to develop out of finance into broader areas, thinking in wider vein with a high degree of success. Same thing applies at a Trust, I'll need communication and interpersonal skills at that level" (functional manager, purchaser, board level).

For others the future was unclear, and moves from local to regional level were more of a problem:

"I do not have clear path because of what I do, the only jump is into general management but I enjoy what I do in HR - I would be happy to move if the right thing came along. I would have been happy to go to Region but those career paths have disappeared now" (functional manager, provider, board level)

These managers clearly felt that they needed some help to bridge the barriers between functions and between organisations, and it is to this we turn in the next section, using the analogy with the climbing frame.

The Climbing Frame as a tool for career management

Findings from our study illustrate how respondents have made sense of the organisational changes in the NHS in terms of their careers. For some, organisational change has opened up opportunities, for others it has closed doors. Many respondents were asking themselves "where do I go from here?" and "how do I get the experience I need to take me to different jobs, different levels and different organisations?". In order to address the needs of all groups, it is important to be able to illustrate links between career opportunities within and between organisations and individual career aspirations. In this section we introduce the concept of the 'climbing frame' to link the shape of individual careers to the organisations in which the careers are made (Gunz 1989 (a) & (b)).

It is possible to conceptualise both vertical and horizontal career tracks (Arthur et al. 1989, Tyson & Jackson 1992). Vertical careers reflect movements up through the management layers of an organisation and are based on formal authority. Horizontal careers may involve movement between different types of work and may be based on increments of prestige, expertise or experience. Using the climbing frame as metaphor, people usually enter at its lower levels and move from rung to rung as vacancies arise. Sometimes the rungs are higher, sometimes they are at the same level but in a different part of the frame, and sometimes they may be lower. Schein's (1978) model of careers adds a movement towards the centre, termed 'the inner circle' or the core of the occupation or organisation. Together these models can help us to conceptualise the increasingly multi-dimensional nature of careers in and between organisations.

Understanding the shapes of career climbing frames within organisations, helps senior executives to make sense of the possible career patterns open to them and to others and can thus provide a framework for career planning, career counselling and succession planning. Charlwood (1994) has shown in outline the relevance of the climbing frame metaphor to the NHS.

The outline of a climbing frame has been constructed for the NHS in Figure 3.1. It is three dimensional. The first two dimensions: professional qualifications and background, and location within different organisations within the NHS, illustrate the existence of the barriers which derive from the boundaries between professions, functions and organisations. The third dimension is of demonstrable competence. In many ways it is on the basis of this third dimension that movement is most likely to be facilitated between organisations, between levels and between professional and functional groups.

Each dimension will be briefly discussed.

i) **Professional qualifications, background and experience**
People's positions on this dimension (i.e. to which columns in Figure 3.1 do they have access?) is answered by the question "in which areas do you have professional qualifications or experience?". The choice of senior employees in the NHS on this dimension is dictated by their qualifications and experience. For example, a consultant with an MBA with experience as a clinical director would locate herself in both the Doctor and General Management columns and could arguably be ready to take positions which depended on either or both these qualifications. Whereas a consultant with only medical qualifications or experience would be firmly placed within the medical column.

Movement between these columns is facilitated by acquiring different professional qualifications or experience. Whilst it is easy to define entry barriers to medicine and nursing, management is less easily defined and can be entered through experience alone, without qualifications. But as we saw earlier, people participating in this research felt, that in the NHS, management qualifications help to make such moves. Figure 3.1 is intended to be illustrative; not all professional and functional backgrounds are included, for example, columns could be added for PAMs, information management, human resource management and other managerial functions. Furthermore, it is acknowledged that a significant number of

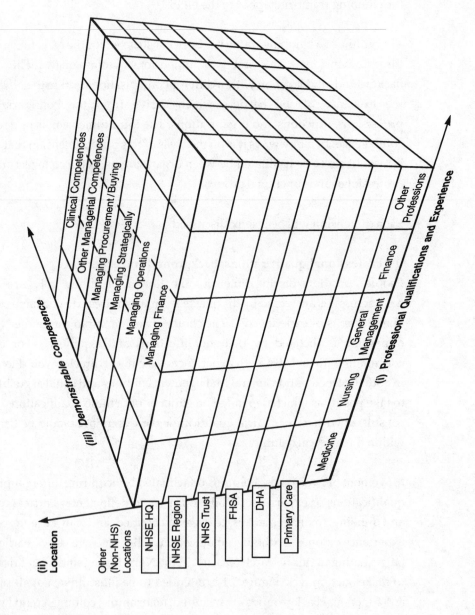

Figure 3.1 *A Career Climbing Frame for the NHS*

(i) Professional Qualifications and Experience

- Medicine
- Nursing
- General Management
- Finance
- Other Professions

(ii) Location

- Other (Non-NHS) Locations
- NHSE HQ
- NHSE Region
- NHS Trust
- FHSA
- DHA
- Primary Care

(iii) Demonstrable Competence

- Clinical Competences
- Other Managerial Competences
- Managing Procurement/Buying
- Managing Strategically
- Managing Operations
- Managing Finance

jobs require a combination of professional backgrounds e.g. medicine or nursing and general or functional management.

In looking to the future, it would be advisable to consider the relevance of professional backgrounds which have traditionally not been represented in the NHS, since it may be that a background in social work, voluntary agency administration or public relations may become increasingly relevant for some NHS jobs in the future.

ii) **Location of job**

People's positions on this dimension (i.e. to which rows in Figure 3.1 do they have access?) is answered by the questions "where do you work now?" and "where have you worked in the past?". Executives in the NHS may work in general practice, health authorities, Trusts, or the Executive. (There will be changes in the designation of health authorities, if DHAs and FHSAs are merged as planned and RHAs disappear). We saw that only a small minority of our respondents had experience of work at regional or national level. A further and probably bigger boundary here is between the NHS and private or overseas health care systems or indeed non- health care sectors. The world outside the NHS is the periphery of this frame and was not the subject of this research. However, we would suggest that movement between the NHS and other parts of health and social care is likely to become more frequent and therefore the implications of such developments need to be considered by both individuals and organisations.

iii) **Individual skills and competences**

People's positions on this dimension (i.e. to which slices in Figure 3.1 do they have access?) is dependent upon their areas and levels of demonstrated competence, which derive, but are distinct from, their experience, training and location. The distinction is that qualification is sometimes a necessary, but never a sufficient condition for actually being able to put knowledge and training into effective practice. The slices are illustrated in Figure 3.1 in generic terms of managing financial resources, managing people, managing operations, managing strategically, managing procurement and buying. Other managerial competences could, of course, be added and then there are also all the clinical vocational competences which may be demonstrated by doctors, nurses and PAMs. As this study was not concerned with specialist clinical professional career paths, these are not elaborated in Figure 3.1 or in the text.

Within the context of particular NHS organisations, the interpretation of generic competences could be more specific, both in respect of focus and level. Each of the cubes which are created by the three dimensions of profession, organisation and competence could be drawn showing distinctions between focus and levels of competence. For example, using the five levels of management competence defined by the Management Charter Initiative (1990). However, the diagram was kept relatively simple as an illustrative tool at this stage.

The climbing frame can be used to consider the basis for recruitment to particular jobs by plotting the essential and desirable characteristics which are sought in applicants for any particular job. In this way recruiters may be encouraged to cast their nets more widely to other professional groups or organisations. They need to look especially at how competences demonstrated in one professional or organisational sphere are transferable. The climbing frame can also be used by individuals to identify in which cells they currently appear and at what level and to ask themselves (preferably with the help of a guide or mentor) about the dimensions of profession, organisation or competence which they would like to develop. Attempts can then be made to find ways of putting wishes and plans, once evaluated, into practice.

It is, of course, probable that individuals considering future plans or employers considering recruitment to a particular job would look for presence in more than one column, row or slice. Thus the climbing frame for any individual – or job – is likely to indicate presence to a particular level in a variety of cubes.

On the basis of the findings of this research, example commentaries are given on how doctors, nurses, general and financial managers have moved within the three dimensions of the climbing frame, and of where they have encountered difficult barriers.

Doctors face the option of whether they see themselves playing a predominantly professional role or one with a strong managerial element. If they identify themselves as predominantly professional, they are likely to take a career path that leads them to being a consultant in a local provider. If they see themselves as developing managerially they may opt for a career in public health in a DHA or as a clinical director in a Trust, or within the NHSE or the office of the chief medical officer. For doctors wishing to develop managerially the main barrier is in gaining management development or initiating self-development, such that they can increase the range and depth of their competences.

People with a nursing background similarly face the option of whether they wish their career to be predominantly professional or predominantly managerial. In the former case they may become a team leader or chief nurse in a Trust. Alternatively if they see their career as predominantly managerial, posts to which they go at present include locality manager or service manager in a Trust. At the local level in purchasing, nurses' managerial roles are less clear – some for example become quality managers, others locality managers. There are also opportunities to move to the NHS Executive as a regional or national adviser or to the Office of the Chief Nurse. Whereas when doctors assume managerial roles they normally do so in combination with medical work, it is more usual for nurses to forsake their clinical work and move wholly into management, albeit often in roles that require that they have an intimate understanding of nursing practice. This difference is underpinned by differences in the terms and conditions of employment, including pay for doctors and nurses.

In the preceding pages we have seen that in DHAs and Trusts, nurses are not breaking through to the top levels of management in significant numbers. This is in spite of considerable will and investment from the centre to encourage such movement for example through the National Bursary Scheme. Movement should come through a concentration on helping nurses to increase the range and depth of their managerial competences and to gain entry into other professional columns, notably general management, through obtaining a DMS or MBA. It will be recalled that a barrier for nurses in management is seen to be the transference of status inequalities between doctors and nurses from the professional to the managerial sphere.

Someone with a general management background will clearly be located in the managerial columns, and may enter NHS Trusts as a business manager and proceed to roles such as care group manager and manager of operations. On the purchaser side they may be locality or performance managers. At the regional level there are roles in performance monitoring and evaluation as well as the major managerial functions. Someone with a background in finance may aspire to a specialist career. Should they wish for a wider managerial brief they can become commercial or marketing directors and eventually CEOs through expanding their range and level of competences or moving between organisations. The regional and national roles in financial advice, monitoring and regulation are changing; as the restructuring proceeds, opportunities will be available at these levels but their exact nature cannot be yet determined.

The descriptions given above are drawn from our research data and they are descriptive rather than normative. We believe that at the national, regional and local level, organisations need to give careful consideration to roles which are currently available, to inform people of the options available, to take action to remove unnecessary barriers and obstacles and to put in place management development activities to facilitate appropriate movements and the development of required competences. Barriers should only be insurmountable with reason. For example, no- one would want someone without a medical background performing heart surgery or someone without an accounting qualification undertaking financial audit. In many cases however, barriers and hurdles are the unintended consequences of restructuring or historical accident. It is important that a commitment exists to challenge such barriers, to question their necessity in order to increase morale, allay fears about the future, and secure a more effective service.

The responsibility for career development must lie with both individuals and organisations. Gunz (1989) argues that there are limits to how much an individual can take charge and that it is important for both the individual and the organisation to recognize those limits. Whilst the centre will not and cannot plan individual careers in a general or specific way it can take action to ensure that an infrastructure is in place to help people identify the range of possibilities and to move from post to post. This means having champions in organisations who are prepared to be more directive in taking ownership of climbing frames for the organisation as well as for individuals. Leadership is needed to suggest ways in which a combination of self management as well as management development and organisational development can equip individuals to move and organisations to be ready both to develop and to receive individuals as they move.

In the project conference which provided feedback on the findings to interested parties a career profiling exercise using the climbing frame was undertaken. Figure 3.2 describes the exercise and lists the questions which provided the basis for discussion about various movements, between professions and functions. Senior executives may wish to undertake some career planning discussions using such a checklist in order to identify where the barriers exist which prevent movement within, out of, or into, their organisations; to question the validity of the barriers; and to ask what organisations or individuals need to do to secure greater lateral as well as vertical career moves.

Figure 3.2 *The Climbing Frame: Career Profiling Exercise*

The aim of the exercise is to use the concept of the climbing frame to map a route through and between organisations showing how knowledge and skills may be developed via appointment to particular posts and engagement with a variety of learning and development projects, including learning sets, mentoring, secondments and self-development as well as more formal management development.

For any pathway you should undertake the following tasks:

1. What are the transferable skills and competences between the posts?

2. What new skills/competences need to be developed?

3. How can the skills be acquired and the competences demonstrated?

4. Identify interim posts providing opportunities for developing additional skills, competences and experience that may be required.

5. Action for organisation: what does the organisation need to do?

6. Action for individual: what does the individual need to do?

7. Identify the key requirements for making the move.

8. Identify the main barriers, if any, for a person wishing to make this sort of career move.

9. Are these barriers – necessary?
   – surmountable?

10. If barriers surmountable, what needs to be done to facilitate change?

In this way NHS organisations need to carve out and advertise new paths and possibilities for individuals, and provide them with development opportunities to bridge any competence gaps – this is something the individual cannot do alone. Positive steps need to be taken to foster a self development culture within the NHS; a point which is explored further in Chapter 8.

Opportunities to develop skills and knowledge and a mind set which acknowledges the relevance of competences demonstrated in one job, as a basis for recruitment into another, will not occur "naturally". They need to be the subject of managerial action. The literature shows that for career management systems (Stamp 1989, Mayo 1992) to operate successfully there needs to be mechanisms such as developmental appraisal systems and information provided by the organisation about career paths, to help individuals take responsibility for their own careers and respond successfully to change. More co-ordination, information and management development is necessary to help individuals become more aware of their own role in securing their own self development whilst, at the same time, the barriers need to become the object of creative scrutiny to understand their meaning and to validate their necessity.

Without positive action senior people and those lower in the NHS will feel stranded and uncertain over how to make the next move and what their future holds. The losers from unnecessary barriers and career deadends are not only individuals but also organisations which lose valuable talent and do not see the benefit of cross fertilisation of ideas between locations and professional groups. Such exchange aids collaboration and joint working as well as creating improved conditions for information exchange which is an essential part of good market structures. Identifying alternative career paths and facilitating them must be an important aspect of NHS management.

3.6 Summary

- Thirty five per cent of respondents held executive director positions. Twenty six per cent of respondents holding executive director positions were female and 74% were male. 55% of executive directors were aged under 45. Twenty five per cent of executive directors had work experience at RHA level at sometime in their careers, compared with only 8% of non-board executives.

- A number of factors were found to influence career choice. Family influences were important for both doctors and nurses, whereas 'chance' or 'luck' was identified more by general or functional managers. Public service values were identified by all groups, but were particularly noticeable amongst general managers who were working in purchasing organisations.

- There were a variety of reasons for clinicians' involvement in management: promotion, interest in management or wish to be involved in decision making, being 'next in line' in terms of seniority, previous experience and default (that there was no one else) or encouragement from others.

- Thirty eight per cent of respondents felt that the recent restructuring in the NHS had had a positive effect on the way they thought about their career. Only 16% felt the effect had been negative on their career. More respondents from purchasers (47%) thought the effects were positive, compared to respondents from providers. Twenty nine per cent of clinical managers considered the effects positive, 36% that they had no effect and 23% that the effects were negative. More of those at director level were positive (46%) about the effect of the reforms than those at other levels (30%).

- Career aspirations among respondents tended to reflect a managerial/ professional divide. Forty five per cent of those with a background in general management said they will 'aim for the top'. Thirty eight per cent of those with a nursing background felt they would like to move out of the NHS, and a higher proportion of women (28%) compared to men (16%) voiced this view. Thirty four per cent of those with a medical background wanted to move out of management. Twenty one per cent of all respondents would like to move out of the NHS and 14% to move to another NHS organisation.

- The changes occurring within large, complex organisations, such as the NHS, to flatter managerial structures, together with shifts in emphasis from vertical to horizontal relationships and networks, mean career development is becoming less obvious. In the NHS context of decentralisation and the internal market, career development is made more opaque. Tensions arise as a result of the restructuring. In particular, our findings point to a clear perception of a dual career structure emerging between purchasing and providing.

- The three dimensions of professional qualifications and experience, type of organisation and demonstrable competences can be used to construct a climbing frame in which individuals can locate themselves and consider their next moves, and employing organisations can map their staffing requirements and consider how best to fill them.

- Constructive and creative approaches to career planning are of benefit to individuals and employing organisations. Barriers to movement between location or functions need to be scrutinised in order to check their validity. Individuals need to be given opportunities to develop the nature and range of their demonstrable competences. This will not happen naturally of its own accord, it needs to be a focus for organisational investment.

Chapter 4 Managerial Activity: Competence, Roles and Responsibilities

Restructuring in the NHS has taken the form of flatter organisations with fewer managerial levels and greater decentralisation of service provision. The business orientation and performance culture implied by decentralisation (Colling & Ferner 1992, Fulop 1991) and reinforced by 'new wave management' (Morgan 1989, Wood 1989, Osborne & Gaebler 1992) has ramifications for the expected competence of the three groups at the centre of our study: the general, functional and clinical managers in purchasing and providing organisations.

In this chapter we describe managerial roles and responsibilities in the organisational context of purchasing and providing in the NHS and draw out the implications for management competence. The chapter is divided into the following sections:

- Researching Management Competence

- Management Responsibilities

- Typical Job Profiles: Similarities & Differences

- Support for Management Positions

- Managing Time

- Managerial and Organisational Competence

- Summary

4.1   Researching Management Competence

Management development and its practical implementation became the subject of considerable debate in the 1980s. Particular attention was focused on the concept of management competence, its definition and measurement, and the extent to which it should be evaluated on the basis of inputs, process activities or outcomes (DOE

1981, DOE and DES 1984, 1988, CNAA 1992). 'Inputs' of knowledge, skills and understanding are attributes of individuals (Mansfield 1989). 'Processes' are concerned with how managers make things happen, for example, planning, decision-making and networking; they are embedded in corporate culture (Jacobs 1989). 'Outcomes' concentrate on performance in the workplace environment, for example, decisions made, services delivered, people appraised and so on.

As Figure 4.1 illustrates, each of the three foci imply different things for the assessment of managerial performance and each has its limitations.

Figure 4.1 *Approaches to Management Competence.*

Focus	Inputs: knowledge, skills and attributes: e.g. self-confidence, communication, efficiency, ability in team work.	Processes: what managers do: e.g. planning, decision-making, networking, developing new markets, organising teams.	Outcomes: what managers achieve: e.g. decisions made, budgets allocated, people recruited, services delivered.
Orientation	Person	Job	Job
Assessment	Qualifications. Psychometric testing.	Difficult to assess other than longitudinally, or through simulations.	Outcome criteria: e.g. commercial, financial, resource utilisation.
Limitations	Having the above does not guarantee individual or organisational performance.	How do you know what is required and whether the person is being effective?	The individual manager may be sacrificing means to ends or over concentrating on the short-term.

There is disagreement over the relative emphasis which should be given to input, process and outcome. In our view each approach is partial and complementary to the others. Hence all three competence foci (inputs, process and outcomes) were explored in the individual interviews as shown in Figure 4.2.

This Chapter concentrates on management competence in the form of managerial processes. It describes the findings on managerial tasks and responsibilities and managerial support which derive from analysis of Section B of the interview schedule. The findings relating to Section A have already been discussed in the previous chapter, Sections C, H & G are discussed in Chapter 5, D in Chapter 6 and E in Chapter 7.

Figure 4.2 *Approaches to Management Competence in this Study*

Inputs	Processes	Outcomes
Education (A)	Managerial tasks/ responsibilities (B)	Performance evaluation (C)
Qualifications (A)	Managerial Support (B)	Critical incident (G)
Career experience (A)	Part played in management team (D)	
Personal qualities they bring to the job (H)	Internal and external networks (E)	

Note: The letters in brackets refer to appropriate sections of the interview schedule.

There is also debate on the emphasis which should be given about the generic or specific competences and about the appropriate balance between analysis of jobs or people, [Boyatzis 1982, Burgoyne 1988, Canning 1990, Collins 1989, Cockerill 1989, Day 1988, Devine 1990, Fondas 1989, Greatrex and Phillips 1989, Hay 1990, Hopfl and Dawes 1993, Jacobs 1989, MCI 1990, Shelborn 1990, Stewart 1989, Storey 1990].

In this research we have aimed to analyse the requirements for different types of jobs which carry senior managerial responsibility, as well as to understand our respondents in terms of their own individual experience and needs. We have also attempted to address the issue of managerial competence at an organisational as well as an individual level. Indeed it is our contention that decisions can only be made about the nature of managerial jobs and thereby the needs for management development within a context set by the organisation's strategy, objectives and key tasks.

Figure 4.3 is a schematic illustration of the research project and the levels of analysis addressed. It shows the range of tasks which are implicit in any attempt to determine the needs for management development within an organisational context. The research design reflected this need by ensuring that the study of senior executives was set within a study of organisational context.

The interviews resulted in descriptive data about activities undertaken by people in senior posts in general, functional and clinical management in the reformed NHS. The data collected are subjective in that they rely on managers own

Figure 4.3   *Management Development within the Organisational Context*

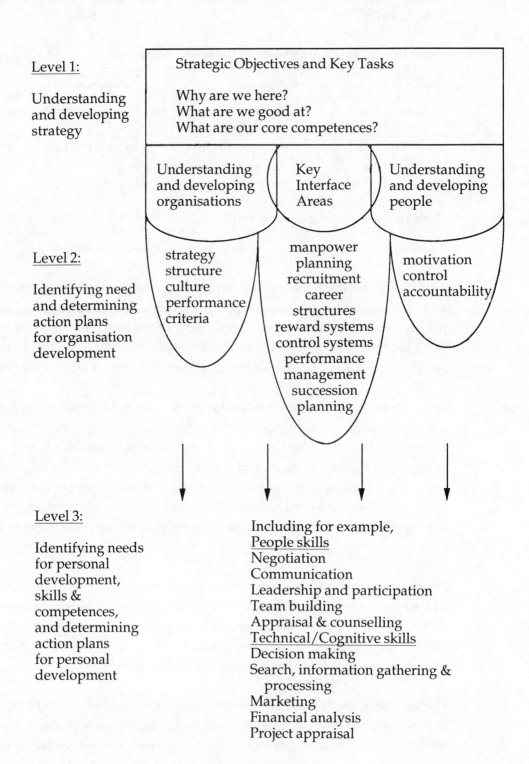

Level 1:

Understanding
and developing
strategy

Strategic Objectives and Key Tasks

Why are we here?
What are we good at?
What are our core competences?

Understanding
and developing
organisations

Key
Interface
Areas

Understanding
and developing
people

Level 2:

Identifying need
and determining
action plans
for organisation
development

strategy
structure
culture
performance
criteria

manpower
planning
recruitment
career
structures
reward systems
control systems
performance
management
succession
planning

motivation
control
accountability

Level 3:

Identifying needs
for personal
development,
skills &
competences,
and determining
action plans
for personal
development

Including for example,
People skills
Negotiation
Communication
Leadership and participation
Team building
Appraisal & counselling
Technical/Cognitive skills
Decision making
Search, information gathering &
     processing
Marketing
Financial analysis
Project appraisal

perceptions of their roles and responsibilities; this was matched by deductive work based on an understanding of the organisational and environmental context of the NHS.

Figure 4.4 provides another schematic for considering managerial competence. It has two dimensions of competence. The first ranges from a minimum level to ... ...city for growth. For any one job there are a set of competences in development within ... .ion. However, within that same job there is likely to ...s and outcomes which must be demonstrated by anyone which people may be helped to move ...d to ...ment. For individuals interested in their introduced in the previous chapter. ....to develop and retain their own ...pacity for growth and ...the basis through ...hich was

The second dimension in Figure 4.4 derives from the distinction that can be made between competences which are relatively generic, e.g. team working, strategic thinking, identifying and working to milestones or achieving budget, and others which maybe more specific, e.g. management accounting techniques, creation and analysis of patient satisfaction questionnaires, or techniques of vascular surgery. However, even specific competences will have some wider application e.g. patient satisfaction techniques are generic to market research. When appointing to a job, managers need to understand not only the specific and general competences which are required for any job (in segments A & B of Figure 4.4), but they should also identify competences in segments C & D which will provide the basis for personal development.

The approach illustrated in Figure 4.4 is relevant to the discussions in the previous chapter about the extent to which competences demonstrated in Trusts are transferable to DHAs and vice versa. This is an issue to which we return at the end of this chapter.

Figure 4.4 *Placing Competence in a Framework for Growth*

COMPETENCE

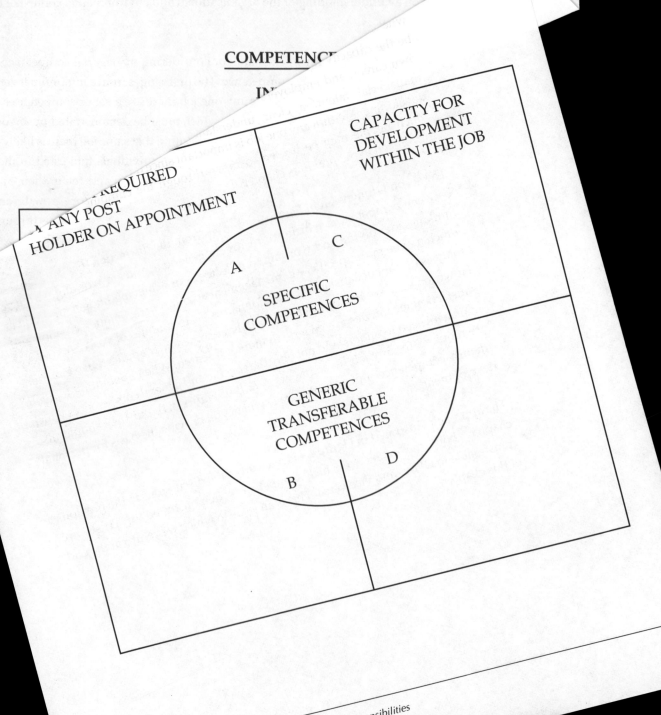

CAPACITY FOR
DEVELOPMENT
WITHIN THE JOB

REQUIRED
ANY POST
HOLDER ON APPOINTMENT

A

C

SPECIFIC
COMPETENCES

GENERIC
TRANSFERABLE
COMPETENCES

B

D

4.2   Managerial Responsibilities

All respondents were asked in an open-ended question to describe their managerial responsibilities. The results are summarised in Table 4.1 which shows the responses of all respondents, as well as the division between purchasing and providing respondents.

The categories listed in Table 4.1 were derived from an analysis of the text of the interviews. They give an indication of the ways in which the language of management is used in the NHS, and thereby the ways the task of management is conceptualised. There are no absolutely dominant categories. The largest single group was the 59% of respondents in provider organisations who spoke about their responsibilities for operational management, that is for all the activities concerned with securing the delivery of services to patients or programmes for health promotion or disease prevention.

Forty per cent of respondents talked about their responsibility for **'strategic planning'**, whereas only a small proportion (6%) talked in terms of **'managing change'**. The distinction between these two categories is important. Talking about 'strategic planning', respondents were describing responsibilities and activities which they saw as fairly distant from the sharp end of operations. They were activities involved in considering and charting the future, which may in the course of time be translated into action. In contrast when talking about 'managing change', they were describing a more active, pragmatic involvement in which the changes are created within the organising unit, as well as or even instead of, being imposed upon it. Something of these more dynamic and creative aspects of management is also captured in the responses (19%) which identified leadership as a main management responsibility.

The functional areas of contracting, business planning, managing finances, human resources, marketing and information are all represented to some moderate or small extent in the responses. The provision of medical advice was cited by 21% as a management responsibility and 15% drew attention to their role in quality. Purchaser rather than provider respondents drew attention to some specific aspects of their management agenda in terms of the Health of the Nation, primary care developments and multi-agency working. In the main providers were less specific.

Table 4.1 *Management Responsibilities*

Could you describe the responsibilities of your managerial position (Qu.B.3)

Dominant Responses	Purchasing Respondents (n=103) %	Providing Respondents (n=165) %	All Respondents (n=268) %
a) leadership*	12	24	19
b) strategic planning*	47	35	40
c) managing change	6	5	6
d) operational management*	16	59	43
e) business planning	14	19	17
f) financial management	18	15	16
g) information	12	6	8
h) marketing	8	9	8
i) contracting*	37	14	23
j) human resources	10	17	14
k) medical advice	16	24	21
l) quality*	23	10	15
m) Health of the Nation*	19	–	8
n) primary care*	20	4	10
o) multi-agency working	38	4	17
p) projects	10	4	6

* statistically significant differences were identified between purchaser and provider respondents at p < 0.05

Notes:
1. Respondents could mention more than one responsibility.

The concept of **leadership** was mentioned more frequently in provider organisations and particularly by those with a clinical background, although general managers in provider organisations also featured in this group. For example, one respondent described the role of the clinical manager as:

"Providing strategic leadership and initiating change, not day to day administration" (clinical manager, provider).

Functional managers were, however, less likely to describe their managerial responsibilities in terms of leadership. In purchaser organisations, executive directors were more likely than lower levels to refer to their role in leadership. Proportionately more older (45–54) than younger respondents and more men than women expressed their managerial responsibilities in terms of leadership.

Proportionately more purchasers than providers described **strategic planning** as part of their job. For example,

"Strategic planning, looking forward to what will happen within the HC on a five year cycle and making people aware of that" (functional manager, purchaser, level below board)

Within purchasing organisations, strategic planning is more likely to be described as part of managerial responsibilities by those with a medical background, ie. those in public health. For example,

"Public health has a wide role, influencing the attitude towards and the shape of services" (clinical manager, purchaser, level below board)

A present job and background in general management, particularly in providing organisations and a position at director rather than lower levels is more likely to lead to a view of being involved in strategic planning.

Proportionately more provider than purchaser respondents and particularly those with a medical background and those involved in clinical management described themselves as having **operational management** responsibilities. For example,

"I have to match the resource represented by a sizeable group of consultants and small group of juniors to the multifaceted requirements of providing service including quality, safety, education of junior doctors and on-going development of staff and colleagues" (clinical manager, provider)

Executive directors were less likely to describe operational management as part of their responsibilities.

Proportionately more men than women and more of those with a general or functional rather than a clinical management background described **business planning** as part of their responsibilities, for example,

"Business planning means understanding the market on a daily basis and feeding back to the organisation what it is that purchasers want in the marketplace. Our responses and adaptations are presented via a business planning framework. In this way we are clear what our objectives are and the action required to take them forward. Business planning is bottom up and we have produced frameworks and a timetable" (general manager, provider, board level)

Gender was significant with more men describing responsibilities for business planning than women.

Marketing was only identified as a managerial responsibility by relatively small groups in both purchasing or providing organisations, yet as the discussion of

Table 8.1 will show it is felt by respondents to be a major skill development need. Perhaps if more respondents felt confident to undertake it, it would assume more importance in their jobs.

Contracting responsibilities were identified by proportionately more functional managers in purchasing organisations than other groups. For example,

"I provide professional advice and lead corporate responsibility on a number of issues outside finance. I am responsible for contracting and contracts management" (functional manager, purchaser, board level)

In providing organisations, general managers and executive directors were more likely to cite it as part of their responsibilities.

As one would expect **financial management** was identified as part of their responsibility by more functional managers than other managers in both purchasing and providing organisations.

Similarly, **information** was seen as largely the responsibility of functional managers, particularly at director level. However, as Chapter 7 notes, only seven of the twenty-one sites comprising the study had an Information or IT Director at senior management level.

Similarly, giving **medical or clinical advice**, as part of managerial responsibilities was only identified by those with a clinical background. For example,

"Job is hard to define but in essence I am responsible for medical advice to the Trust Board and the executive team" (medical director)

Quality was identified as a managerial responsibility by proportionately more respondents in purchasing than providing. In provider organisations, those with a nursing background but doing a general management job tended to describe quality as part of their managerial responsibilities. For example,

"I act as resource person to a lot of people within the quality component of the job, networking and putting people in touch across departments" (executive director)

Whereas in purchaser organisations, proportionately more of those below rather than at director level were more likely to describe quality as part of their managerial responsibilities, the opposite was true for providers. Gender was significant with proportionately more women than men describing quality as part of their job; a finding which is strongly related to the relative dominance of nurses in this category.

Addressing **Health of the Nation** issues was described by proportionately more purchasers than providers, and more of those in clinical rather than general or functional management as part of their managerial responsibilities. Proportionately more respondents in purchasing rather than providers, and below rather than at director level, identified dealing with primary care as a managerial responsibility.

Human resource management

Given the overall concern of this study with the development of individuals and organisations, areas which functionally come within the remit of human resources, more space is given to the discussion of the way in which the sample of senior executives talked about their involvement in **human resource management** in comparison to other areas. In fact few general or clinical managers identified **human resources** as part of their managerial responsibilities. Although there was discussion about the requirement for greater vision in the development of human resource strategies and policies particularly at the provider unit level, our research shows that the human resource function is not yet fully developed at local level, nor are many general or clinical managers aware of their own key role in its development. These findings are consistent with a recent study of personnel effectiveness in the NHS (Guest and Peccei 1992) which shows that effectiveness is most highly rated for personnel administration issues rather than in areas of professional and more strategic human resource management, with personnel departments having high levels of influence over day to day personnel decisions, but less over major Trust policy decisions.

We found great differences between human resource managers in how they defined their activity, and this reflected their diverse background and routes into human resource management. These ranged from beginnings in non-graduate secretarial and administrative posts or general NHS management, to graduate human resource specialists some of whom started outside the NHS. Different interpretations of their jobs also reflected historical development of their own organisations, and in particular whether the human resource manager has achieved board level status. The following quotes describe the very different foci for human resource activity.

First, those organisations where human resources is not represented at board level and where the role is very much that of "personnel administrator and support".

"I'm responsible for staff in my own department; recruitment, development, discipline; the provision of support for managers; staff mix; advice to the chief executive and the board on broader perspectives for human resource management". (human resource manager, provider, level below board).

"Human resources is an umbrella function [covering] industrial relations, recruitment and welfare; management development and training, and day nurseries". (human resource manager, provider, level below board).

Some HR managers in purchasing articulated their isolated position:

"Sometimes I feel very isolated, with very few human resource people in commissioning there is no network within the region for sharing ideas with others. I need to invest time building networks external to the organisation". (human resource manager, purchaser, level below board)

Some of the smaller purchasing organisations did not have an internal manager clearly defined as being in the human resource area. Here the human resource expertise sometimes came from outside the organisation (such as from consultants), from non-executive directors with particular expertise or was spread through other roles in the organisation. In one instance a director of corporate strategy who was also responsible for marketing and planning, had human resources within his remit:

"One of my roles is human resources, – personnel and health and safety including occupational health. On the people side there is a split between my own department and also those contracts I run for training and occupational health and so on. ... I see the HR side of the job as developmental, it helps the broader, wider brief and helps succession for the CEO. HR is a means to an end – to justify my salary I have to take the wider perspective than just HR eg. health gain and planning, employment comes at the end of that and follows the 5 year strategy". (human resource manager [corporate strategy manager] provider, board level).

Where human resource managers were in the tier below the board many were pushing to gain board level status:

"The human resource area should have a place on the management board so that we can begin to be built into the business planning for next year" (human resource manager, provider, level below board)

Second, are the organisations where human resource directors have achieved higher status and defined their role as "architects of change". In this context issues of change management, management and organisational development, and performance management are highlighted:

"I am primarily concerned with strategic activity although I oversee extensive operational activity. The strategic activity includes training and development; issues which are increasingly related to performance and how we can identify it; and another key area is communications. Also downsizing the human resource department – we are becoming a small specialist support and advisory service". (human resource director, provider, board level)

"My main areas of work are 1. skills, people and resources for effective commissioning of health services. 2. Organisational development of the corporate team, board and executive, and the initiation of joint working with other organisations such as social services. 3. Management development, broad staff development, ensuring the possession of skills and clarifications of roles appropriate to outcomes. 4. Individual career development, pathways into the organisation and development of career pathways. 5. Maintenance of the human resource function and system – IPR, objective setting, personnel policies, staff development, discipline. 6. Change management – merger and the effects on different culture and individuals priorities". (human resource director, purchaser, board level)

"My HR role is setting strategic direction and targets, monitoring performance against the targets ensuring viability, gathering senior and clinical managers for clinical management groups. Also segment into manpower planning, recruitment and retention, education, training and development. Also staff communications, employee relations, staff support and welfare, reward and other benefits. ... I am supported by a performance manager, the HRM planning manager, the training and development manager and also by external networks – there is a regional HR network which meets informally as a group of trust personnel directors.... A barrier to doing the HR work well is integrating personnel management with business management – this is important to the operation of the trust but there is a lack of time and little knowledge and experience of strategic HRM". (human resource manager, provider, board level)

Interestingly another director identified the informal role of the human resource director in change management and broadening the management view:

"His HR knowledge of personnel issues is important and he is good at pulling the team back to what they are looking at. Also on day to day running issues has been his ability over the last three years of keeping people together during times of great stress". (general manager, provider, board level)

Overview of management responsibilities

Following the open-ended question about managerial responsibilities, all interviewees were given a list of 27 managerial duties and responsibilities and asked to pick from it the managerial duties and activities that their job involved and then to proceed within the interview to indicate their degree of importance by means of a self completion sheet. This technique allowed the researchers to ensure that they were securing comparative data from all respondents, whereas the previous open-ended question had allowed an exploration on the basis of categories the respondents themselves thought important. As it was, the open-ended question generated similar categories to those identified for respondents in the closed option question B.7.

The scale of importance on the self completion sheet ran through 5 points as follows: very little, some, moderate, highly, extremely. If their job did not include one of the activities, they were asked to tick the N/A (not applicable) box. Table 4.2 shows the percentages within each job category (general, functional and clinical manager), within purchaser and provider organisations, of those who rated each activity highly or extremely important.

The following statistically significant different responses to Qu.B7 (at $P < 0.05$) are identified when the data is analysed by the key characteristics of type of organisation, background, present job, gender and age.

strategic planning: identified by
- proportionately more of those at director than other managerial levels.

business planning: identified by
- proportionately more provider than purchaser respondents.

evaluation of overall organisational performance: identified by
- proportionately more respondents with background as functional managers than other backgrounds
- proportionately more in present jobs as general and functional managers than clinical managers
- proportionately more executive directors than those at other levels.

negotiation of service contracts: identified by
- proportionately more respondents with backgrounds as functional and general managers than other groups
- proportionately more in present jobs as general and functional managers than clinical managers

Table 4.2 *Managerial Duties and Activities*

Activity rated highly or Extremely important (Qu.B7)

	GM (n=117)			FM (n=45)			CM (n=106)			ALL (n=268)
	Pu	T	Pr	Pu	T	Pr	Pu	T	Pr	%
a) strategic planning	70	79	89	65	69	72	80	70	68	74
b) business planning	44	58	76	65	69	72	05	56	68	59
c) evaluation of overall organisational performance*	52	63	77	79	66	56	30	45	48	56
d) negotiation of service contracts*	41	45	51	50	42	36	20	24	25	36
e) developing new services	52	58	66	58	46	36	58	62	63	58
f) health needs assessment	24	18	11	20	13	08	70	25	14	20
g) evaluating service delivery	55	61	68	30	40	48	60	60	60	57
h) evaluating contract performance*	56	62	68	60	52	46	30	42	45	52
i) managing service delivery*		52	53		24	24		60	60	52
j) managing contract performance	50	44	38	47	43	40	16	40	45	42
k) marketing your service*	27	40	55	05	23	36	11	27	31	32
l) allocating financial resources*	47	47	47	85	78	72	20	41	46	50
m) controlling financial resources*	40	50	64	70	80	88	05	57	69	58
n) recruitment and selection	27	27	26	40	31	24	10	41	48	33
o) promotion	25	23	21	30	29	28	15	24	26	24
p) succession planning*	36	36	36	30	36	40	15	31	35	34
q) allocating performance related pay*	25	27	29	30	40	48	10	05	04	20
r) individual performance review and appraisal	56	61	66	45	62	76	32	35	36	51
s) training and development	48	53	59	40	53	64	45	44	44	50
t) grievance, discipline and dismissal	13	20	28	20	29	36	00	20	25	21
u) job design	27	26	25	45	38	32	20	24	24	27
v) organisation of your team	81	82	83	85	87	88	70	72	72	79
w) motivation of your team*	84	88	93	90	93	96	80	76	76	84
x) external liaison and networking*	92	82	70	75	76	76	90	62	56	73
y) internal liaison and networking*	95	97	98	95	93	92	85	74	72	87

Notes:

* statistically significant differences were identified between respondents by present job at p < 0.05

The results are given within each job category in terms of –

Pu (% of purchasing respondents)

T (% of all respondents)

Pr (% of providing respondents)

Key:

GM = general manager FM = functional manager CM = clinical manager

developing new services: identified by
- proportionately more female than male respondents

health needs assessment: identified by
- proportionately more purchaser than provider respondents
- proportionately more female than male respondents

evaluating service delivery: identified by
- proportionately more respondents with backgrounds as nurses than other backgrounds
- proportionately more female than male respondents

evaluating contract performance: identified by
- proportionately more respondents with backgrounds as functional and general managers than other backgrounds
- proportionately more respondents in present jobs as general rather than functional and clinical managers
- proportionately more respondents at executive director level than lower in the organisation

managing service delivery: identified by
- proportionately more respondents with backgrounds as nurses than other backgrounds
- proportionately more respondents in present jobs as clinical rather than general and functional managers
- proportionately more respondents at director than lower levels in the organisation
- proportionately more female than male respondents

managing contract performance: identified by
- proportionately more respondents with background as nurses than other backgrounds

marketing your service: identified by
- proportionately more provider than purchaser respondents
- proportionately more respondents in present jobs as general rather than functional and clinical managers; even so only 40% of general managers see marketing services as a highly or extremely important managerial activity.

allocating financial resources: identified by

- proportionately more respondents with backgrounds as functional than general or clinical managers
- proportionately more respondents in present jobs as functional rather than general or clinical managers
- proportionately more respondents at director than lower levels

controlling financial resources: identified by

- proportionately more respondents from provider than purchaser organisations
- proportionately more respondents with backgrounds as functional managers than other backgrounds
- proportionately more respondents in present jobs as functional rather than general or clinical managers

In passing it is interesting to note that 80% of functional managers, but only 50% of general managers and 57% of the clinical managers gave allocating and controlling financial resources as important aspects of their job. Financial management is still seen by over half of those in general or clinical management as activities which can be left to "the specialists".

recruitment and selection: identified by

- proportionately more respondents from provider than purchaser organisations
- proportionately more respondents below, rather than at, director level

succession planning: identified by

- proportionately more respondents with backgrounds as nurses than other backgrounds
- proportionately more female than male respondents.

Interestingly comparatively few (34%) of our sample thought succession planning was highly or extremely important in their managerial activity. The group who features larger than others for this dimension were those with a nursing background and women.

allocating performance related pay: identified by

- proportionately more respondents with backgrounds as functional or general than clinical managers
- proportionately more respondents with present jobs as functional than general or clinical managers
- proportionately more respondents at director than lower levels

individual performance review and appraisal: identified by

- proportionately more respondents in present jobs as functional or general than clinical managers
- proportionately more respondents at director than lower levels
- proportionately more female than male respondents

training and development: identified by

- proportionately more respondents with backgrounds as nurses and other health professionals than other backgrounds
- proportionately more female than male respondents

grievance, discipline and dismissal: identified by

- proportionately more provider than purchaser respondents
- proportionately more responses from nursing and other health professional backgrounds than other backgrounds
- proportionately more female than male respondents

job design: identified by

- proportionately more female than male respondents

organisation of your team: identified by

- proportionately fewer respondents with backgrounds as doctors than other backgrounds
- proportionately more respondents at director than lower levels

motivation of your team: identified by

- proportionately more respondents in present jobs as functional than general or clinical managers
- proportionately more respondents at director than lower levels

external liaison and networking: identified by

- proportionately more purchaser than provider respondents
- proportionately fewer respondents with backgrounds as doctors than other backgrounds
- proportionately more respondents with present jobs as general than functional or clinical managers
- proportionately more respondents at director than lower levels

internal liaison and networking: identified by

- proportionately more purchaser than provider respondents
- proportionately fewer respondents with backgrounds as doctors than other backgrounds

- proportionately more respondents in present jobs as general or functional rather than clinical managers
- proportionately more respondents at director than lower levels
- proportionately more female than male respondents

The responses shown in Table 4.2 reveal that once again strategic planning is rated as very important by the majority (74%) of the respondents. The managerial activities which are deemed highly or extremely important by more than 60% of this group of senior executives are largely concerned with internal management issues, as follows

- (v) organisation of your team (79% of all respondents)
- (w) motivation of your team (84% of all respondents)
- (y) internal liaison and networking (87% of all respondents)

The only other activity to fall into this overall high scoring group in addition to (a) **strategic planning** was (x) **external liaison and networking** (73% of all respondents).

A focus on internal management issues was not translated into high scores for the detail of human resource management (i.e. n-u of the list), but was more concerned with the broader issues of managing people, with an emphasis upon the importance of internal communication and motivation.

The systematic approach of the self-completion sheet concerning management duties and activities has produced results that accord with intuition. Beyond the 'shared by all' activities each group has its different focus with areas of overlap. Thus, for instance, the clinical managers are very much the operational arm focusing on service development, management and evaluation. Interestingly they share with functional managers (who were in the main finance based) the duty of financial control, the devolved nature of which is a prime focus of organisational development.

Gender differences were found in developing new services, health needs assessment, evaluating service delivery, managing service delivery, individual performance review and appraisal, training and development, grievance, discipline and dismissal, job design and internal liaison and networking suggesting an over-representation for women in aspects of operational management including personnel issues and their under-representation in areas of financial management and strategic planning. This reflects the relationships between gender, present job, background and level, with proportionately more women and nurses being in middle rather than higher managerial positions.

4.3 Typical Job Profiles: Similarities and Differences

Our research has looked across purchasing and providing organisations to examine the nature of managerial work in the restructured NHS. In order to give examples of different job profiles within and between purchasing and providing, responses to Qu.B7 on managerial activities have been analysed by the job categories shown in Figure 4.5. Responses for all those who indicated that any given category was a major part of their job, were collated for that category and the constituent managerial activities ranked in order of the frequency with which they were mentioned by a particular group as being highly or extremely important in their job. The lists were compiled using managerial activities identified by over 50% of respondents in each job category. Job categories where respondents numbered less than 10 were not included. In some cases respondents occupied more than one category. For example, a director of finance may also have major responsibilities for information.

Figure 4.5 *Coding for individual respondents by job category*

CEO

Finance

Public health

Medical Management

Nursing Management

HR/Personnel

PR/consumer affairs

Quality

Information

Operations

Corporate strategy/planning development

Commissioning

Contracting

Performance review/management

Business management

Primary care development

Figures 4.6 – 4.9 deal with job categories which are only found in either purchasing or providing organisations. Figure 4.6 shows the key managerial activities identified by those in purchasing with jobs in primary care development and illustrates the high priority given to 'liaison and networking' in their job. Figure 4.7 shows the key managerial activities of business managers in providing organisations, where the focus is strongly on internal management. Figure 4.8 shows the key managerial activities identified by doctors in management in provider organisations and Figure 4.9 shows the key managerial activities for their medically qualified colleagues who are working in public health in purchasing organisations. The largest proportion of both sets of doctors identified strategic planning as a key activity. Both groups were strong in the emphasis they gave to internal management. In addition, doctors in provider management placed great emphasis on financial and operational management, whereas public health doctors in purchasing attached importance to developing and evaluating new services and health needs assessment.

Figure 4.6   *Typical Patterns of Managerial Activity: primary care development*

Purchasing Only: Primary Care Development (n=13)
motivation of your team
external liaison and networking
internal liaison and networking
organisation of your team
strategic planning
developing new services
allocating financial resources
business planning
health needs assessment
managing contract performance
individual performance review and appraisal
training and development

Figure 4.7 *Typical Patterns of Managerial Activity: business management*

Provider Only: Business Manager **(n=33)**
motivation of your team
organisation of your team
controlling financial resources (meeting budgets)
internal liaison and networking
business planning
developing new services
evaluating service delivery
managing service delivery
training and development
external liaison and networking

Figure 4.8 *Typical Patterns of Managerial Activity: medical management*

Provider Only: Doctors in Management **(n=60)**
strategic planning
motivation of your team
internal liaison and networking
organisation of your team
business planning
controlling financial resources (meeting budgets)
developing new services
evaluating service delivery

Figure 4.9 *Typical Patterns of Managerial Activity: public health*

Purchaser Only: Doctors in Public Health **(n=15)**
strategic planning
internal liaison and networking
external liaison and networking
motivation of your team
organisation of your team
health needs assessment
developing new services
evaluating service delivery
training and development

Figures 4.10–4.15 deal with profiles for job categories which are found in both purchasing and providing organisations. The figures distinguish between those activities which were identified as common between purchasing and providing and those activities which were frequently rated by respondents in either purchasing or providing organisations.

Figure 4.10 shows the managerial activities found to be common, purchaser-specific and provider-specific for the job of Chief Executive Officer. Figure 4.11 repeats the exercise for finance, Figure 4.12 for human resources, Figure 4.13 for contracting, Figure 4.14 for corporate strategy and Figure 4.15 for quality.

Figure 4.10   *Typical Patterns of Management Activity : Chief Executive Officer (n=21)*

Common

evaluation of overall organisational performance

organisation of your team

motivation of your team

external liaison and networking

internal liaison and networking

strategic planning

individual performance review and appraisal

allocating financial resources

business planning

Purchaser Only:	**Provider Only:**
recruitment and selection	developing new services
training and development	evaluating contract performance
promotion	marketing your services
succession planning	controlling financial resources
allocating performance related pay	evaluating service delivery

Figure 4.11   *Typical Patterns of Managerial Activity : Finance (n=28)*

Common

allocating financial resources

internal liaison and networking

motivation of your team

organisation of your team

controlling financial resources (meeting budgets)

business planning

evaluation of overall organisational performance

external liaison and networking

strategic planning

evaluating contract performance

negotiation of service contracts

Purchaser Only:	**Provider Only:**
developing new services	individual performance review and appraisal
	training and development
	allocating performance related pay

Figure 4.12   *Typical Patterns of Managerial Activity: Human Resources (n=14)*

Common:
individual performance review and appraisal
training and development
organisation of your team
motivation of your team
external liaison and networking
internal liaison and networking

Purchaser Only:	**Provider Only:**
recruitment and selection	controlling financial resources
job design	(meeting budgets)
	strategic planning
	business planning
	evaluating service delivery
	allocating performance related pay
	grievance, discipline and dismissal

Figure 4.13   *Typical Patterns of Managerial Activity: Contracting (n=11)*

Common:
internal liaison and networking
external liaison and networking
negotiation of service contracts
evaluating contract performance
developing new services
evaluation of overall organisational performance

Purchaser Only:	**Provider Only:**
organisation of your team	strategic planning
motivation of your team	business planning
managing contract performance	marketing your services
controlling financial resources (meeting budgets)	
allocating financial resources	
evaluating service delivery	
individual performance review and appraisal	

Figure 4.14   *Typical Patterns of Managerial Activity: Corporate Strategy (n=12)*

Common:
strategic planning
external liaison and networking
internal liaison and networking
developing new services
evaluation of overall organisational performance
evaluating service delivery
organisation of your team
motivation of your team
evaluating contract performance

Purchaser Only:	**Provider Only:**
managing contract performance	business planning
allocating financial resources	marketing your services
	negotiation of service contracts

Figure 4.15   *Typical Patterns of Managerial Activity: Quality (n=11)*

Common:
external liaison and networking
internal liaison and networking
evaluating service delivery
evaluating contract performance
strategic planning
organisation of your team

Purchaser Only:	**Provider Only:**
managing contract performance	evaluation of overall organisational performance
negotiation of service contracts	marketing your services
	motivation of your team

These job profiles show what different groups of staff perceive as important in their present managerial positions. Such an approach can be used in several ways.

It provides those responsible for management development and organisational development with a basis to evaluate areas for development. For example, given an organisational context and environment do people in particular job categories need to be encouraged to alter the balance of priorities about what activities are more or less important in a job? What skills and knowledge underly activities which arguably should have greater representation as important? How can skills and knowledge be developed to facilitate competence in particular activities? What activities which are important in one area are transferable to other areas where they may be under-represented?

For individuals the approach can give them insight into what groups of peers, superiors or subordinates see as important in a particular job category, and allows them to consider the extent to which, for their present or any future jobs, they should be seeking to develop skills and knowledge in different areas.

It is interesting to note the similarities as well as the differences between the patterns of managerial activity identified in purchaser and provider organisations. These profiles suggest that there are some important bridges as well as barriers between the two parts which may be useful in facilitating movement between the two.

4.4   Support for Managerial Positions

Respondents were asked in an open-ended question, to describe the support they receive to do their managerial jobs. Tables 4.3 and 4.4 summarise their responses and show the difference between general, functional and clinical managers. Table 4.3 covers purchasing and 4.4, providing.

Line management was identified as a source of support by more than a third of all respondents. The most popular form of support was undoubtedly respondents 'own team', by which they meant the group of people working in their function, service or department. This was mentioned by 83% of purchasers and 72% of providers and by proportionately more general or functional than clinical managers. However, nearly all the clinical managers in purchasing (which largely means public health physicians) identified their 'own team' as a means of support. Overall, the identification of 'own team' by more functional and public health than other clinical or general managers suggests that where functions are clear and separate, team support is perceived as very important. 'Own team' was also seen as important by proportionately more directors than those lower in the organisation and by proportionately more female than male respondents. This primary emphasis upon functional and departmental groups, suggests that career development or organisational development which depends on cross-functional working will be relatively difficult to orchestrate.

A sizable proportion of clinical managers in provider organisations and particularly those who are doctors rather than nurses, identified the support they received from service and business managers, who often have a nursing background. Nothing comparable in terms of specialist support was recorded for other groups. Colleague support was mentioned only by 8% of clinical managers in providing organisations, compared to 11% of all providing respondents and 15% of all purchasing respondents.

Table 4.3 *Managerial Support in Purchasing*

What support do you receive to do your job? (Qu.B5)

	Purchaser Respondents by Present Job			
	General Managers (n=60) %	Functional Managers (n=21) %	Clinical Managers (n=19) %	All (n=100) %
Internal Sources:				
(a) Line Management	50	24	26	40
(b) own team*	77	86	95	83
(f) colleagues	12	19	21	15
External Sources:				
(i) RHA	22	19	37	24
(j) Regional networks	7	14	11	9
(k) professional networks	7	2	16	7
(l) informal networks*	20	5	5	14
(m) other purchasers	12	5	5	9
(n) providers	7	5	5	6

*statistically significant differences were identified between respondents by present job at p <0.05

Table 4.4 *Managerial Support in Providing*

What support do you receive to do your job? (Qu.B5)

	General Managers (n=54) %	Functional Managers (n=24) %	Clinical Managers (n=84) %	All (n=162) %
Internal Sources:				
(a) Line Management	33	38	30	32
(b) own team*	83	84	61	72
(c) clinical director/manager	2	4	11	7
(d) business manager*	0	4	21	11
(e) service manager*	0	0	34	17
(f) colleagues	11	16	8	11
(g) none	4	0	8	6
External Sources				
(i) Trust Outpost	2	12	0	3
(j) RHA	8	16	2	6
(k) Regional networks	4	8	6	6
(l) professional networks	2	2	4	3
(m) informal networks*	11	8	6	8
(n) purchasers	2	0	0	1
(o) other providers	2	0	1	1

*statistically significant differences were identified between respondents by present job at p <0.05

Turning to external sources of support no single dominant source of support emerged. The RHA was mentioned by 24% of purchaser but only 6% of provider respondents and by proportionately more executive directors than those lower in the organisation.

Support from informal networks was identified by proportionately more general than functional or clinical managers.

A general impression was gained particularly from the provider respondents below board level, that they felt they were operating fairly much alone and without any obvious sources of external support. This was particularly marked amongst respondents in sites which were 1st and 2nd wave rather than 3rd or 4th wave Trusts. This was not regarded negatively or positively; merely as a matter of fact.

4.5   Managing Time

It is well known that people in the NHS work long hours. In reply to a question about the number of hours worked, Table 4.5 shows that the responses were typically of 46 to 55 hours a week, increasing to over 55 hours a week at director level.

Doctors acting as clinical managers were asked about the proportion of time they spent on management per week. The results are shown in Table 4.6. Sixty per centspent between 6 and 15 hours per week on management. The small proportion spending over 21 hours refers to the medical director posts included in this sample.

Table 4.5   *Hours Worked*

On average how many hours a week do you work? (Qu.A24)

Purchaser Responses by Level

	Level 1 (n=38) %	Level 2 (n=51) %	All (n=89) %
Hours p. week			
36 – 45*	16	35	27
46 – 55	42	43	43
56 – 65*	42	22	30
	100	100	100

Provider Responses by Level

	Level 1 (n=35) %	Level 2 (n=60) %	Level 3 (n=18) %	All (n=113) %
Hours p. week				
36 – 45*	6	12	33	13
46 – 55	37	58	61	52
56 – 65*	57	30	6	35
	100	100	100	100

*statistically significant differences were identified between respondents working at different levels in provider organisations at p <0.05

Key: Level 1 = Executive Board Members
      Level 2 = Directors & Managers Reporting to Board
      Level 3 = Managers Reporting to Level 2

Doctors were also asked whether they would like to spend more, the same, or less time on management. While a third would like to spend less time on management, a half of the sample were content with the proportion of their time now devoted to managerial activities, 20% would like to spend more time.

We know that many of our interviewees felt overloaded and pushed for time. It is therefore interesting to begin to gauge which aspects of managerial work in the NHS are most time consuming. Each respondent was given a card on which the five areas of management listed in Table 4.7 were printed. Each area was amplified in a few lines, which are printed in the interview schedule (Appendix 1:Qu.B8).

Table 4.6   *Numbers of Hours per week spent on management: (doctors in providers only)*

What proportion of your time do you now spend on management (approximate hours per week)? (Qu.A25)

Hours per week	*Doctors (n=52) %
Under 5	19
6 – 10	37
11 – 15	23
16 – 20	15
21 and above	6
	100

*refers to clinical directors and medical directors in provider organisations

Respondents were asked to consider, given this range of activities, which were the two areas that take up most of their time.

Responses are summarised in Table 4.7, which shows the different patterns of response for general and clinical managers and all respondents in purchaser and provider organisations. The separate responses of functional managers are not shown since most of their time is devoted to their own particular functional area, for example managing financial resources for finance managers and managing people for human resource managers. These differences would be lost if responses were aggregated into one group. Their responses are, however, included in the 'all respondent' category to show the overall distribution of managerial time within purchaser and provider organisations.

TABLE 4.7 *Time given to Managerial Activities*

Given this range of managerial activities which are the two areas which take up most of your time as a manager? (Qu.B8)

Purchaser Responses

		General Managers (n=53) %	Clinical Managers (n=14) %	All Respondents (n=86) %
(a)	managing strategy*	72	93	69
(b)	managing services*	38	21	30
(c)	managing financial resources	4	8	20
(d)	managing people	26	36	33
(e)	managing liaisons and networks*	60	57	55

Provider Responses

		General Managers (n=48) %	Clinical Managers (n=58) %	All Respondents (n=128) %
(a)	managing strategy	67	57	62
(b)	managing services*	42	47	41
(c)	managing financial resources	23	35	32
(d)	managing people	50	48	49
(e)	managing liaisons and networks	38	31	34

*statistically significant differences were identified between respondents working in provider or purchaser organisations by present job at $p < 0.05$

Note:
1. Each respondent could mention 2 aspects.

In purchasing and providing approximately two thirds of all respondents said that **managing strategy** was one of the areas which took up most time. In purchaser organisations, this response was given by more executive directors than others and was an almost unanimous response from public health physicians.

The area to get the second highest support as one of the two areas which takes up most managerial time, was **"managing liaisons and networks"** for purchasing and **"managing people"** for providing. These differences reflect directly on the different nature of purchasing and providing activities. For **managing services** differences were identified by present job with more general and clinical rather than functional managers. The lowest score in both sorts of organisations was given to **'managing financial resources'**, although not surprisingly this activity received scores from proportionately more functional managers (all finance managers) and indeed came second in their rankings in providing and first in purchasing organisations.

4.6   Managerial & Organisational Competence: Discussion

Studies of managers in public and private sector organisations indicate that middle management jobs have become more generalist with greater responsibilities over a wider range of tasks (Kanter 1989(b), Dopson and Stewart 1990). These changes require new skills: greater flexibility and adaptability are stressed together with more generalist skills which include financial knowledge, an ability to manage staff of different backgrounds, a wider understanding of their environment in terms of other departments and beyond the organisation's boundaries, a greater marketing and strategic orientation and a capacity actively to manage change. Yet the results reported here suggest that for many NHS managers these are relatively uncharted waters.

Harrison and Thompson (1992) argue that for middle managers in the NHS the internal market has had the effect of producing flatter organisations that require middle managers to 'act horizontally', and thus to develop the skills and capabilities to support their new roles. For example, in this research we found that purchasing is as much about mobilising agencies and networks as about managing in organisations. The managerial skills the purchasing team need are those concerned with influencing, communicating, negotiating and networking as a complement to their knowledge of finance, epidemiology, health services and health economics. General and functional managers in purchasing have to chart a careful path through a number of constituencies: professionals, providers, politicians, pressure groups and the public (May 1992), and be prepared to challenge the overall distribution of resources and, perhaps, to shift the balance between care groups and treatments available (Heginbotham et al 1992). This means that each manager needs a combination of generic and specific competences appropriate to the context.

Whilst the possession of specialist functional skills is important it is no longer a sufficient basis for senior executives in the NHS. They must learn to manage across functions and professions and indeed, particularly in purchasing, across organisations. Some of our respondents were well aware of this imperative, although somewhat unsure of how to achieve it:

"We wear functional hats still, the question is how to muster resources in an appropriate way, in terms of skills rather than functions". (general manager, purchaser, board level)

Another respondent explained how strong functional identity is often founded on defensiveness:

"We've got to learn to take off our functional hats, people don't want to give away things that would be always theirs in a more functional organisation. It's only recently become clear that by "our team" I don't mean the functional group, and people are worried." (general manager, purchaser, board level)

The challenge of building on specialist skills to develop other broader ways of working was discussed by a nurse who had recently entered management:

"Yes, I used to think that if I became a senior management person it would be because I was a good nurse. I now feel its skills that I have to offer, some are connected to nursing, others are not. I have to be able to articulate other values, but I know I run the risk of alienating myself from my background". (service manager, provider)

The movement of managers from functional areas like personnel, finance and information into general manager positions is a well-trodden career development path in most organisations, and it is an area that will probably become increasingly important for managers in the NHS. There are also opportunities for commercial or marketing managers. Some of these are coming from the ranks of the general managers, others bring in specialist marketing skills from other sectors (Sheaff 1991) Human resource management is another area that has come to the fore in the re- structured NHS. The traditional personnel model that evolved in the health service was one of "administrative support" with managers located in district and regional health authorities servicing the directly managed units (Tyson 1985). It is only recently that many of these personnel administrators have moved into provider units to develop a more strategic role with greater power for local decision-making (Stock, Seccombe & Kettley 1994). New roles have thus emerged in purchasing and providing and it is likely that in the future there will be greater emphasis on the functional management route into general management. For clinical managers the change in focus from individual practitioner to management team member with responsibilities to the corporate whole contains its own contradictions.

Issues surrounding the link between managerial effectiveness and organisational performance are especially pertinent to organisations undergoing rapid change. Recent work in the strategy area uses the concept of 'core competences' at the organisational level. In this context, the attention of the senior executives is drawn to what are termed core organisational competences. Executives are advised to consider what collectively they are really good at, what they know well and the variety of applications to be exploited via these core competencies (Prahalad and Hamel 1990). Newly created purchasing and providing organisations need to give careful thought to what their core competences really are in order to provide a central benchmark for strategic decisions and management development.

In our approach to the concept of managerial competence we drew attention to the importance of context. The identification of individual managerial competences presuppose that core competences at any organisational level have been identified. In discussions with senior executives it was clear that in some organisations little thought had yet been given to establishing and then seeking to develop organisational competences, even though they are crucial in determining the context for managerial activity and defining the criteria for the assessment of organisational effectiveness. This must represent a major area of management activity for all NHS organisations.

4.7   Summary

- Managerial competence is approached in this study through a consideration of three complementary aspects: the inputs, processes and outcomes of managerial activity. The relative emphasis which should be given to each continues to be debated. It is important that people at local, regional and national level in the NHS are aware of the differences and limitations of adopting any one single approach.

- Care must be taken to locate the identification of required competences within an organisational context which reflects the organisation's strategic objectives and key tasks, which in turn require consideration of the organisation's environment.

- Competences can be identified as generic or specific, and their application to jobs may be essential (being the minimum required) or provide capacity for development. An analysis of these competence characteristics can aid career and succession planning.

- An open ended question on managerial responsibilities gave an indication of the ways in which the language of management is used in the NHS. There was considerable talk in the interviews about the importance of formal strategic planning, but there was comparatively little talk about actively managing change in a flexible way in order to take advantage of opportunities as they occured, albeit within a framework of well defined strategic objectives. This suggests that more work needs to be done in encouraging senior staff to adopt a more active, pragmatic and creative managerial role.

- Many respondents spoke about their management tasks in ways which suggested they felt themselves in a battle with their circumstances. They were considerably preoccupied with the immediate tasks of holding the fort, whilst at the same time making plans for a distant future when the seige might be lifted. Only occasionally however, did they talk about what they could do actively to change their approach or their operating circumstances.

- In the description of managerial roles and responsibilities, the dominant concerns of the senior staff who are engaged in managing the purchase and provision of health care are somewhat focused on internal management issues. This is strongly the case for doctors, nurses and other health professionals newly come to management, but it is also a theme which runs through many of the other responses.

- Typical job profiles were constructed from the managerial activities identified as important by different groups of staff. Similarities and differences between functions which are found in purchasing and providing were identified. This approach can be used by those responsible for management development and organisation development to consider the appropriateness of present priorities of groups of staff and to give indications of where there may be skill or knowledge deficits or surpluses. It can also help to identify where competences are common between purchasing and providing and thereby suggest ways in which people can move within the career climbing frame constructed in the previous chapter. For individuals it can give them insight into how their priorities compare with peers, superiors and subordinates and provides them with a basis for considering their own personal development.

- When asked about the support they receive to do their jobs, the most popular response was to identify respondents' 'own team", that is the group of people working in their function, service area or department. Just over a third of all respondents mentioned "line management" as a support.

- In reply to a question about the number of hours worked, the responses were typically of 46 to 55 hours a week. Seventy nine per cent of doctors in provider management spent 15 hours or less a week on management, with 19% spending under 5 hours per week on this aspect of their work.

- In answer to the question 'which aspect of management takes up most of your time' approximately two thirds of respondents in purchasing and providing identified "managing strategy". The second area identified as taking up most managerial time, was "managing liaisons and networks" for purchasing and "managing people" for providing.

- Whilst the possession of specialist functional skills is important it is not sufficient for senior executives in the NHS. They must develop the capacity to manage across functions and professions, and, particularly within purchasing, across organisations.

- The link between managerial effectiveness and organisational performance is especially pertinent when organisations are undergoing rapid change. It is vital for organisations carefully to identify their core competences (what they are really good at, what they know well and the range of ways in which they can use their knowledge and expertise) as a benchmark for strategic decision making and management development.

Chapter 5 Individual Performance Management and Review

Part of the thrust of the NHS reforms in 1991 was to increase the sense of personal and corporate accountability within providing and purchasing organisations. Various schemes for individual performance review (IPR) have been in existence for managers since the introduction of general management in 1983. The present IPR scheme was introduced in 1987 for general managers when for the first time there was a universal scheme. In addition, since that time senior management remuneration in the NHS has had an element of 'Performance Related Pay'. This pay element is awarded in terms laid down by a national scheme which details the way in which awards can be made, and the ceilings which apply for individuals, districts and regions. Clinical staff, on the other hand, have not, as yet, been formally involved in any national schemes for performance review or performance related pay, apart from the merit and distinction awards for doctors.

Once established as a trust, each provider could choose whether to stay within national schemes or whether, with each new appointment and promotion, to move staff onto trust terms and conditions. Many trusts have moved their senior managers and executives to new terms, and all trusts were in 1994 advised to develop their own systems for local pay determination. In addition the NHSTD has given support to local initiatives through funding consultancy advice for seven provider units developing pilot schemes for performance management and measurement. Most DHAs, at the time of fieldwork were operating within national systems, but anticipating changes. It is against this background of change that issues of performance management and review were discussed with our respondents.

This chapter is divided into the following sections:

- Mechanisms for Performance Review
- Personal priority setting
- Personal effectiveness evaluation
- Barriers which prevent personal effectiveness
- Summary

5.1 Mechanisms for Performance Review

IPR System in Use

All of the organisations in our study operated some variant of the senior management IPR system which essentially relies on the process of objective setting and evaluation. Formal annual reviews are performed with the appraisee's line manager, supplemented with half yearly reviews and ongoing informal progress reviews. Likewise all organisations reported use of the national senior management PRP system which operates through bands. The percentage of staff that can be placed in each band is rationed and band ratings relate to the percentage of performance pay received.

Although all the organisations had IPR, there was considerable divergence in its use. In some organisations its use was very patchy with little top management commitment and enthusiasm, but in others, despite acknowledged problems, it was given a high profile. In the latter there was strong support from the top, an awareness of the CEO's role in developing the organisation's mission, strategy and objectives and often a human resource manager committed to both performance management and organisational development.

Who evaluates?

All respondents were asked whether any one was formally accountable for evaluating their individual performance. Summary results are given in Table 5.1. This shows that 15% of all respondents said that 'no one' was formally accountable for evaluating their performance.

The response 'no-one' was disproportionately found amongst clinical managers, 37% of whom reported 'no one'. This proportion rose to 44% of clinical managers when we only considered provider respondents. Both these differences between clinical and other managers are significant at $p < 0.01$. The few general and functional managers who said 'no one' was formally accountable for evaluating their performance, all said that nonetheless this was done informally. Some doctors also said they were evaluated informally but more than 25% of all doctors in our sample were in the group of those who said they were neither evaluated formally or informally.

Table 5.1 *Performance Evaluation*

Is anyone formally accountable for evaluating your individual performance? (Qu.C.1)

	Purchaser respondents (n=95) %	Provider respondents (n=152) %	Total (n=247) %
(a) CEO	51	39	43
(b) Chair	8	6	7
(c) Other	39	32	35
Someone (total)	**98**	**77**	**65**
(d) No one	2	24	15
	100	**101**	**100**

Note:
1. Differences between cells in Table 3.1 were significant (p <0.01)

In line with the national system, generally it was respondents' "line managers" who conducted the performance evaluation in consultation with them. More of our sample in purchasing were evaluated by the CEO than those in providing. This simply reflects that proportionately more purchaser respondents were at board level. Those who identified some one other than the Chair or CEO as their evaluator were, as one would expect, drawn disproportionately from those at more than one level below the board.

The evaluation process

Having established who, if any one, was involved in evaluating individual performance, the interviewer sought to establish from those who had been evaluated, how the evaluation was carried out. Table 5.2 shows that the majority of respondents when answering this question (and who cited some system) were thinking about their formal IPR, as the means of performance evaluation.

Table 5.2   *System of Performance Evaluation*

How is your evaluation done? (Qu.C.5)

	General Manager (n=94) %	Functional Manager (n=37) %	Clinical Manager (n=60) %	Total (n=191) %
(a) Formal IPR	83	78	55	73
(b) Informal chat	9	11	25	14
(c) Not happened yet	6	5	12	8
(d) Other	2	5	8	5
	100	99	100	100

The IPR system is based on the traditional system where a manager reviews subordinates individually. However if we look outside the NHS to both other organisations and the literature we find a number of recent innovations in performance review. One of the most important is in the use of multi-source and multi-level appraisal (as discussed, for example, in Fletcher 1993, Redman and Snape 1992, Winstanley 1992). There are a number of factors which makes it seem sensible for the NHS to look beyond the use of only "downward appraisal":

–   the high professional base in the NHS,

–   the push for better team working across directorates and towards more of a "seamless" care for the patient,

–   the introduction of quality management systems and patients' charters which push the perspective away from the manager and towards the patient as a customer or client and as a judge of performance,

–   downsizing and delayering where hierarchical relationships become less important than lateral and networking ones

Possible innovations could be the incorporation of more team based appraisal (self appraisal and appraisal by peers) and upward appraisal.

The advantage of having **team based appraisal** is that for many managers in the NHS, their work is not contingent on their own success, but on their success as a member of a team which may be cross functional and multi-disciplinary. Many respondents saw their own effectiveness as crucially dependant on successful team working, and identifying, agreeing and being committed to working towards common goals. This was reflected in many of the critical incidents which respondents gave to illustrate their own effectiveness (reported in section 5.3), and was also reflected in the strong arguments which were advanced for a more team based performance management system:

"A better system would be team objectives and team monitoring, no one achieves things alone" (chief executive, purchaser)

"I would like to see a balance between individual performance and team performance - combined total for being a good team-player. We need greater acceptance of team performance in the organisation and to ensure that people who carry out IPR have the skills to do it." (functional manager, provider, board level)

"The system is individually focused and we need it to be more part of a team and more about behaviour, not just outcomes and achievements." (general manager, purchaser, board level)

"The philosophy is designed with individual performance review in mind and does not help with the development of corporate objectives and team working. It compartmentalises and is divisive, it does not encourage cohesion and is very mechanistic, it is easy to slip into doing it that way and not recognise the environment, team IPR is more attractive." (clinical manager, purchaser, board level)

"I am interested in the idea of pursuing the notion of peer review for managers, and review of my performance by my own staff – this is equally as important as the formal performance review, but we don't do it" (clinical manager, provider, level below board)

"I am not satisfied with the way we set objectives because it does not bring together a corporate approach or look at the way the department works together which is as important as the individual bit – for evaluation we need corporate organisation objectives measured against individual." (general manager, purchaser, level below board)

The advantage of having **"upward appraisal"** or at least feedback, would be to redress the gulf which we have highlighted in our research which exists between on the one hand many managers claiming that their own effectiveness has been radically improved by the help of a sponsor, mentor, coach or role model at some time in their career, and yet on the other the lack of importance many (although not all) managers attach to developing their subordinates (as shown in the descriptions managers provide about their job, duties and responsibilities).

Despite the push for more "patient" focused performance systems, supported by the Government in their publication of The Patients Charter, the identification of performance targets and feedback on performance for individual managers as perceived by the perspective of the patient is most likely to be channelled through others, for example staff dealing with quality or complaints, who interpret their experience.

Performance Management Systems

Recent research has highlighted a shift in interest and activity away from "stand alone" appraisal systems, and towards individual performance review being part and parcel of "performance management systems" (PMS) (for example see Neal 1991). The most comprehensive piece of research is the latest of the research surveys conducted by the IPM in this area, which includes detailed case studies as well as a national survey (see Bevan and Thompson 1992 and Fletcher and Williams 1992)

Bevan and Thompson's conditions for PMS are:

1   communication of a vision of organisational objectives to all employees,
2   the setting of departmental and individual performance targets which are related to wider objectives,
3   the conducting of a formal review of progress towards these targets,
4   the review process is used to identify training, development and reward outcomes,
5   the organisation evaluates the effectiveness of the whole process in order to improve effectiveness.

Bevan and Thompson found that just under 20% of organisations in the UK claim to operate a formal PMS. Our research showed a wide variation within the NHS in the extent to which the development of IPR systems could be seen to constitute performance management systems in practice.

Very different experiences were reported with respect to the existence and communication of a shared organisational vision (point 1). In some sites it was poorly developed, in others we found chief executives who saw this as a core part of their role:

"We are keen within the organisation to identify business objectives in explicit terms and to link what the individual is doing with the corporate objectives. The mission dictates the objectives which dictates the strategy. We identify from corporate statements of intent key personal objectives for the CEO and executive directors. The process is wrapped up tightly in strong IPR including management and monitoring issues, and developmental issues, handled in a tight framework that we share in common." (chief executive, purchaser)

"I am responsible for injecting judgements which are exclusively the CEO's on the order in which goals are set and should be tackled. Once priorities are set I ensure the systems are in place to enable development to occur and bring them to a conclusion..". (chief executive, provider)

Although IPR does allow for the formal review of progress based on objective setting (point 3), the extent to which this is actually put into practice is patchy. Some of our respondents experienced difficulty in linking their objective setting to the wider organisational context (point 2), and there was considerable dissatisfaction with the balance between consideration of training, development and reward outcomes (point 4). Little reference was made to the extent to which the effectiveness of the process was evaluated (point 5).

Experiences of Performance Review

Respondents were asked to identify the criteria which they thought were used in their performance evaluation. Table 5.3 shows that respondents in purchasing referred only to individual or organisational objectives. In providing, respondents referred also to financial targets and to operational targets set by management, for such things as activity and service levels.

Table 5.3 *Criteria Used in Individual Performance Evaluation*

What criteria do you think they use (in performance evaluation)? (Qu.5b)

Criteria	Purchaser respondent (n=34) %	Provider respondent (n=57) %	Total (n=91) %
(a) Financial	0	21	13
(b) Operational management targets (eg activity)	0	11	7
(c) Meeting individual objectives	47	46	47
(d) Organisational objectives, deriving from business plan, etc	53	33	41

Note:
Respondents could identify more than one criterion.

When asked if they would like to change any aspect of the way their performance is evaluated, 69% of all respondents replied 'yes' (Table 5.4). Those wishing to change were found disproportionately in purchasing and reflecting that, in general and functional management positions. Proportionately more younger (88% of those below 45) than older (50%) respondents wanted to see a change. All these differences were statistically significant at p <0.05.

Table 5.4 *Wish for Change in Performance Evaluation*

Would you like to change any aspect of the way your performance is evaluated? (Qu.C.6)

	Purchaser respondents (n=69) %	Provider respondents (n=111) %	Total (n=180) %
Yes	80	63	69
No	20	37	31
	100	100	100

Note :
1. Differences between cells in Table 5.4 statistically significant (p <0.05)

Past research has highlighted some inadequacies with IPR systems (see IHSM 1991, Nalgo survey 1992, Sheldon 1992 for example). Perceived problems with IPR for performance review largely revolve around five issues:

1   It is too time-consuming,

2   It is not taken seriously,

3   People have difficulty in setting objectives,

4   The link between individual and organisational performance assessment is tenuous,

5   Its link with performance pay undermines its developmental objectives, and does nothing to consolidate individual with organisational performance.

Our research confirms these problems in the NHS, although it shows that in general the processes of objective setting, of having an opportunity to reflect on ones work, and securing feedback on performance, are valued aspects of the system. The following points were raised by managers who reported negative experiences of their performance review:

–   **time:** lack of time given to process

–   **bureaucratic,** cumbersome and time consuming

–   **not taken seriously:** perceived lack of importance by reviewer, delays, cancellations, postponements of reviews

- **lack of skill** by appraiser in conducting appraisals
- **not systematic:** too ad hoc, no follow through, formal reviews not supplemented by informal ongoing support and review
- **developmental side is underdeveloped**
- **objective setting:** concentration on objectives doesn't allow balance of total workload, the objectives don't reflect the intangibles, lack of **flexibility** in allowing objectives to change.
- **lack of linkage of individual to corporate performance:** the individual focus is not meshed with team and corporate objectives.

Indicative comments relating to the points above include:

"The system does not work well and we are concerned to review it, it is not sufficiently linked to corporate objectives, it is cumbersome and time-consuming to apply, it cannot adequately account for the link between the individual, the team and the whole organisation." (human resource director, provider, board level)

"It is a very bureaucratic approach here – ticking boxes but not looking at the process eg. it looks to see if people are meeting objectives but it disenchants and demotivates staff." (clinical manager, purchaser, level below board)

"It is a fiction that one has to go through. It fails abysmally in what it attempts to do, it is run by its own paper system, and although it may be a good system for defining goals, financially it is meaningless." (general manager, purchaser, board level)

"There are periodic formal reviews but they get sacrificed due to time constraints" (functional manager, purchaser, board level)

"You need to ensure the people who carry out IPR have the skills to do it – there are training needs here – the system is only as good as the people who work it." (functional manager, provider, board level)

"I have no experience and training in IPR and how to do it with my own staff. My manager has helped but he has had no formal training." (functional manager, purchaser, level below board)

"It is a difficult situation because I am more experienced and have been around longer than the director." (clinical manager, purchaser, level below board)

"No one tells you that you are doing a good job." (general manager, provider, two levels below board)

"There is little emphasis on personal development whether through MD or through the work that we do, this happens because of the goodwill and commitment from individuals and not because of the system." (general manager, purchaser, level below board)

"We don't use IPR to develop people enough. Because we are a flat organisation I do a lot of IPR but I don't get involved in training and development much. It is seen as about bandings and quotas of bandings." (functional manager, purchaser, board level)

"The trouble with evaluation is that despite the time taken to critically think about how to improve performance, ... there is no support for your improvement – you need a tutor or mentor." (clinical manager, provider, level below board)

"I would be more motivated if there was someone out there to check it with, a mentor rather than the isolating, pressurising effect of the present system." (general manager, provider, two levels below board)

"The problem is IPR is seen as a substitute for continuing management, there is little time spent on motivating between IPRs, you need a formal appraisal but it should not be a substitute." (general manager, purchaser, board level)

"I would like to see the IPR system take account of external barriers more. We have to get contracts signed by 31st March deadline – this is impossible, but politically, we have to sign up to it." (general manager, provider, level below board)

"There is a problem of timing because the job has changed and the director has changed so a lot of the objectives are no longer relevant by the time of the next appraisal. It is not adjusted within the year so it really is an arbitrary kind of assessment." (general manager, provider, level below board)

"Objectives are always changing, especially in response to national initiatives such as waiting lists." (general manager, provider, board level)

"The objectives are reviewed at the end of the year but the goal posts have moved to a different pitch, and we are without an in year review that could change objectives." (functional manager, provider, board level)

"The system is fine but it is not implemented very well, I get frustrated by their not putting more time and effort into training people around objective-setting, if we have no training then performance review is not proper because there are no proper objectives." (general manager, purchaser, one level below board)

"We need the key results areas to be well-focused and top down otherwise some of the objectives set may be peripheral and may not link with others." (functional manager, provider, level below board)

Table 5.5 summarises the way in which respondents would like to see changes in their performance evaluation. A third, drawn disproportionately from functional managers and those at the top of the organisation, would like to change the criteria.

They would like to see a greater linking of individual to organisational objectives, together with a broader concern to establish whether, within constraints, individuals had done a 'good job'. They felt they were often held accountable for delivery on targets over which they had little or no control, hence the 22% who complained that the evaluation process was inflexible and coped poorly with changes in circumstances. This was a view held by proportionately more general managers than others. Another 31% of respondents had problems with the process. Here the focus was on their feelings that the evaluation was often hurried and not given sufficient importance by the evaluator. This view was held particularly by younger respondents and those who were clinical managers.

Twenty one per cent, drawn disproportionately from the more senior respondents, wished for a change in the reward element. They felt that the standard IPR system did not allow sufficient flexibility, or bonuses of sufficient magnitude, to act as a strong basis for motivation. Many others criticised the PRP system, and this is discussed below.

Table 5.5 *Suggested Changes in own Performance Evaluation (Qu.C.7)*

	Purchasers respondents (n=55) %	Providers respondents (n=70) %	Total (n=125) %
(a) Change evaluator	18	23	21
(b) Change criteria	33	33	33
(c) Change reward element	26	17	21
(d) Problems with process of evaluation	33	30	31
(e) Copes poorly with change, inflexible	22	23	22
(f) Other	2	7	5

Note:
1. Respondents could mention more than one area

A number of differences in response to QU C.7 were found to be significant at $p < 0.05$ level. With reference to changing criteria, more functional managers than clinical or general managers, and more directors than lower level people wanted to change the criteria. More directors rather than others wanted to change the reward element. More younger (below 45) than older wanted to change the process reflecting the perceived greater requirement for feedback and help in performance development earlier on in careers.

Clinical managers and those from a nursing or medical background were more inclined to seek to change the evaluator, and more clinical managers were inclined to change the process than general or functional managers. This reflects both the lack of skills in performance appraisal and feedback and lack of importance given to this process by this group's line managers, suggesting some development help and awareness programmes are necessary here. This suggests an inappropriateness for this approach for these groups; they appreciate feedback and objective setting but not within the context of this mechanism and process, and it is to this we turn in the section below.

Clinical Managers and Performance Review

With the exception of doctors merit and distinction awards, clinical staff have not, as yet, been formally involved in any national schemes for performance review or performance related pay, although appropriate supervision and peer support is an integral part of any clinical professional's work.

Some trusts are moving to examine performance review aspects of clinical professional staff. There are, for example, developments with consultant job plans as a basis for discussion about activity and performance. The pay of doctors, nurses and other health professionals thus far has been determined on the recommendation of Independent Pay Review bodies according to national scales and terms and conditions of employment, but at the time of fieldwork there was some movement within trusts to secure more locally based arrangements. As yet the 'merit' and 'distinction' awards for medical staff are determined at regional and national level with little local managerial input. Furthermore, there is no clear link between such awards and performance. Indeed expectations of clinical performance are difficult to determine and define and the place of management performance in the evaluation of medical staff is unclear.

In the future it is possible, but not very likely, that medical and clinical audit could provide a vehicle for the evaluation of individual performance. At the present time it is concerned only with general issues of performance and effectiveness and there is great resistance to moving towards individual audit. The Royal Colleges, the GMC and the UKCC, amongst other bodies, all have a role in evaluating individual clinical performance, but it is a role which only comes into play when performance is considered to be unsatisfactory. There are no formal mechanisms for the positive evaluation of individual clinical performance.

Given this and the fact that a proportion of doctors involved in management consider they are undertaking their managerial duties almost 'as a favour' to the organisation, the issue of performance evaluation and appraisal for clinical managerial staff is highly charged.

The situation is in part different in purchaser organisations where directors of public health are more fully integrated into the managerial world, but some problems which arise are the same, particularly when it comes to general managers evaluating public health performance.

A number of points came out of this research which relate to 'doctors as managers' experiences of the use of management systems for performance evaluation and development.

- Time constraints, for example,

"I haven't the time"

"I have no objection to an occasional discussion but a regular review would be very irksome"

- Cultural and status constraints relating to their own perceptions of their profession, for example,

"I cannot be accountable to people earning half as much as I am"

"part of me says I do not want to learn to play the management game"

- Suspicion over how the system would be used, and in particular the fear that it would be used to control rather than help, for example,

"it is potentially quite threatening"

"the problem is to overcome the suspicion of professionals who deliver the healthcare"

- Lack of knowledge by potential appraiser of appraisee's job

"It is very difficult for the CEO to evaluate professional performance. There is a need for peer review. I have a lot of power in that what I say is difficult to contradict because I am a doctor. I try not to use it but I do, there is a problem with complacency." (public health physician, purchaser, board level)

However, despite these comments, a significant proportion of clinical directors say they would welcome more support and opportunity to discuss and develop their objectives (so long as the system was designed sensitively), and this particularly applies to those not currently in the IPR system, for example,

"I would appreciate finer guidelines and direction to meet the overall hospital strategy".

"I could do with more feedback in relation to managerial skills, but I am unlikely to find the time for managerial appraisal."

It was not just the clinical managers who resisted being appraised by general managers, as the latter also had problems when being appraised by the former, and this again was related to the gap in knowledge and understanding of each other's role and sphere of work – a theme which emerges from our study. These instances are drawn from business managers who are appraised by their clinical directors from clinician backgrounds:

"The clinical director finds it very difficult to appraise me, because he has a lack of knowledge of the full range of tasks and management in general."

"My appraisal really needs to be done by someone with management experience. Currently they don't actually know how well you are doing, it just depends on how well you get on with your consultant director"

"I don't feel the clinical director has enough knowledge of the development of clinical services management, for career planning."

"the clinical director doesn't see the totality of my role, just how to handle the staff at the unit, it is such a multi-facetted job."

"I would like more regular feedback from the clinical director and would prefer feedback from the general management side also."

These quotes illustrate the importance of

- choosing an appropriate person to conduct the evaluation

- providing management development to enable the evaluation to be conducted effectively

- facilitating better dialogue and understanding between the spheres of clinical and general management.

One question remains: why so many clinical directors, who say they would like more help in setting objectives, and feedback on their accomplishment, don't get it. Possible reasons could be that current systems are inappropriate, managers do not want to "take on" clinical directors or worry that if not done sensitively, it may be misinterpreted due to suspicion and the lack of trust, or there is no one available to provide leadership in these matters.

Experience of Performance Related Pay

Whereas the experience of IPR was mixed with evidence of successful and unsuccessful use, there was nearly a unanimous view over the national scheme for PRP for senior managers. In this scheme individuals subject to IPR are placed in one of five bands of achievement with 1 as the highest. The total PRP paid in any one year is subject to an overall limit expressed as an average percentage increase for any one group. Only four respondents expressed support or satisfaction with the system. All others who expressed a view, were dissatisfied with it. Their attitude is represented in the following comments:

"I am keen on the idea of management by objectives, but not keen on the way it is related to employees pay (clinical manager, purchaser, board level)

"I like the setting objectives but I am not sure whether the reward system is worth the hassle, we need a separate reward system and objectives." (general manager, purchaser, board level)

"IPR is discredited by PRP because it drives everything down to cash, and with regional quotas, we end up with everyone getting disgruntled" (functional manager, provider, board level)

"the link to PRP is horrible and should be dumped ... the model is badly flawed, it demotivates and blurs issues around IPR and objective setting, it is difficult for people to see the developmental objectives. Also it is not managed well. . it is not consistent and fair. The PRP framework has an average tendency so it is impossible to have brilliant teams – you cannot reward collective high performance – if you give 2 people the top rating then you have to give 2 people the bottom rating – this is stupid when linked to objective setting process. You should be able to reward achievement of objectives through bonuses etc. ... Nat West do it separately" (chief executive, purchaser)

"PRP is a waste of time as a system in terms of the incentives it provides. .. and PRP is no motivation factor." (general manager, purchaser, level below board)

"PRP is a farce because of the quota system so there is no incentive." (functional manager, purchaser, level below board)

"I have a lack of confidence in PRP as a valuable tool for motivating. The quota system makes it very devalued, "you are a 2 but I can't give you a 2". People are motivated from doing the job well." (general manager, provider, level below board)

"I have criticism of PRP as a negative motivator, if you score highly, you do not necessarily get it, the money is rationed – this is extremely demotivating for staff." (chief executive, provider)

"The trust is moving away from the PRP system to a base pay level one, subject to annual review, it is not so mechanistic" (chief executive, provider, board level)

"PRP is very difficult ... for ensuring equity. People's expectations that if they have done well they get a 1 or a 2, but maybe they have done a good job and that would give them a 4, so there is disappointment and unrealistic expectations. PRP could focus on fringe benefits and not just the money side. For example Boston have a matrix of fringe benefits – extra annual leave, flexible working, crèche facilities and you agree what suits you best, so it is possible to reward people in other ways, for example, organisational support to go on training courses." (general manager, provider, level below board)

"It is de-motivating because money is available on a quota system, you have to stand up and shout out about how wonderful you are, it is unable to pick up on more invisible work, and my manager doesn't have the age and wisdom to do that." (nursing manager, provider, two levels below board)

The criticisms of the national scheme for PRP for senior managers were of four kinds:

- **Appropriateness:** it is inappropriate to professional staff

- **Works against team working:** because it is impossible for everyone to do well (because of the ratio bandings); it is divisive and encourages competition rather than collaboration to improve performance overall.

- **Unfair application:** it is applied in an unfair, subjective and biased way

- **Irrelevance and ineffective:** it does not help organisations and individuals to meet their objectives or result in any positive performance improvement.

Of these comments perhaps the most important is the relationship of PRP with team working and the perceived view that an individual based performance reward goes against the culture and ways of working which the NHS is trying to encourage – particularly team working. A number of respondents suggested that performance rewards achievable by everyone would be more appropriate, particularly if they were related to success of the organisation (or team) overall, rather than just to the individual's success at meeting their own objectives. Although the PRP system was intended to be based on organisational objectives cascaded down to the individual level, the perception is that this doesn't happen.

Many local schemes for PRP now address these issues, but were not in place at the time of fieldwork.

5.2   Personal Priority Setting

Senior executives do not, of course, simply respond either to circumstances or to objectives established in consultation with others, they are also involved on an individual basis in setting their own priorities. Table 5.6 summarises responses to the open-ended question "By what criteria do you set priorities in your job?"

Nearly half the respondents identified the 'corporate or business plan' as the basis for their own priorities. This response came from significantly more executive directors than those beneath them and from more general than functional or clinical managers and, surprisingly, from more younger managers (below 45). The next two most popular priorities were seen to derive from 'regional or national' targets on the one hand and 'personal objectives' on the other. Both of these were significantly more popular with purchasers than providers, particularly the "Health of the Nation" agenda, and with more general or functional than clinical managers. Significantly more provider respondents and especially clinical managers, identified clinical targets as a primary source of their personal objectives. 'Firefighting the daily crisis' was the basis of priority setting for a quarter of our respondents, with significantly more clinical than other managers citing it.

Priority setting was not found to be an easy process. In reality managers found many difficulties in getting the time to set their own priorities, and felt they lacked the ability to do so. Such points were made in discussions over their performance evaluation and the IPR process, and over barriers to their own effectiveness.

Table 5.6   *Priority Setting*

By what criteria do you set priorities in your job? (Qu.B.4)

Criteria	Purchaser respondents (n=97) %	Provider respondents (n=157) %	Total (n=254) %
(a) Corporate objectives, business plan	45	46	46
(b) Corporate, regional, national timetable and deadlines	55	18	32
(c) Personal objectives (IPR), agenda, capacity, judgement, experience	43	24	32
(d) Daily basis of what needs to be done, firefighting	22	28	26
(e) Clinical timetable/priorities	0	29	18
(f) OD/MD requirements	9	13	12
(g) Financial pressures, VFM and cost effectiveness	3	12	9
(h) Health of Nation, Public Health report	20	0	8
(i) The CEO, boss, line manager	6	3	4

Note:
1. Respondents could identify more than one criterion.

When asked about their own effectiveness, barriers to it, and ways they set priorities in their own job, a big issue for managers was "the size of their agenda" and the difficulty they had in balancing the many and varied demands on their time. Most managers reported working long hours (see data on hours worked in Table 4.5), yet a significant proportion of managers reported that their workload exceeded their capabilities. As well as help with time management, they needed help with reconciling the demands of patients, purchasers, their own managers, region, the government, not to mention their own agenda. This makes the need for priority setting even more important; if they cannot work any longer perhaps they can work more effectively.

Typical comments from managers on their difficulty with setting their own objectives are:

"the problem is not fully knowing what is expected...."

"the problem is a reluctance by some colleagues to be serious about prioritising"

"there is a lack of direction and clarity for my area"

"the barrier is the wide scale on which I could get involved, being focused and clear about what the priorities are, butterflying on projects, not getting to grips with projects, I am missing a clear sense of purpose."

"I am unable to divest myself of the day to day trivia.'

"I don't really set priorities – it feels like I am chasing my tail.'

"a development issue for me is defining within the organisation what our corporate job is and then defining the way we should achieve it'

"I would like to see more collaboration on setting objectives."

"It is very much crisis management ... it is very frustrating. I need relief from other duties and I need a spell out.'

Some also identified the need to retain an element of flexibility in priorities and objectives, a point already made earlier with respect to IPR:

"You have to plan but you also have to be flexible because things crop up." (general manager, purchaser, two levels below board)

A positive intervention mentioned by some was the taking of time out from the day to day "firefighting" to reflect on their priorities. For example,

"Away-days among directorates looking at how to reach changes necessary in organisational and cultural terms, and make the organisation more appropriate for the task is an on-going essential process". (general manager, provider)

It appears that what is wanted is some management development help to support objective and priority setting such as away days, facilitators and extra guidance from either internal or external experts or mentors.

5.3   Personal Effectiveness Evaluation

In this section, we explore the answers to three areas of questioning on personal effectiveness: a critical incident, an open question on attributes leading to personal effectiveness, and a closed question requiring respondents to choose the most important from a list of personal attributes. Altogether, this data provides an overview of managerial inputs as a basis for identifying and evaluating managerial competence (as discussed in Chapter 4).

Respondents were asked to:

"describe an incident in which you were particularly effective in your job, for whatever reasons" (Qu.G.1).

Given the varied nature of their jobs, it is not surprising that respondents raised a very wide variety of activities (see fig. 5.1).

However despite the variety of types of critical incident there was much greater convergence over why they thought that they had been particularly effective in this instant. Figure 5.2 identifies the factors which were explicitly cited by respondents as the means to their success.

The message that comes across so clearly from figure 5.2 is that in order to achieve success, respondents felt they generally needed one of two things. The first critical skill is the need to work through and with others – and in particular the ability to network and teamwork with those in ones own area of work, with those in other departments, and for many, with those outside of the organisation.

Examples of the type of thing that managers were saying about the importance of teamwork, networking, generating enthusiasm and participation are quoted below. Many included reaching out or working in a new way which resulted in

Figure 5.1 *Subjects Identified in Critical Incidents and Their Popularity Qu.G.1*

In descending order of popularity, respondents mentioned incidents involving:

* reorganisation and development of services (24% of critical incidents)
* human resource and staff development issues (16%)
* improving information and IT (12%)
* improving service quality initiatives (11%)
* getting contracts and bringing in funding (8%)
* development and communication of strategy (6%)
* changing culture and increasing team working (6%)
* budget management (5%)
* communication with stakeholders / patients / purchasers (4%)
* vision / leadership (2%)
* getting trust status (2%)
* improving image and public relations (1%)
* setting up a policy (0.5%)
* personal progression (0.5%)

Notes:
1. Rounding figures up and down has resulted in total not = 100%,
2. n = 190 critical incidents

benefits from ongoing participation and team- working, and many talked of the importance of "keeping people on board" and "getting doctors together to talk":

"The hospital used to be a very institutionalised unhappy place with bullying and low standards of care, high turnover of significant groups of staff. I ran an organisational development programme and completely turned that around using staff changes, training, consumer research, recruitment, team-building with external facilitators, working with relatives and other families to begin to talk about the problems, and staff talking together so changed the culture, and the standards of care are still rising. For example we have a more equitable distribution of resources, the overview of care is so much better with skill mix teams, and we have achieved enough flexibility to offer proper delivery of care, and we have improved relations with GP practices." (functional manager, provider)

Figure 5.2 *How People Achieved Success in Their Critical Incident of Personal Effectiveness Qu. G.1*

Working with others/team working/networking/ taking people with them/collaboration/ participation/consultation	(43%)
Persuasion/influence/negotiation/lobbying	(23%)
Communication – openness/clarity/giving out information "getting message across"	(13%)
Hard work/effort/use of own skills and expertise	(10%)
Coaching/developing others/enabling/ empowering/training	(10%)
Working against others/battles/struggles/ overcoming resistance/coercion/applying pressure	(9%)
Recruitment	(8%)
Having information/research/monitoring information	(8%)
Strategy/vision/good leadership	(6%)
Restructuring/reorganisation	(3%)
Setting up a pilot scheme	(2%)
Managing staff exits	(2%)
Culture change	(2%)

Notes:
1. No score: ie. respondent didn't explain in sufficient detail – 9%
2. Percentage is scored out of number of respondents answering this question citing this factor, thus respondents can cite more than one method used and so percentages do not total 100%.
3. Only where respondent cited criterion explicitly is it scored, thus implicit scores are not included.
4. n = 173 critical incidents

"I'm pleased that I've been able to turn around the image of the unit - three years ago it was not rated very highly by the region, we had a long history of over-spending and trade union problems. I'm impressed with what happens here - the co-operation ... and a lot of enthusiasm. Getting back into shape has been very tough for everyone. Nothing has been done single-handedly, (it has been as a result of) excellent teamwork." (chief executive, provider, board level)

"the introduction of electronic results reporting to GPs and our clients (was the critical incident). ... Grabbing GPs because there are wider implications of the electronic link so the underlying aim is strategic for our hospital. What was involved in this was selling ideas, costs, what was suitable and the people involved. We had to cut across all the departments ... and required the director to create enthusiasm among the heads of department, also the GPs, FHSA, suppliers of GPs equipment and we needed agreement to use the systems before even thinking about the problems of technical feasibility." (clinical manager, provider, level below board)

"I shifted emphasis this contracting year. Last year I went to units and talked to professionals. This year I talked to patients. I talked individually to a group of 25 patients over the year. This was a significant shift in direction. I took the decision to get to the people we serve. Access was difficult. I had the naïve idea that people would be delighted to talk. I got to them through GPs. ... Also randomly picked a service such as x and rang patients up to talk to them. The key points came out concerning discharge back to the community and admission to hospital. We took the approach of 'give us the next 3 people admitted to your ward' – and then we rang them up" (general manager, purchaser)

The second critical skill relates to the art of persuasion and the ability through communication or negotiation or even "selling" to get others to generate some sort of agreement from which action can be taken which results in positive outcomes. Examples here are:

"(the critical incident was) the commissioning of a new building ... This was about involving and negotiating about what the service should work like and including users – clinicians, GPs etc. From the planning level of working through to being involved in the project team decisions." (general manager, provider)

"(the critical incident was) a selling job which was useful to the organisation. To sell to colleagues and GPs the idea that GPs should comment on individual consultant performance in clinical terms by means of a questionnaire. This was fairly threatening for consultants. The impetus was - however good you are, you can always improve ..." (clinical manager, provider)

To support the negotiation and generation of a consensus and teamwork, many cited the importance of giving out clear information in an appropriate way. Examples here are:

"(the critical incident was) waiting lists. Moving patients needs advocacy skills ... Had to develop it, manage it, market it, go on TV about it." (general manager, purchaser)

"pulling together (various activities) involving all staff leading to two mega two hour sessions. (They were the) key event in setting out quite publicly what was important. The style is – we are a non-hierarchical, non-status, learning organisation. If you don't believe us try us, test us." (chief executive, purchaser, board level)

"(critical incident was) the presentation of information to the Hospital Management Group – making it as clear as possible, overcoming confusion – on review of annual performance. Open Board meetings are a chance to find out what is going on. Communication helps to keep a good team of staff together." (functional manager, provider)

Although less common, there were examples of working with people in a less positive way, and usually these instances were where a clinical manager was trying to get consultants "on board". A number cited great "battles" and "struggles" and some even resorted to coercive tactics. For example:

"I am involved in fighting a battle to recover the service, and have nearly succeeded ... this has involved long battles on all sorts of levels" (clinical manager, provider)

"I was instrumental in (overcoming) the geriatric problem, ... overcoming bed blocking problem ... Surgeons were very resistant ... the shift in resources was a "hell of a struggle" and last Winter was a nightmare for the department and I had to keep banging on the door." (clinical manager, provider)

"Introducing a new system of management – no one wanted to do the CD job. There was no directorate culture, (everyone) was acting as individuals. It was a rocky beginning so used it to black spot when people were being difficult. We tried to agree a policy. If someone can't then the person is given the black spot which is meaning that you can do the job yourself." (clinical manager, provider)

There were a few who felt that they had succeeded through their own effort and hard work or specific skills and expertise, but these generally were in the areas of setting up information systems or finance systems:

"Doing the financial work for the trust application changed the world I live in. It was a terrifying time ... I felt a personal sense of achievement on the day we became a trust. I'd done the work and succeeded, not just on "front of the house". The workers were being paid, bills being paid, computer system going. I felt I'd achieved the most." (functional manager, provider)

However comments on success through working alone were not typical. The general message is that general, clinical and functional managers think that successful management in the NHS is about working with and through others, and success depends on developing such skills and requires the positive support, consent and involvement of others. Many cited additional satisfaction from the process, developing positive working relationships, and team and networking which outlasted the incident itself.

For those who couldn't identify a critical incident (4) it was either because they were too new to the job, or they somehow felt they weren't quite coping enough to lift up their head and identify anything tangible. A typical comment here is:

"Not as yet, it has been a bit of a struggle so far".

In explaining their critical incident, many respondents mentioned their criteria for judging it a success. In general respondents mentioned some criteria of effectiveness in the sense that the outcomes had met their objectives, for example "improved quality", "achieved results", "saved money", "resulted in better communication, working relationships" "attitudes" "better team working", "waiting lists reduced"; and efficiency improvements such as "more work for the same cost", "increased referrals". Two other sorts of response also featured. First, some respondents mentioned reputational measures of effectiveness, such as "good feedback from users", "customer satisfaction", "improved the reputation of the department", "won awards". Second, some perceived the success in the way it had developed their view of the world, and interpreted success in terms of its effects on them, for example "it changed the world I lived in", "it was a watershed for me". Generally, people seemed satisfied by seeing some tangible results or quality improvement, or could identify some development or change to which their action was attributable.

The critical incident was not the only way the study elicited people's comments on personal effectiveness. They were also asked about their personal attributes in a more general way. All respondents were asked in an open-ended question to identify the three most important attributes which they personally possessed which they felt led to their own effectiveness (Table 5.7). Following this exercise they were given a list of attributes and asked to rate them in importance. (Table 5.8).

Table 5.7 presents a summary of the responses which were relatively homogeneous both between purchasers and providers and across most of our other demographic variables. Three significant but expected differences are worthy of note. Significantly more women (78%) than men (62%) rated their interpersonal and communication skills as being one of the three of their most important personal attributes. More executive directors than those in levels one or two below them, cited interpersonal and communication skills, whereas more respondents at lower levels highlighted organising skills. More younger people (25–34) cited organising skills whereas more older people (55–64) cited the importance of a knowledge base. The most frequently mentioned attributes were interpersonal and communication skills, leadership and strategic vision and individual personality traits which underlie both of these characteristics.

Table 5.7 *Personal Effectiveness Evaluation*

In your opinion what are the most important attributes you personally possess which lead you to being an effective executive (Qu.C.1)

Attributes	Purchaser respondents (n=102) %	Provider respondents (n=162) %	Total (n=264) %
Individual personality traits	40	45	43
Leadership/strategy abilities	40	40	40
Interpersonal/communication skills	60	73	68
Team building, working, motivation	16	7	11
Analytical skills	28	20	23
Organisation skills, ability to get things done	17	19	18
Knowledge base, technical background professional competence/expertise	30	26	27
Accept change, flexible, willingness to learn	13	6	9
Stamina, energy, hard working	6	6	6

The human side of management received significantly greater emphasis than the technical or knowledge base of management.

Having answered the open-ended question on managerial attributes, all respondents were then given a self-completion sheet on which 14 personal attributes were listed (Table 5.8). They were asked to indicate the degree of importance they attached to each attribute for an effective executive in their position to possess.

Table 5.8 shows the proportion of each of the three 'present job' groups who rated the given attribute as "Highly Important". Top scores, receiving assent as 'Highly important' by more than 70% of all respondents, were:

- communication skills (82%)
- ability to get things done (81%)
- personal integrity (77%)
- ability to provide leadership (75%)

The lowest scores were:

- willingness to take risks (32%)
- creativity (31%)

This response profile is interesting in that the lower scores are for attributes which in the contemporary business and commercial world are seen to be critically important for managerial success. However within the NHS, where senior executives are trustees of public money, there is apparently less emphasis on risk taking and creativity.

This demonstrates some of the contradictions with which senior executives in the NHS are grappling. On the one hand they are exhorted to act more like the private sector and yet on the other they are required to manage public funds within tight financial constraints and on an annual break even basis. With such a regime it is indeed difficult to put too much emphasis on risk taking and creativity.

The emphasis on the importance of communication and leadership accord with earlier findings presented in Chapter 4. The emphasis upon 'ability to get things done', relates to the difficulty of managing complex organisations in circumstances where systems for evaluating organisational and individual performance are underdeveloped. Thus it is possible to spend a great deal of time and energy on decision making and planning, only to find that there is little systematic 'follow through' to secure that the intentions are developed into a coherent reality.

In commenting on the differences encountered in responses from different groups for Table 5.8, it is interesting to note that both in terms of present job and in terms of background, there were few significant differences between the groups. Significantly more general managers attach high importance to 'skill in using alliances and networks' and to 'willingness to take risks'. The question was asked in terms of each respondent replying for "an executive in their position'; nonetheless there was only one statistically significant difference when the data was analysed by level; proportionately more of those reporting to the board, rather than those above or below this level, rated the attribute of 'creativity' highly. In terms of gender, female respondents were significantly more likely to cite "ability to develop others" than male respondents.

Table 5.8 *Views on Important Managerial Attributes*

Please indicate the degree of importance you attach to the following personal attributes for an effective executive in your position to possess (Qu.C.1)

Highly rated "Highly Important"	General Manager (n=117) %	Functional Manager (n=45) %	Clinical Manager (n=102) %	Total (n=264) %
(a) Efficiency	39	47	45	42
(b) Ability to get things done	85	89	74	81
(c) Self confidence	56	60	43	52
(d) Skill in logical thought	49	56	47	49
(e) Skill in the use of alliances and networks*	74	62	48	62
(f) Ability to develop others	47	56	42	46
(g) Adaptability	56	75	52	57
(h) Ability to work in a team	65	73	60	64
(i) Ability to provide leadership	75	73	76	75
(j) Willingness to take risks*	41	27	23	32
(k) Creativity	32	36	28	31
(l) Communication skills	86	84	76	82
(m) Personal integrity	74	78	81	77

Notes:

Statistically significant differences in response to Qu.I.l were found between general, functional and clinical managers

* statistically significant differences p <0.05

5.4   Barriers Which Prevent Personal Effectiveness

Respondents views, identified in Table 5.6, that their performance is adversely effected by circumstances beyond their control, not least by the rate of 'top-down' imposed change, are to some extent also reflected in Table 5.9. This summarises the responses to an open-ended question about the main barriers to personal effectiveness. 'Operational overload', with too many imposed targets was identified by 33% of all respondents, 'the pace of change' by 13% and 'financial constraints' by 19%. 'Operational overload' was experienced by all levels, types of job and in all organisations. There were no significant differences between groups in their response. The 'pace of change' was identified by significantly more purchasers and 'financial constraints' by more respondents in providers organisations, where it was particularly expressed by clinical or functional rather than general managers.

However, the greatest barrier to change was identified as internal management problems. This was significantly more likely to be identified by respondents in purchasing and by those who were in the middle rather than at the top of the organisation. In discussing this as a barrier to effective performance, respondents spoke of 'lack of clarity', 'confused roles and responsibilities', 'relations between departments', 'poor communications' and 'defensive attitudes'. Lack of skills and knowledge, lack of information and the operation of the internal market were each identified by just 15% of the total respondents. Executive directors were significantly different to those lower down the organisation in that more of them identified the political environment, and aspects of the internal market as barriers, whereas less of them mentioned financial constraints and internal management problems.

Table 5.9 *Managers perceptions of barriers to personal effectiveness (Qu.B.6)*

What do you identify as the main barriers, if any, that prevent you from doing your job in the way that you would like to do it?

	Purchaser respondents (n=97) %	Provider respondents (n=159) %	Total (n=256) %
Political environment, bureaucratic centralisation	16	9	11
Pace of change*	19	9	13
Aspects of internal market	19	13	15
Financial constraints*	7	26	19
Operational target overload	30	35	33
Internal management problems*	52	35	41
Lack of skills/knowledge* (personal and others)	24	9	15
Professional/managerial differences/conflicts*	3	26	17
Lack of information	16	15	15
Working with other groups, problems of multi-agency working	6	3	4

Notes:

1.   Respondents could identify more than one reason

2.   * Statistically significant differences in replies to Qu.B.6 were found for these items between purchasers and providers at p <0.05

Barriers to Effective Working Facing Doctors in Management

Analysing the responses to Qu.B6 of 59 professionally qualified medical doctors who, whilst retaining important roles as leading clinicians, at the same time had designated senior managerial responsibility in provider organisations, we found that forty per cent of these doctors in provider management cited operational overload, followed by 33% who cited internal management problems and 31% who identified financial constraints and lack of resources.

A cautious, often ambivalent and occasionally very negative approach from doctors in management accords with the findings of other studies (Burgoyne and Lorbiecki 1993, Mahmood and Chisnell 1993, Simpson 1993). It will be recalled from Chapter 3 that a third of doctors in management wanted to relinquish their managerial roles in due course.

At the time of fieldwork the doctors in management in our sample were strongly preoccupied with internal management issues and were paying comparatively little attention to the management challenges which were, even then, strongly evident in the environment of the internal market. The concerns of clinical directors identified in the research focused, as is shown below, on issues of time, succession, their colleagues, budgetary responsibilities, human resource management and the means of securing what they see as appropriate support and terms of reference.

Time. Clinical directors are concerned about the extent to which their managerial tasks encroach on the time they have for their clinical activity. Their concerns relate to professional credibility, to the clinical demands of their job, and for some to their capacity to undertake private work. Some clinical directors undertake their managerial duties entirely on a 'non- sessional' spare time basis. Others may have negotiated one or even two sessions. Table 4.6 showed that 60% of doctors in management in this sample spent between 6 and 15 hours a week on management.

Succession. Many of the first wave of clinical directors are concerned about succession. They look at their colleagues and see personality and motivational reasons why many of them were not 'chosen' for this job. Some feel trapped into what they think should ideally be a 'rotating' job.

"If I felt happy about any of my colleagues I'd hand over but I don't and they don't have confidence of rest of the hospital. One is paranoid and flies off the handle. The other is clinically excellent but hopeless as a communicator. I was tempted by another job – clinically a bigger department and yet none of the management hassle. I didn't go because of family."

Others are concerned that they are finding the managerial part of their job too beguiling and may be unhappy to give it up; they then fear that if they become institutionalised into the job they will lose the freshness of appreciating the tensions which in a sense are inherent to their success.

Managing their colleagues. The thing clinical directors find most difficult to do in practice is to manage, direct or cajole the colleagues whom previously they could ignore if they encountered major areas of disagreement. An important part of the clinical director's power base is the continued support of colleagues who may well believe the rationale for representative clinicians is to defend clinical and sectional interests against managerial encroachments. However some of the newer, younger clinical directors, perhaps from relatively 'unfashionable specialties' that previously were not high in the 'pecking order' of hospital consultants, are eager to embrace what they see as an alternative source of power in the organisation.

The appointments process is often opaque. Sometimes there is a formal appointments procedure, but often the designated consultant emerges as the 'agreed' choice which will be acceptable to both sides. Undoubtedly, their corporate role is easier to accomplish if clinical directors have both the support of their colleagues and yet are appointed or at least supported by the corporate executive so that there is a degree of shared understanding of their role.

"I'll only accept another 3 year term if there's clear evidence of colleagues backing me."

"We're in two camps and its difficult to please everyone, especially clinical colleagues. Its easy to get alienated from clinicians who see you as tarred with the management brush. You're all the time trying to keep a balance but its difficult."

In seeking advice and help on developing their managerial roles, questions of the following sort frequently arise –

"How do I get my colleagues to do something which they don't want to do? ... This has never been my problem before, its always been somebody else's. Of course I know that doctors can be difficult, and that they are appointed for their clinical and intellectual skills. They're not appointed for their commitment to an organisation which in many ways they see as a 'necessary evil'.... They've often got where they are by being strongly individualistic and fighting their corner... They're not inclined to change now, just because I – another doctor – suggest they should." (clinical director, provider)

An example of a particularly difficult issue is when there is an acknowledged corporate need to reduce medical staffing in order to achieve competitive costs, and yet also a corporate need to reduce junior doctor's hours to comply with national agreements, to reduce and restructure the trainee grades as well as to comply with patient charter initiatives to have a more consultant led service. Some clinical directors reported feeling ineffective and isolated in trying to find a means of, as someone said, "squaring this circle".

Budgetary responsibility. The extent to which clinical directors have responsibility for staff and non-staff budgets and are entering into internal and external service contracts for clinical services such as pathology and radiology and non clinical support such as laundry and waste disposal, vary widely. One of the barriers to budgetary devolution is the information systems which are found in trusts. There are difficulties with data input, with the systems and with data access. Some of the input difficulties reflect the fact that many consultants still do not stress to their staff the importance of securing a valid data base. The clinical director is called upon to seek to ensure his/her team is taking this seriously. Issues concerned with information management are explored more fully in Chapter 7.

Human resource management. Trust status accords greater flexibility in negotiating terms and conditions of employment. Clinical directors see more personnel issues devolving to their level. They welcome the flexibility it affords but fear the time it will consume and would prefer to avoid the difficult situations which are sometimes encountered, and avoid becoming active in fields wherein they feel they lack expertise and interest. At the time of fieldwork we found clinical directors giving relatively low priorities to routine human resource management activities, which they tended to leave to others.

Appropriate support and terms of reference. Given that clinicians are filling the role of clinical director precisely because they retain their medical position and yet combine it with managerial responsibilities, it is important to consider where the boundaries between medicine and management lie and what managerially needs to be placed directly in their remit, and what can be delegated and where they need support. It is here that the role of business and service managers are crucial.

Acting in the market place. The new market structure creates the opportunity for clinical directors to seek to influence purchasers and to find out their current thinking. However, we have yet to encounter clinical directors in more than a few sites who have really begun to give careful consideration to this part of their role. Whilst clinical directors said in response to our question about job activities that 'strategic planning' and marketing of their services are important aspects of their job, most of them at the time of field work had done little to establish dialogue with purchasers or GPs, other than about individual patients. There is a determination by the NHSE and Ministers to secure greater involvement of clinicians in contracting and a movement was launched in January 1994 by the Minister for Health under the title 'Involving Local People and Clinicians in Purchasing Health Services'. This is therefore an area in which there are likely to be significant developments.

5.5   Summary

- All participating organisations operated some variant of an Individual Performance Review system at the time of study. In all these systems line managers were expected to review subordinates individually both formally, at regular intervals and informally through on-going feedback and review. There was much support for the existence of mechanisms which facilitate objective setting for individual managers and which enable these to be linked to corporate objectives and priorities, and ones which promote feedback. However, the operation of current IPR systems were not found fully to meet these needs.

- In some sites, there was little top management commitment to systems of individual performance review, whereas in others they were given a high profile and considerable support.

- A small minority of respondents, largely composed of doctors in provider management, said no one was formally accountable for evaluating their performance.

- Criticisms of the operation of the present systems of performance review focused on the lack of opportunities to review team rather than individual performance, to relate individual to corporate performance and to provide opportunities for informal evaluation and feedback. They were also seen to lack flexibility in dealing with changing objectives and to suffer from lack of commitment and inadequate implementation in some places. On the whole there was support for change to systems which were more developmental and provided more opportunities for coaching and mentoring and for collective objective setting, than those which are more judgemental.

- The issue of performance evaluation and appraisal for clinically qualified managerial staff, particularly doctors in provider management, is highly charged and its practice is undeveloped. Respondents spoke of difficulties of shortage of time, cultural and status differences and a lack of trust between doctors and managers, as blocking developments in this area. Nonetheless many clinical directors expressed a view that they would welcome the opportunity to discuss and develop appropriate objectives.

- There was widespread dissatisfaction with the current managerial performance related pay (PRP) system, particularly with respect to its inability to reward good team performance and corporate success as a whole. We conclude from the data collected in this study that the current PRP system does not in general work to improve motivation and performance. There is currently a movement to secure local pay systems in Trusts but the DHAs will still operate the PRP system.

- When questioned about the basis for priority setting in their job, the dominant responses were in terms of corporate objectives, external deadlines, personal objectives and daily firefighting. The great majority of respondents felt they had difficulty in balancing and meeting the many and varied demands on their time.

- In describing critical incidents in which they felt they had been particularly successful, respondents drew attention to two critical skills. The first is the ability to work through and with others, within and beyond departments, professional groupings and organisations. The second is skill in communication, persuasion and negotiation, to secure agreement and commitment from others.

- In summarising their own view of the attributes which led to their being effective, respondents again drew attention to the human side of management rather than its technical side or knowledge base.

- Comparatively little importance was attached to willingness to take risks or creativity as a basis for effective management in the NHS at local level.

- In reviewing the main barriers to doing their jobs as they would wish, the largest groups of respondents noted internal management problems, operational overload and financial constraints.

- Doctors in management in provider organisations identified seven areas which presented problems for them in their managerial work. These were
  - conflicting and unmet demands on their time,
  - issues of succession when their term of office finished,
  - managing independent, autonomous colleagues with divergent views,

- ill-defined or unsupported budgetary responsibilities,
- meeting increasing demands for human resource management,
- securing appropriate support and terms of reference,
- finding the time and developing the capacity to act in the marketplace.

Chapter 6 **Contributions to Teams: Sources of Conflict and Consensus**

One of the requirements for effective management in both purchasing and providing organisations is that people from a variety of clinical and managerial backgrounds will be able to work together. Each type of organisation requires input from people of different backgrounds and experience. Providing needs input from all the clinical professions, general and functional managers, as well as those who take special responsibility for operations, quality, and corporate development. In purchasing there is a need to engage with people who are sensitive to local issues, equipped to evaluate clinical work, skilled in negotiating contracts, financial management, needs assessment and sustaining dialogue with other statutory agencies and the voluntary sector. In addition to complementary areas of expertise, there is also the issue of developing teams which have complementary personal and managerial styles (Belbin, 1993). Each organisation should therefore be concerned to develop a strong and cohesive top executive team capable of effecting strong and inspirational leadership which is built upon diversity of experience and strength in performance.

This study is focused on the views and roles of senior executives in DHAs and Trusts. No direct consideration is given to the board as a whole, including non-executives, except insofar as they are mentioned by the respondents. Reference should be made to recently completed studies by the Centre for Corporate Strategy and Development at the University of Warwick into the membership and operations of whole boards of health authorities and trusts for consideration of the role of chairs and non-executive directors (see, for example, Ashburner et al. 1993, Ferlie et al. 1993).

Each of the organisations studied was in a sense newly created, even if several of the top team had long been associated with the institutions in which they worked. In this project, we were interested in exploring respondents' views on membership and process in the top team, the extent to which respondents felt they were part of 'teams' and their views on the strengths and weaknesses of teams in which they were participants. One particular interest was in respondents' views on the varying contributions which they felt were made by those with a clinical compared to a managerial background.

This chapter is divided into the following sections:

- Views on the 'Top Team'

- Parts played in Teams

- Sources of Conflict in Teams

- Differences between clinical and managerial contributions

- Summary

6.1   Views on the Top Team

Membership

All respondents were asked whom they saw as part of the top management team in their organisation. Table 6.1 shows their responses.

Table 6.1   *Perceived Membership of the Top Team*

Who do you see as part of the Top Team? (Qu.D.1)

	Purchasing respondents (n=91) %	Providing respondents (n=147) %	All respondents (n=238) %
(a) The Whole Board * (non Executives & Executives)	8	18	13
(b) Executive Directors	35	30	32
(c) Senior Management Group * (broader than (b))	37	23	29
(d) Clinical Management Group	n/a	7	4
(e) Other groupings which do not fit above – usually combinations of executive directors and one level below	20	22	22

Notes:
* Differences between purchasing and providing respondents significant at p <0.05

Beyond generalities, respondents were specifically asked whether they saw themselves as part of the 'top team'. Of the 238 respondents who answered this question, 52% saw themselves as part of the 'top team', (Table 6.2). This amounted to 59% purchasing respondents and 48% of providing respondents (Table 6.2a).

The most commonly identified composition of the 'top team' was built around the whole group of executive directors, with the occasional inclusion of the chair and non board directors or senior managers. Those who identified just the executive directors as the top team (category (b) in Table 6.1) were drawn disproportionately from director level, compared to respondents below director level. Those in the inner circle tended to see themselves as constituting the top team whereas others in the organisation were more likely to perceive the top team to be more widely drawn.

Significantly more provider (18%) than purchaser (8%) respondents identified the whole board (including the chair and non-executives) as the 'top team', whereas significantly more purchaser (37%) than provider respondents (23%) saw the top team as including a wider group of senior executives than that of the executive directors. This suggests that purchasing organisations are perceived by more participants as 'flatter' organisations with a broader group at the top, than is the case in providing organisations. The chair and non executive directors are seen to be part of the 'top team' by more provider than purchasing respondents. One possible explanation is that as providing organisations and activities have a long history, and a more defined and familiar set of tasks, it is easier to perceive the role and influence of the whole Board. In contrast the corporate role of the Board in purchasing may appear less obvious and defined, particularly at the stage at which field work was completed for this project.

Interestingly, the perceived division between those who saw themselves as in the top team and those who saw themselves outside it, did not always reflect a division between those who were, and those who were not, executive directors (Table 6.2). Nineteen percent of executive directors (13% of those in purchasing and 23% of those in providing) did not see themselves as part of the top team. In such cases this was because they saw the top team as being more narrowly defined, usually including the CEO, finance director, sometimes one other executive director and occasionally the chair. This more 'limited' definition was found more frequently in providing than purchasing organisations. In cases where the top team was seen to include more than the executive directors, the inclusions were usually the 'other directors' who although reporting to a member of the Board, had significant independent functional or operational responsibilities. Thirty six percent of all respondents (40% of purchaser, 34% of provider respondents) who were not executive directors saw themselves as part of the top team.

Table 6.2   *Respondents: In or Out of the 'Top Team'*

Who do you see as part of the Top Team? (Qu.D.1)

Table 6.2a: *by Purchaser and Provider*

	Purchaser respondents (n=91) %	Provider respondents (n=147) %	All respondents (n=238) %
Saw self as member	59	48	52
Did not see self as member	41	52	48
	100	100	100

TABLE 6.2b: *by Position*

	Executive Director (n=85) %	Below Executive Director (n=153) %	All respondents (n=238) %
Saw self as member	81	36	52
Did not see self as member	19	64	48
	100	100	100

Strengths and weaknesses of the Top Team

All respondents, whether they perceived themselves to be members of it or not, were asked open-ended questions about the perceived strengths and weaknesses of the top management team. Responses are shown in Table 6.3 divided between purchaser and provider respondents, and Table 6.4 divided between those who saw themselves as part of the top team and those who did not. Evaluation of team performance is highly subjective, but nonetheless extremely powerful in influencing attitudes and behaviour.

Overall the strengths of the top management team were perceived predominantly to be in terms of their ability to work as a team, their capacity to act as a forum in which different groups and interests were represented, the personal strengths of individuals, and the team's capacity for good leadership and vision. A medical director of a first wave trust contrasted this positive experience of the trust executive team with the old district management team.

"If I think back to the District Management Team, each would be plugging their own corner, so nothing got done, Now our team has a single motive, to make the place work and deliver good care – no one has a different scenario and everyone is pulling in the same direction, informality is also a strength." (medical director, provider)

Other comments highlighted the importance of trust and yet the confidence to disagree as team strengths.

"It's essential to have different views. Decisions are better for an increase of information and views. We ought to have robust organisations. We deal with difficult complex issues all the time. We need people who are able to handle conflict and not take it personally. We're getting there – and when we've arrived, it will be a strength". (executive director, purchaser)

The strengths of (a) showing good leadership, (b) being a good team and (e) bringing together personal strengths of individuals were mentioned by significantly more executive directors compared to others in the organisation. In purchasing organisations significantly more respondents cited the personal strengths of individuals whereas in providing organisations, significantly more respondents identified the team's capacity to act as a liaison between groups and as a representative forum for discussion. This last view was more noticeable amongst male rather than female respondents and amongst the functional managers rather than general and clinical managers, however these differences were not statistically significant. Very few respondents spontaneously identified the team's capacity to act as a communicator or conduit for the rest of the organisation as a strength of the top team.

Table 6.4 shows that whereas the relative distribution of responses between those who saw themselves as members of the top team and those who did not, is similar, proportionately smaller percentages of non members identified each strength. This was particularly noticeable in terms of the responses that a strength of the top team was to act as a representative or liaison focus for different groups; proportionately more members than non members identified this as a strength. Thus, whilst this may be seen within the team as a strength proportionately less of those who perceived themselves to be outside the team share this view.

Table 6.3 *Perceived Strengths of the Top Team within Purchasing and Providing Organisations (Qu.D.2)*

Dominant Responses	Purchaser respondents (n=87) %	Provider respondents (n=142) %	Total (n=229) %
(a) good leadership and vision	12	13	12
(b) a good team, complementary skills	33	36	35
(c) representative, liaison, focus for different groups*	8	24	18
(d) communicator/conduit to rest of organisation	2	4	3
(e) personal strengths of individuals	25	10	16

Note:

* differences between purchasing and providing respondents significant at p <0.05

1. Respondents could mention more than one strength

2. Mentions with frequencies less than 3% excluded

Table 6.4 *Perceived Strengths of the Team by Top Team Membership*

Dominant Responses	Sees self as Member (n=117) %	Does not see self as Member (n=107) %	Total (n=224) %
(a) good leadership and vision	14	8	11
(b) good team, complementary skills	38	30	34
(c) representative, liaison, focus for different groups	22	12	18
(d) communicator/conduit to rest of organisation	2	5	3
(e) personal strengths of individuals	17	12	15

Notes:

1. Respondents could mention more than one strength

2. Mentions with frequencies less than 3% excluded

In turning to respondents' identification of weaknesses identified in Tables 6.5 and 6.6., over 20% of respondents identified the top team's 'separation' from the rest of the organisation, speaking in terms of it being seen as 'closed off' and a 'cabal'. This complements the low rate of respondents identifying communication with the rest of the organisation as a strength. This view was offered by significantly more of those who were lower in the managerial hierarchy and within provider organisations, by those who were clinically qualified, younger and those who did not see themselves as part of the top team. For example, one clinical director said he and his colleagues were *"the cannon fodder" of the Trust – "not much consulted, but given clear orders on what to do to deliver financial and activity targets."*

Another clinical director commented in similar vein,

"There's a small group at the top and a big difference between those who are in and those who are out, this ostracises certain groups – cliques are formed – and it's not good for bringing down barriers between professional groups and managers."

Table 6.5 *Perceived Weaknesses of Top Team (Qu.D.2)*

Perceived Weaknesses of Team within Purchasing and Providing Organisation

Dominant Responses	Purchaser respondents (n=87) %	Provider respondents (n=142) %	Total (n=229) %
(g) lack of leadership, vision	9	3	5
(h) lack of team/integrative * approach	47	14	27
(i) poor organisation and * management in team	21	33	28
(j) poor communication with, closed off from, organisation	18	29	25
(k) personal weaknesses of * individuals	17	7	11

Notes:
* Differences between purchasing and providing respondents significant at p < 0.05
1. Respondents could mention more than one strength
2. Mentions with frequencies less than 3% excluded

Table 6.6 *Perceived Weaknesses of Team by Top Team Membership*

Dominant Responses	Member (n=117) %	Non Member (n=97) %	Total (n=214) %
(g) lack of leadership, vision	7	3	5
(h) lack of team/integrative * approach	33	20	27
(i) poor organisation and management, don't get the benefit	25	35	2
(j) poor communication with, closed * off from, organisation	20	31	25
(k) personal weaknesses of individuals	15	7	11

Notes:
* Differences between those who saw themselves as members of 'top team' and whose who did not significant at p < 0.05
1. Respondents could mention more than one strength
2. Mentions with frequencies less than 3% excluded

Whereas a weakness of the top team for some clinical managers is that they felt themselves excluded; from an alternative perspective as a finance director, a weakness is a lack of leadership in driving change,

"Sometimes we have to make compromises to keep the clinical directors on board, we have to give sweeteners to help the castor oil go down."

To yet another participant, the ability to compromise was cited as a strength rather than a weakness.

Two other types of weakness were identified by a considerable proportion of respondents. Significantly more respondents from purchasing organisations (47%, compared to only 16% of provider respondents) identified a lack of an integrative team approach, alluding to different interests and perspectives pulling the top team apart and making it less effective. This was a response from significantly more younger (below 45) than older respondents and from significantly more functional rather than general or clinically qualified managers. The following comments illustrate this view,

"as with many top management teams, there's difficulties in working out the practical terms of reference, people want defined frameworks, their territory and there's demarcation disputes, a lot of navel gazing and trying only to talk about their role or contribution." (executive director, purchaser)

Significantly more provider (37%) than purchaser (21%) respondents spoke of poor organisation and management creating weaknesses in the top team. This was particularly found in respondents who were below director level in the hierarchy, especially clinical directors. A smaller proportion of respondents spoke of poor leadership and individual weaknesses as team weaknesses. These ideas were voiced by significantly more of those in purchasing than providing and by more of those who saw themselves as members of the top team than those who did not.

An 'inside' view of the top team thus increased the likelihood of identifying individual weaknesses or a lack of a team approach, but decreased the likelihood of identifying the team as it being 'closed off' from the rest of the organisation. Members of top teams would be advised to ask themselves how others see them and to address these feelings of 'poor communication' which are held by those who feel 'outside' the top team.

Membership of other teams

Those who did not identify themselves as being a member of the top team, were asked to identify a team of which they felt a part. The results are shown in Table 6.7.

Table 6.7   *Team Membership for Respondents who did not identify selves as part of the Top Team (Qu. D.4)*

	Purchaser respondents (n=47) %	Provider respondents (n=88) %	Total (n=135) %
(a) Whole organisation	7	5	5
(b) The senior managerial group * (not seen as 'top team')	0	20	13
(c) Team based on own function/directorate	66	67	67
(d) * Cross functional project teams	51	19	30
(e) Teams involving people from other organisation	6	1	3

Notes:

1. Some respondents identified membership in more than one team

* Differences between purchaser and provider respondents significant at p<0.05.

The more frequent response from those who did not consider selves part of the top team was to identify their own functional or departmental team. Interestingly, 51% of the 47 purchaser respondents (who did not consider selves part of the top team), identified with membership of crossfunctional project teams, this was significantly more than the 19% of the comparable group of 88 provider respondents.

6.2   Parts Respondents Played in Teams

Respondents were asked to identify the parts they felt they played in teams. Those who had said they felt they were part of the top team, answered in terms of this experience; those who did not feel they were part of the top team answered in terms of their membership of the teams identified in Table 6.7. Owing to pressure of time this question was only asked of about 50% of respondents. This was an open-ended question and the responses shown in Table 6.8 reveals the categories which were mentioned. There were only quite small differences in the range and pattern of responses when one compared purchaser and provider responses.

The most frequently mentioned team role was one of **'leadership'** and this was identified by proportionately more respondents who were women than men, and who were currently in general or functional management rather than in clinical management.

Roles concerned with 'liaison and communication' and 'advice' were the next most frequently mentioned. **'Liaison and communication'** were more popular responses from respondents in providing organisations, from those whose 'roots' were doctors or general managers, and from those who were below director level. It was also identified by proportionately more women than men and was a dominant response for clinical directors.

'Advice' was more popular with functional than with general or clinical managers and with more men than women. The role of 'managing performance' was more popular amongst younger respondents and those at the top of the organisation.

Table 6.8 *Parts played in the Top and other Teams in Purchasing and Providing Organisations (Qu. D.5)*

		Purchaser respondents (n=54) %	Provider respondents (n=67) %	Total (n=121) %
(a)	leadership	39	40	40
(b)	representative	6	5	5
(c)	liaison/communication	18	23	21
(d)	team builder	11	–	5
(e)	manage performance	17	11	13
(f)	advice	22	21	22
(g)	lay view	4	–	2
(h)	innovator	4	6	5
(i)	pragmatist	4	2	3
(j)	antagonist	8	11	9
(k)	varies	4	9	7
(l)	other	11	9	10

Notes:
1. Respondents could identify more than one response
2. Mentions with frequencies less than 3% excluded

Table 6.9 *Parts played in top and other teams (Qu.D.5)*

		Top Team Membership (n=56) %	Membership of other Teams (n=57) %	All Respondents (n=113) %
(a)	leadership	39	39	39
(b)	representative	2	7	4
(c)	liaison/communication	16	24	20
(d)	team builder	4	5	4
(e)	manage/secure performance	18	9	13
(f)	advice	23	20	22
(g)	lay view	2	2	2
(h)	innovator	7	4	5
(i)	pragmatist	4	2	3
(j)	antagonist	13	7	10
(k)	varies	2	12	7
(l)	other	11	9	10

Note:
1. Respondents could identify more than one response

6.3   Sources of conflict in teams

In response to Qu.D.9, 'Do you detect recurring sources of disagreement and conflict between members of any groups in the (specified: top or other) team (of which you are a part)?', 82% of purchasing respondents and 70% of providing executives responded positively. (Table 6.10). There was no significant difference in responses between those who answered in terms of their membership of the top team and those who answered in terms of their membership of other teams.

Table 6.10 *Recurring sources of disagreement and conflict between members of the team (Qu.D.9)*

Detecting disagreement & conflict	Purchaser Respondents (n=81) %	Provider Respondents (n=107) %	Total (n=188) %
Yes	82	70	75
No	19	30	25
	101	**100**	**100**

Statistically significant responses were identified between purchasing and providing respondents p<0.05.

Respondents were then asked in an open-ended question to say how this disagreement or conflict showed itself (Table 6.11). In providing organisations almost half the 77 people who responded, identified disagreement recurring on the basis of differences between a medical or clinical professional perspective and a managerial perspective. Proportionately more clinically qualified than other managers answered in this way. A third of provider respondents identified the battle for resources and other priorities as being the basis for recurring disagreement. Proportionately more of those with roots as doctors rather than as managers answered in this way, which was also more characteristic of managers below, rather than at, director level.

Other sources of disagreement featured strongly in responses from purchasing interviewees, over half of whom focused on lateral conflicts between departments and functions, and 19% drew attention to difficulties at the institutional boundaries between the DHA and FHSA. It may be remembered that all but two of our purchasing organisations had some form of shared working

"with all the change and all the jockeying for position, the potential for conflict and organisational chaos is increasingly strong." (general manager, purchaser, below board)

Table 6.11   *Manifestation of Conflict*

How do recurring sources of disagreement and conflict between members of the team of which you are a part show themselves? (Qu.D.10)

Dominant Responses	Purchaser respondents (n=67) %	Provider respondents (n=77) %	Total (n=144) %
(a) medical or clinical vs managerial conflict*	6	44	26
(b) allocation of resources & priorities*	2	31	17
(c) personal conflicts	18	10	14
(d) status between 'top' and 'middle'	12	5	8
(e) internal conflict between departments/ functions/directorates	54	14	33
(f) geographical differences	6	3	4
(g) institutional boundaries (DHA/FHSA)	19	–	9

Notes:

1. Respondents could mention more than one source

2. Mention with frequences less than 4% excluded

* Differences between purchasing and providing respondents significant at p<0.05.

Personal conflicts on the basis of individual differences, differences between levels in the organisation and geographical differences were also mentioned by respondents. Status differences were more frequently mentioned by those below, than at, director level.

Respondents commonly alluded to the rapid pace of change and the frequent restructuring, as having created a climate of fear and insecurity which made people more defensive and eager to cling to 'any territory' they could secure. This, they felt, inhibited the development of coherent structures and strategies to meet the new missions of purchasing and providing,

"We've got to get departments working together, more team working and sharing objectives between departments ... There's still a fair bit of mistrust and a fortress mentality." (general manager, purchaser)

In looking across purchasing and providing organisations, it was apparent that the newness of purchasing and the fact that many of the purchasing respondents felt relatively insecure about the prospect of further institutional change, created a personal edge to conflicts. Several respondents referred to conflicts arising from personal insecurities and defence of territories. This was less common in providing organisations probably reflecting the fact that their corporate tasks have had longer to become established, are more clearly focused and more easily translated into identifiable roles. Even though the internal market has created new pressures and challenges in providing organisations, the definition of roles, responsibilities and remits has considerable continuity in providing with the past. This, of itself, creates further anxieties for senior purchasing executives who have often been recently engaged in providing, the 'stock in trade' of the NHS. In discussion some purchasing executives revealed that they have found it difficult to adjust to the lack of a big providing empire, in terms of numbers of people employed, even though they now command a large empire in terms of financial budget.

6.4 Differences between Clinical and Managerial Contributions

Given our interest in the differences in views between those who have medical and those who have managerial roots, and between those who now occupy general or functional managerial positions as compared to those who occupy clinical managerial positions, we asked a direct question about the different contributions which were experienced from those with a clinical and those with a managerial background. It is important to note that this question was asked after the general question on sources of conflict and disagreement in order to avoid 'leading' the respondents to this particular line of thought.

In reply to the question 'Do you think that people with a clinical professional background make a different contribution to the management team than those with a managerial background?' 84% of the respondents replied 'yes'. (Table 6.12). The minority who disagreed were drawn disproportionately from general and functional managers rather than from clinically qualified managers. However, these differences were not statistically significant. Doctors were almost unanimous in believing that the clinical and managerial contribution was different.

Table 6.12   *Different Contributions of Clincians and Managers to the Management Team*

Do you think that people with a clinical/professional background make a different contribution to the management team than those with a managerial background? (Qu.D.11)

	Purchaser Respondents (n=83) %	Provider Respondents (n=121) %	Total (n=204) %
Yes	82	85	84
No	18	15	16
	100	100	100

A follow up question asked respondents to say in what ways the contributions were different. Responses are shown in Table 6.13. Those who thought the contributions were different but complementary came disproportionately from purchasing rather than providing and from general and functional rather than clinical managers. Respondents from providers, and particularly doctors, focused on the special and unique contributions of clinicians, which they felt derived from their training, experience and independent way of working.

Some saw the differences in a negative light,

"Yes, there is a different perspective – it's the professionals who should be listened to. Contracts are based on numbers and not complexity, age, urgency and so on. The system for contracting is totally immature. Managers and doctors have totally opposite drives. Doctors treat patients and managers control the way patients are treated. Its called rationing health care and its not any better than in the past." (Clinical director, provider)

For some the difference of perspective created considerable dissonance.

"Clinicians are being asked to do what's not compatible with the other half of their job. We're trained to be doctors and then asked not to be doctors for two sessions a week to do something we're not trained for and are not as good at as what we're trained for ... it's bizarre. Clinical

directors are consultants put in the role of cash register and budget book ... deep down the whole thing is a bit of a front, managing is still done by the manager but when it suits them, the clinical directors are "involved in making the decisions". (clinical director, provider)

Other views were, in contrast, very positive.

"I do it because I like it, it's interesting and especially here, we've got a good visionary kind of executive, we want to introduce a new management system to derut the NHS, it's very emancipating and intellectually stretching". (clinical director, provider)

Amongst managers, particularly in provider units, there was a significant but minority negative view that clinicians were unable to take a corporate managerial view.

The clinical-managerial divide is easily and often stereotyped. For example, one typical view is indicated as follows,

"On the whole clinicians are not good managers. They are 'needs' led not 'resource' led. They see only what people should have not how they are going to be paid for giving it ...." (executive director, provider)

"The differences are inevitable, based on experience clinicians are inclined to be parochial and its a job to make them think more widely" (business manager, provider, two levels below board)

From the other side, the clinical stereotype of a manager can be encountered,

"Managers are more likely to be 'yes men', lacking a detailed understanding, interested only in meeting deadlines. Clinical professionals are more careful in their deliberations and have their eyes on what's best for the patient". (clinical director, provider)

Some respondents emphasised that it was possible and desirable to ensure a balance,

"To keep professional integrity and to make a real contribution". Others want to ensure "a good mix.. both have valid view points......" (clinical manager)

Some respondents wished to play down the professional differences and emphasise similarities between people once they enter the top team,

"Management is more than taking a professional perspective, there's not a difference between professional and managerial issues. The point is we all share a responsibility to deliver and get everyone on board – and try to get people to work for the Trust, as well as the NHS." (executive director, provider)

Table 6.13 *The contributions of clinical and managerial backgrounds to the managerial team (Qu.D.12)*

In what ways are the contributions different?

	Purchaser Respondents (n=79) %	Provider Respondents (n=108) %	Total (n=187) %
(a) different but complementary skills	22	12	16
(b) clinicians have a special contribution which managers cannot have	61	65	63
(c) special mention of patient focus for clinicians	3	13	9
(d) clinicians cannot take corporate/managerial view	9	18	14
(e) depends on individual	13	8	10

Notes:
1. Respondents could mention more than one response
2. Responses with frequencies lower than 5% were excluded

"They're not as different as people perceive; they come from different pasts but are all working to the same goal; its just that one is nearer the patient than the other." (business manager, provider, two levels below board)

Some respondents strongly supported the involvement of doctors in management, seeing it as having helped to effect significant change

"traditional debate between managers and doctors was all about resource constraints. Now its different its about .. given the resources let's talk about how we're going to deliver ... purchasers have got a set of levers to pull and the changes have set in motion a whole set of change mechanisms and whole value system is changing – and its better." (chief executive officer, purchaser)

"Its been a success in getting issues tackled which are on the medical management agenda. These issues are better shared than not, even though they're very sensitive, e.g. value for money or clinical freedom." (medical director, provider)

Our study showed that in both purchasing and providing organisations, great value is placed on building on the differences, establishing mutual trust and respect between clinicians and managers and valuing the special contribution that clinicians can bring to management. This is the case in providing (Dawson et al 1994) and in purchasing (Dawson et al 1993). For a minority, however, there remains great scepticism about whether the gains made are worth more than the difficulties encountered. Factional defensiveness is not beneficial for either Trusts or purchasers. New ways of working together will not necessarily emerge 'naturally' but will have to be the focus of particular programmes of organisation development as well as of individual development.

This conclusion accords with the consensus statement issued by the BAMM, BMA, IHSM and RCN (1993), which concluded that the critical success factors for effective clinical management were as much to do with developing organisations to emphasise quality and innovation, and to facilitate involvement and influence from all staff, as they were to do with developing skills and experience of individuals.

6.5   Summary

- Each of the organisations studied in this project was in a sense newly created. The interviews explored the extent to which respondents felt they were part of teams and their views on the strengths and weaknesses of the teams in which they participated.

- All respondents were asked to identify whom they saw as part of the 'top team'. The most common response was to see the executive directors as forming the core of the top team. For people lower in the organisation and those who did not see themselves as part of the top team, there was a greater likelihood that they would see the top team as wider than the executive directors. Provider respondents were more likely to include the chair and non-executive directors, whereas purchasing respondents were more likely to include other senior directors as well as board members.

- The strengths of the top teams were seen to lie predominantly in their ability to work as a team, their capacity to act as a forum in which different groups and interests were represented and the personal strengths of individuals. There was proportionately little mention of the top team providing leadership or vision.

- The weaknesses of the top teams were seen to lie in their own poor organisation, in their lack of a team or integrative approach and their poor communications with the rest of the organisation. These weaknesses were mentioned by significantly more of those who saw themselves as 'outside' rather than 'inside' the top team.

- At the time of fieldwork, top teams were seen at best in terms of bringing together different interests and at worst as being poorly organised and cut off from the rest of the organisation.

- When asked what roles each respondent played in teams, the most frequently mentioned was leadership. This contrasts with the comparatively small mention 'leadership' received as a strength of the top team.

- A large majority of respondents said they detected recurring sources of conflict and disagreement between members of the team.

- In providing organisations recurring conflicts were mainly seen to arise from differences between a medical or clinical professional perspective and a managerial perspective. In purchasing disagreements were also seen to arise largely from differences of function and discipline. Institutional differences between DHAs and FHSAs in areas where joint commissioning was developing were also notable.

- Respondents referred to the rapid pace of change and experience of recurrent restructuring, as creating a climate of fear and insecurity, which encouraged people to be defensive about their own functional interests, and to inhibit the development of strong, cohesive teams with diverse membership.

- There was a commonly held view that people with a clinical background made a different contribution to managerial work when compared with those of a general or functional management background. The latter group tended to talk in terms of different but complementary approaches, whereas doctors focused their discussion on the special and unique contributions of clinicians.

- The majority of respondents believed there was mutual trust and respect between managers and clinicians. However, amongst a minority of general and functional managers there was a negative view that clinicians were unable to take a corporate managerial view and amongst a minority of clinically qualified managers some disdain was expressed about managers being narrowly focused on achieving their own deadlines and objectives which were not always seen to contribute to patient care or health status.

Chapter 7 Contacts, Networks and Information

In the new world of the internal market, managing through contracting, competition and co-operation in the market place for health has turned a spotlight on contacts, networks and information. The contracting process relies on two key components: internal and external liaison and networking and information systems support. This chapter describes managers' contacts and networks and then focuses on the use of information from the perspective of purchasers and providers.

The chapter is divided into the following sections:

- Patterns of Internal Communications
- Patterns of External Communications
- Information Issues in Purchasing and Providing
- Information in the NHS: Discussion
- Summary

7.1 Patterns of Internal Communication

This section is based on respondents' descriptions of their contact with others. They were each asked to name their three most important internal and the three most important external contacts. Responses were aggregated to give an overall picture of the most important types of contacts for purchasing and providing managers operating within the internal market.

Tables 7.1, 7.2 and 7.3 summarise the pattern of important internal contacts in terms of their distribution between whether they are lateral (within or between functions at approximately the same level) or vertical (up or down the hierarchy, regardless of function).

Across the whole population of 'three most important internal contacts', just under half (43%) are lateral contacts within or between functions and just over half (56%)

are vertical contacts up or down the hierarchy. Table 7.1 shows that the pattern of internal communication for purchasers and providers are not greatly different. Proportionately more internal contacts are made across functions within purchasing and proportionately more 'top down' contacts are made in providing organisations.

Table 7.2 shows the division of contacts between general, functional and clinical managers, and Table 7.3 the division between different levels. Proportionately more important internal contacts for clinical managers are within their own function (11% compared to 3% for functional and 6% for general managers). This also reflects differences in 'level' in the organisation. Proportionately more of those 2 levels below the board (13%) have more contacts within their own function than those above, whereas at director level a third of important internal contacts are across functions. Proportionately more functional managers (41%) and as one would expect, proportionately more of those at the top of the organisation (in any function), are making important contacts across functions.

As far as vertical contacts are concerned, as one would expect, executive directors are making proportionately more downward contacts, whereas those lower in the hierarchy are making proportionately more contacts upwards. Proportionately more functional managers identified upward contacts and proportionately fewer (compared to general and clinically qualified managers) identified downward contacts.

In summary, and looking for differences in patterns of 'important internal contacts', one can say that general managers conformed to the 'norm' for the group as a whole, whereas functional managers identified more contacts upwards and sideways, and clinically qualified managers identified more contacts within their functions and downwards. This reflects the tendency for clinically qualified managers to be operating as functional operational managers in a hierarchical fashion. This may pose particular challenges in terms of management development for clinically qualified managers if they are to develop the skills, confidence and knowledge required for effective management at a more strategic level.

Table 7.1 *Internal Contacts by Purchaser/Provider*

Please give the names of the three people within your organisation whom you regard as your most important internal contacts (most important to do your job)? (Qu.F.1)

	Purchaser respondents (n=263) %	Provider respondents (n=368) %	Total (n=631) n	Total (n=631) %
Lateral				
Contact within own function/department (approx. same level)	7	8	46	8
Contact between functions/departments (approx. same level)	40	33	228	36
Vertical				
Contact placed higher in hierarchy (regardless of function)	23	19	129	20
Contact placed lower in hierarchy (regardless of function)	30	40	228	36
	100	100	631	100

Note:
1. This analysis is based on a population of all the contacts identified (n=631)
    i.e. up to a maximum of 3 per respondent

Table 7.2 *Internal Contacts by Present Job*

Please give the names of the three people within your organisation whom you regard as your most important internal contacts (most important to do your job)? (Qu.F.1).

	GM (n=288) %	FM (n=118) %	CM (n=227) %	Total (n=631) n	Total (n=631) %
Lateral					
Contact within function/ department (approx. same level)	6	3	11	46	8
Contact between functions/ departments (approx. same level)	36	41	33	228	36
Vertical					
Contact placed higher in hierarchy (regardless of function)	20	27	18	129	20
Contact placed lower in hierarchy (regardless of function)	38	29	38	228	36
	100	100	100	631	100

Note:
1. This analysis is based on a population of all the contacts identified (n=631)
    i.e. up to a maximum of 3 per respondent
    Key: GM = General Manager FM = Functional Manager CM = Clinical Manager

Table 7.3 *Internal Contacts by Level in the Organisation*

Please give the names of the three people within your organisation whom you regard as your most important internal contacts (most important to do your job)? (Qu.F.1)

	Executive Board (n=231) %	One Level below (n=354) %	Two Levels below (n=46) %	Total (n=631) n	Total (n=631) %
Lateral					
Contact within own function/ department (approx. same level)	3	9	13	46	8
Contact between functions/ departments (approx. same level)	36	38	26	228	36
Vertical					
Contact placed higher in hierarchy (regardless of function)	20	19	33	129	20
Contact placed lower in hierarchy (regardless of function)	41	34	28	228	36
	100	100	100	631	100

Note:
1. This analysis is based on a population of all the contacts identified (n=631)
   i.e. up to a maximum of 3 per respondent.

7.2 Patterns of External Communications

Respondents were asked to name their three most important external contacts. Tables 7.4 to 7.8 summarise the pattern of important external contacts. Having shown the different patterns between purchasers and providers in Table 7.4, the remainder of the Tables show patterns of responses within either providers or purchasers, with respondents divided by present job and level.

In general, the pattern of external contacts shown in Table 7.4 reflects the core areas of importance for the groups examined. Thus, purchasers and providers are each the others most important external contacts. The regional tier is also important for both. Contacts with local authorities (including social services, housing and education departments) were proportionately more frequently mentioned by purchaser respondents (19%) while professional/functional groupings were more frequently mentioned by provider respondents (22%).

The influence of respondents' broad job type is particularly noticeable for providers (Table 7.5) where proportionately more functional managers (36%) mentioned contacts with professional/functional groupings, and proportionately more clinical managers (24%) mentioned contacts with GPs.

In purchasing, functional managers contacts are limited in the main to the regional tier and to providers, whereas both general and clinically qualified (public health) managers identified significantly more contacts with providers, local authorities and GPs (Table 7.6).

Looking at the influence of level it can be seen from Table 7.7 that significant proportions of respondents two levels below the board in provider units are in contact with GPs and their own functional/professional groupings. This group is largely composed of clinical managers with a nursing background. Contact with purchasers is proportionately more frequently mentioned at the executive board level (32%), as is contact with the regional tier (30%).

Table 7.4 *External Contacts by Purchaser/Provider*

Please give the names of the three most important outside organisations with whom you come into contact in the course of your work. (Qu.F.3)

	Purchaser respondents (n=210) %	Provider respondents (n=224) %	Total (n=434) n	Total (n=434) %
National NHS	0	1	3	1
Regional NHS	19	15	73	17
Provider NHS	23	10	72	17
Purchaser NHS	7	24	68	15
FHSA	6	2	16	4
GP/GPFH	15	15	66	15
LA/SSD/Housing etc	19	5	51	12
Voluntary Organisation	4	4	18	4
Professional/Functional Grouping	2	22	52	12
CHC	5	2	15	3
	100	**100**	**434**	**100**

Note:
1. This analysis is based on a population of all the contacts identified (n=434)
   i.e. up to a maximum of 3 per respondent.

Table 7.8 shows that those below the executive board in purchasing identified proportionately more contacts with GPs, FHSAs, voluntary organisations and CHC than those on executive boards who identified proportionately more contact with local authorities, other purchasers and the regional tier.

In summary, and looking for differences in patterns of 'important external contacts' one can note the limited nature of external contacts for those in functional positions in both purchasing and providing. Within purchasing, there was relative infrequent contact with professional/functional groupings and with other purchasers, but more frequent contact with LAs. Respondents at executive board level in both purchasing and providing maintain frequent contacts with the regional tier and their counterpart organisation within the internal market.

Table 7.5 *External Contacts for Provider Respondents by Present Job*

Please give the names of the three most important organisations with whom you come into contact in the course of your work. (Qu.F.3).

| | Present Job | | | | |
| | GM (n=97) | FM (n=44) | CM (n=83) | Total (n=224) | |
	%	%	%	n	%
National NHS	1	2	0	2	1
Regional NHS	16	32	6	34	15
Provider NHS	6	9	16	23	10
Purchaser NHS	27	21	22	53	24
FHSA	2	0	2	4	2
GP/GPFH	14	0	24	34	15
LA/SSD/Housing etc	6	0	7	12	5
Voluntary Organisation	6	0	4	9	4
Professional/Functional Grouping	18	36	18	48	22
CHC	4	9	1	5	2
	100	100	100	224	100

Note:

1. This analysis is based on a population of all the contacts identified by provider respondents (n=224) i.e. up to a maximum of 3 per respondent.

Key: GM = General Manager FM = Functional Manager CM = Clinical Manager

Table 7.6 *External Contacts for Purchaser Respondents by Present Job*

Please give the names of the three most important organisations with whom you come into contact in the course of your work. (Qu.F.3).

| | Present Job | | | | |
| | GM (n=143) | FM (n=33) | CM (n=34) | Total (n=210) | |
	%	%	%	n	%
National NHS	0	3	0	1	0
Regional NHS	17	33	8	39	19
Provider NHS	23	28	24	49	23
Purchaser NHS	7	9	6	15	7
FHSA	6	6	8	12	6
GP/GPFH	15	6	24	32	15
LA/SSD/Housing etc	20	9	24	39	19
Voluntary Organisation	5	3	3	9	4
Professional/Functional Grouping	1	3	3	4	2
CHC	7	0	0	10	5
	100	100	100	210	100

Note:
This analysis is based on a population of all the contacts identified by purchaser respondents (n=210) i.e. up to a maximum of 3 per respondent.

Key: GM = General Manager FM = Functional Manager CM = Clinical Manager

Table 7.7 *External Contacts for Provider Respondents by Level in Organisation*

Please give the names of the three most important outside organisations with whom you come into contact in the course of your work. (Qu.F.3)

| | Executive Board (n=88) | One Level below (n=118) | Two Levels below (n=18) | Total (n=224) | |
	%	%	%	n	%
National NHS	1	1	0	2	1
Regional NHS	30	7	0	34	15
Provider NHS	3	15	11	23	10
Purchaser NHS	32	20	6	53	24
FHSA	0	3	0	4	2
GP/GPFH	11	17	22	34	15
LA/SSD/Housing etc	3	6	11	12	5
Voluntary Organisation	1	5	11	9	4
Professional/Functional Grouping	16	23	39	48	22
CHC	2	3	0	5	2
	100	100	100	224	100

Note:
1. This analysis is based on a population of all the contacts identified by provider respondents (n=224) i.e. up to a maximum of 3 per respondent.

Table 7.8 *External Contacts for Purchaser Respondents by Level in Organisation*

Please give the names of the three most important outside organisations with whom you come into contact in the course of your work. (Qu.F.3)

| | Level | | | |
	Executive Board (n=103) %	One Level below (n=107) %	Total (n=210) n	Total (n=210) %
National NHS	1	0	1	0
Regional NHS	22	15	39	19
Provider NHS	23	23	49	23
Purchaser NHS	9	6	15	7
FHSA	3	8	12	6
GP/GPFH	14	17	32	15
LA/SSD/Housing etc	22	15	39	19
Voluntary Organisation	1	7	9	4
Professional/Functional Grouping	2	2	4	2
CHC	3	7	10	5
	100	100	210	100

Note:
1. This analysis is based on a population of all the contacts identified (n=210)
   i.e. up to a maximum of 3 per respondent.

7.3 Information Issues

The role of information is increasingly at the forefront of discussions about organisational performance. Information-based technologies and the capabilities they offer comprise the infrastructure supporting the organisation. Information strategy refers to attempts to develop strategic frameworks based around information and IT needs. Information systems are the organisational applications, increasingly IT based, which should meet information needs of the organisation (Willcocks 1994). Information systems are a central part of organisation infrastructure and produce ways of differentiating between competitors in terms of internal performance as well as in the services offered to clients and customers (Drucker 1991, Quinn 1992, Harris 1993). For the new purchasing and providing organisations in the NHS the mechanism of the internal market has thrown a spotlight on information strategy and IT systems.

In this section information is discussed from an end-user perspective. In section E of the interview schedule, respondents were asked about the information they used in their jobs and about areas in which they felt they needed more or better information to equip them for their tasks within purchasing and providing healthcare. The findings are based on the subjective judgements of the accuracy and reliability of information which we know will vary according to the user's experience of using the information most relevant to his or her goals (Dockery 1992). Within the NHS, experiences of information systems differ within and between users in purchasing and providing organisations according to the levels of sophistication of their information systems, their information needs and their capacity for understanding and using the systems inputs, processes and outputs.

Nine sites, four providers and five purchasers, out of the twenty-one in our study were developing, or had already developed, a formal information function within their management structure; in seven of the nine sites there was an IT or Information Director at senior level.

Information issues in purchasing

Effective information management for purchasers requires good information sources and communication processes within health authorities and especially between health authorities and a variety of other organisations, notably, secondary care, primary care, local authorities, voluntary organisations, community groups and sources of national, regional and local official statistics. All purchasers were seeking to establish structures and systems to cope with new tasks which are heavily dependent on securing, analysing and utilising sound information. Purchasers have had to define their information requirements as they have struggled to define and develop their role. Figure 7.1 summarises the key information issues which recurred in interviews in all our purchasing sites.

Purchasers are critically involved in securing information from providers, in order that they can better manage the contracting process. All purchasers were seeking to establish an appropriate balance between wanting to 'know everything' and thereby almost perpetuating a 'directly managed unit' approach, and being so distant that they were inadequately informed of what (in terms of cost and quality) they were buying. It is a key challenge to determine the basket of provider performance indicators which are appropriate for successful purchasing.

Figure 7.1   *Key Information Issues for Purchasers*

*   defining information requirements
*   information systems security
*   information systems support
*   integrated development of IT structure
*   information analysis
*   securing accurate information from and to secondary and primary providers
*   generating information to support contracting
*   defining and monitoring provider quality
*   generating information to support evaluation of corporate performance
*   generating information for internal management control
*   market intelligence
*   accessing and using community, environmental and demographic information
*   health needs assessment
*   population profiles

For Question E1 all respondents were shown a card listing the following five headings:

- finance
- quality
- activity
- staffing
- other information

For each heading respondents described the information they used and the information they would like to have. Their responses are summarised in the following sections.

Finance

Finance and activity – based information for contract negotiation is especially important where purchasers are concerned to move from block to cost and volume based contracts. Such changes in the nature of contracts require more detailed and sophisticated financial information systems which are still comparatively rare. Activity is rarely directly linked to financial payments if block contracts still prevail. Some finance departments mentioned using spreadsheet models and information tools such as Healthlinks to manipulate financial and activity information.

General criticisms of financial information were in terms of presentation and the lack of integration of data sets, for example, financial with activity data. It was felt that a lot of effort was still required to secure the sort of effective information integration which would facilitate the development of more sophisticated forms of contracting. It was noted that:

"In the first couple of years of contracting there was no moving forward on what had gone on before, the information systems could not support more than that. The information systems are still not moving fast enough to support even the most small changes we want to achieve". (general manager, purchasing, level below Board)

Quality

Purchasers receive a mass of information on quality from a variety of sources; inspection reports from their own monitoring teams, CHC reports, routine monitoring of complaints, and returns on patient charter standards. Purchasers stress quality as an important part of contracting. Many have a specific department working on quality issues including using patient surveys and GP comments.

Quality is seen by purchasing managers as difficult to define and hard to monitor, particularly with respect to 'soft' information. For example, it is easier to measure waiting times in outpatients than to address 'softer' issues such as privacy and dignity and neither of these touch upon clinical effectiveness. Many respondents felt they were measuring what they could but that they had a great deal more work to do in developing quality information systems.

The paucity of **outcome indicators** is seen as a major problem for purchasers. They stressed the importance of the audit mechanism in provider units and their need to know what, if any, change had resulted from the audit process. They felt generally that this information was not yet adequately forthcoming.

In addition to developing measures of quality in terms of the experience of individual patients, purchasers were aware that a broader quality issue concerns developing a good basis for defining and evaluating changes which are made in terms of the **health of local populations.** One respondent noted

"... it will be at least a year before they have information on service delivery linked to Health of the Nation". (general manager, purchaser, level below board).

More routine access to mortality information, linked to health determinants such as smoking, diet and exercise would complement data on the effectiveness of interventions. Where **health needs assessment** and local health profiling information is available it often requires a labour intensive information hunting exercise. For example, the data on road traffic accidents is good, albeit lacking in detail, but has to be compiled from the police and from city engineers.

Activity

In theory, hospital and community activity data is compiled on a monthly basis and available via management information systems to managers in the DHA. The reality may be different; activity information may be available on a monthly basis but not in respect of the previous month. It is generally agreed that activity information will need to be better particularly in respect of desegregation between and within specialities if contracts are to get more sophisticated. Much thought is being given to ways of evaluating community based work, where we encountered little satisfaction with present information systems as a basis for sound contracting. Some respondents also expressed anxieties about information systems associated with ECRs. Any system so far developed is still very labour intensive.

Where DHAs are working in an integrated fashion with FHSAs, issues were raised concerning information in primary care and the creation of GP practice profiles. Finance and activity data sets are important for budget setting for GP fundholders. In addition, a whole host of financial information is involved in managing prescribing budgets. Primary care information was said to be variable. At the moment, with budgets based on activity, the information is largely geared to financial claims, as one purchaser respondent noted:

'It is easy to see how many GPs have seen how many patients but more difficult to know what they have had done to them".

Staffing

Staffing information is seen as less important now purchasers are no longer responsible for staffing levels in provider units. However with the need to maintain management costs to 1% of their overall budget they still need to pay attention to payroll. DHAs are relatively small organisations, and as one respondent said:

"... not far off the stage where the directors could name everyone". (executive director, purchaser)

Not all sites studied had computerised personnel systems, with much reliance still placed on a manual system for staffing information. Areas where purchasers were looking for improved staffing information and human resource management were in the management of change, particularly that involving mergers between DHAs and between DHAs and FHSAs.

'Other' Information

The pilot work had shown that the main areas of information needs were encapsulated by the headings used above, that is finance, quality, activity and staffing. There were, however, a variety of other needs which are now briefly discussed.

Purchasers require a wide-range of information. In some sites purchasing intelligence projects were underway compiling bibliographic databases of literature relevant to purchasing including, for example, epidemiological data, demographic data , census statistics, household surveys, and literature reviews on the **efficacy of various clinical interventions.**

With an increase in **multi-agency working** around Care in the Community, there is a need for more careful co-ordination of data from different sources – primary care, community care, social services and housing.

Many respondents described their needs for 'soft intelligence' information, in terms of the activities of other healthcare organisations, local authority reviews, general information from the media, and so on.

In a national context there were calls for national and regional databases on the relative costs of providers. This was seen as central to the successful implementation of the internal market. **Market intelligence** was discussed, in terms of comparative waiting times, GPs views on providers, attitudes of provider staff, quality of work, and GP referral patterns. Consumer feedback, patient complaints, information from the Community Health Council (CHC) and results of patient attitude surveys are also important sources of information.

There were calls for more selective **dissemination of information** from the Department of Health, and for information to be summarised and packaged more appropriately and targeted to the relevant people.

In discussions about generating, using and communicating information, respondents in several purchasing sites drew attention to the critical role which **public health** can play in either effectively acting as a conduit for constructive information flows between providers, purchasers and other sources of relevant information or, at the other extreme, obstructing rather than facilitating the flow. Some sites mentioned close working between contracting, commissioning and public health on issues of evaluating and seeking to change clinical practices and setting targets for 'health of the nation'. Other sites were less positive about the role of the public health function, describing their lack of corporatism and willingness to work with other functions and directorates. There was an enormous range between these two extremes.

Information Issues in Providing

Figure 7.2 summarises the key information issues which recurred in interviews in all our providing sites.

Figure 7.2   *Key Information Issues in Providing*

* information management
* under-investment in information systems
* lack of integration of IT-based systems, particularly for finance, activity, payroll and personnel
* need for greater clarity about information needs
* information support for clinical directorates
* improved mechanisms for data collection including quality information
* improved systems for staffing information to enable skill-mix and reprofiling work
* improved marketing information
* comparative provider data
* the development and collection of appropriate outcome data

One respondent commented:

"Information management and management information is poor in the NHS, if any was above average that would still not be saying it was good". (functional manager, provider, board level)

At the time of interviewing, whatever the historical situation, all sites were gearing up their information systems to meet the demands of the internal market. There was a range of experience and investment. The following descriptions by respondents apply to four provider organisations which had made considerable investment:

"We have a good information department and information systems with electronic mailing and case-mix information",

"We have software bought in the USA tailored specifically to the needs of their Trust",

"We use management consultants to help specify the operational requirements for a case-mix management system to be funded later in the year",

"We have a Hospital Information Support System (HISS) bought at the onset of resource management to handle all reports, outpatients, and financial information."

More usually, however, systems of patient administration, case-mix and functional reporting had been established in an ad hoc way. Community trusts reported a history of underinvestment in information systems, and the difficulties of seeking to define appropriate information needs and to build effective systems quickly.

Within provider units there were particular issues associated with developing appropriate information to facilitate and to monitor clinical management. This finding is supported by Gibson (1994) who found that many clinical directors were dissatisfied with the information they receive. Respondents told us that they felt that in some areas they require less information, feeling that they are overloaded with time-consuming unimportant information. On the other hand, there are many areas where they feel they require better quality information, particularly that which relates to financial and activity performance in contracts, costs, and individual, as well as organisational, performance.

Whilst they complained about inadequate information, some clinical directors admitted they were uncertain about their information requirements. They also admitted that it was often poor input from clinical staff that accounted for dubious output.

One clinical manager described the difficulties of coding and identifying costs allocated in a multidisciplinary area such as anaesthetics:

"... last night on-call I was involved in ICU, a caesarian section, and paediatrics. How do you assign costs to all those activities and then assign them to all the different hospital wards?" (clinical manager, provider).

In this way, the value of financial information is impaired because of the problems of classifying and collecting it.

It will be recalled that all respondents were shown a card with the following headings: finance, quality, activity, staffing and other information. They were asked (Qu.E.1) to describe the information they used and the information they would like to have. The responses received in provider organisations are now summarised.

Finance

The amount of change within NHS organisations in terms of management restructuring and departmental arrangements was felt most acutely by information departments concerned to keep up to date management accounts. The majority of provider sites had already computerised the general ledger system, but some still reported difficulties in securing timely monthly statements. One site was still linked to the regional mainframe computing system which meant a six week turnaround for basic information. In a minority of the organisations where financial information was said to be satisfactory, financial information was in the form of monthly budget statements, occasionally linked to activity, showing performance against contracts within 2 weeks of the end of the month. Respondents applauded the accuracy, timeliness and presentation of information. In sites with a formal information function as part of the management structure, special attention was given to executive summary information.

In most cases, information systems were only beginning to address the demands of the internal market and devolved budgets to clinical directorates. General and clinical managers complained of inaccurate financial information, and a lack of trust in the information when it arrived, often later than desired.

Presentation of information was another problem raised by respondents. Financial reports were not seen to be user-friendly, with insufficient analysis and interpretation of the data.

Problems were not confined to revenue information; capital monitoring was described as an area where financial information was weak.

Quality

Information on quality is largely **process-related:** waiting times, complaints, procedures and so on. There is little outcome data. Managers in several provider units were satisfied with their Patients' Charter information and the extent to which they were meeting their Health of the Nation targets. Some mentioned working with the Community Health Council on consumer surveys.

In other sites, quality was described as difficult to determine, often based on guesswork, with only a piecemeal link to clinical audit. The absence of basic mechanisms for collecting quality information was matched by a lack of organisational objectives for quality initiatives. The post of quality facilitator in one site and Total Quality Management co-ordinator in another had been phased out. One respondent noted:

"... this has meant quality issues have been reduced to six monthly ward audits". (clinical manager, provider)

On the subject of clinical audit, one respondent from a purchaser organisation commented:

"... it's easier to get information about the mechanics of service provision, such as, waiting times, than issues involving clinicians' judgements". (executive director, provider)

In their defence, some clinicians argue that standardisation of techniques is necessary if clinical and medical audit are to have wider application. The problem is described as follows:

"Audit may be described as a part of quality control, but whilst we have outcomes for specific services, understanding how the service performs in relation to that is a problem because all patients are different. The resulting measures and statistics only relate to a subset of the overall workload". (clinical manager, provider)

Some respondents were concerned about the sort of quality they should be measuring. One clinical manager described quality measures as naive and crude, arguing that measurement of the complexity of case-mix in terms of demand, not activity, may be more appropriate:

"To take an example, what percentage of the population are not having their varicose veins done because the provider is focussing on other types of interventions? There is a problem with

relating what the population wants with what we think they want, there maybe an overlap but we cannot guarantee it in every case". (clinical manager, provider)

Another clinical manager commented:

"Endless surveys are time-consuming, expensive and do not always help. We need more discussion with clinicians and nurses before we are able to measure properly, we are moving in the right direction, we see the importance of quality over quantity of services". (clinical manager, provider)

This was described as a "bottom-up" approach to quality, combining audit statements, peer reviews, purchaser views, with views from their own staff.

Activity

Activity information is primarily about contract performance. Ideally, sites were looking toward collecting information at sub unit level, in order to compare performance, to compare unit costs, and individual clinical performance.

In all cases, the quality of information is only as good as that input into the information system. At best, activity information is described as accurate, comprehensive and timely, with links to finance, contracts, clinical group working and case-mix. At worst it is described in terms of ad hoc case mix systems combined with inaccurate breakdowns of activity, poor links to contracts and expenditure with little attention being given to its conversion into meaningful management information.

Where activity is monitored against contract target there has been difficulty within and between Trusts in terms of ensuring one is counting like with like. One respondent commented:

"You can never be sure that you are comparing like with like, for example, in outpatients, one patient may visit three departments: is that one episode or three. And between provider units, does everyone count in the same way, for example, chest pains and tests including x-ray and blood is one episode – is everyone doing that?" (general manager, provider, board level)

Activity is measured by FCE (finished consultant episode) in acute sites, yet in areas such as maternity, 70% of the FCE is normally undertaken by midwives. For community units and areas like maternity, activity measured by face to face contact was thought more appropriate, more meaningful and yet undeveloped.

Staffing

Staffing information in the form of staff profiling and skill mix were described as crucial to contract performance. The maintenance of quality standards and activity within budget depends on a comprehensive understanding of staffing issues, for example, what staff are doing, numbers of staff available, taking into account maternity leave, grading structures, and key ancillary staff requirements. Few sites felt they had yet achieved effective systems giving comprehensive information about individual employees and their costs.

Often staffing information relied on a manual system. Where computerised systems were used there were complaints about the accuracy, presentation and relevance of the information. Key information on staff turnover, absence and sickness was hard to obtain, even with computerised personnel systems. This was, however, being tackled in one site which was a pilot site for an integrated manpower payroll system which promised to yield information on staff costs and staff productivity.

Other Information

Managers in providers were concerned to secure more qualitative information from purchasers in relation to contracting and purchasing strategy. Respondents in many of the sites discussed the need to develop better **marketing** information in order to assess their position in the marketplace among GP fundholders and competitor provider units. Several initiatives were described. One site was setting up a forum of community units who are not competitor organisations. Another was in a Department of Health learning set with four other community units for sharing information on prices, contracts and performance. In other sites, partnership arrangements with other units around the country for the exchange of information on ideas and practices facilitated the collection of some comparative national data and information.

Respondents in providing also used this section of the interview to express the need for greater **internal communications,** at present feeling there was little sharing of information either between directorates or within the hierarchy, a point made earlier in Chapter 6.

7.4 Information in the NHS: Discussion

Information-based technologies are a central feature of the broad moves toward New Public Management (Bellamy & Henderson 1992, Margetts and Willcocks 1993, Osborne & Gaebler 1992, Taylor & Williams 1990). Management by contract requires purchasers and providers to exchange robust information on costs, quality and effectiveness of services to a level of detail not previously countenanced in the NHS (Keen 1994). Purchasers need to obtain data from providers which they can integrate with data on their local populations in order to match resources and needs. The new arrangements require the collection of volume, cost and quality data by providers. At every point in the information process our findings show that participants consider there is still much work to be done.

Historically, the public sector including the NHS has a poor record of IT development. During the 1980s, the National Audit Office produced several reports critical of the IT applications in the public sector (National Audit Office 1987, 1989ab, 1990).

The criticisms that were made included the following:

*   a lack of applied IT strategy,

*   inadequate IT project management skills,

*   inadequate evaluation and control mechanisms,

*   inadequate training and staffing in major projects.

Some of these criticisms were addressed by the Department of Health in a document entitled A Framework for Information Systems (Department of Health 1990). This report offered central guidance on technology and training issues, but did not offer an overall information strategy, or much input into the wider issue of understanding the role of information in changing organisations. An ambitious timetable for implementation of IT projects soon gave rise to problems, many of which revolved around basic issues such as the inadequacy of local data collection mechanisms (Pollitt et al 1990).

In 1988 the Resource Management Initiative had been introduced and piloted in six sites. It focussed on the development of information systems aimed at showing the costs associated with treatment activities (Coombs and Cooper 1990). At the same time the Hospital Information Support Systems (HISS) Project involved replacing ageing computers running patient administration systems (PAS), which handle intake and discharge of patients, with packages of integrated systems. Of the original three pilot sites for the NHS HISS project, Greenwich was, at the time of fieldwork, the only one to have completed the planned implementation process and to have subsequently progressed further. According to Bywater (1994) there are two main reasons for this: the Greenwich system was based on tried and proven application software and implementation methods. Second, there was strong commitment on the part of hospital management.

In December 1992 the NHS launched The Information Management & Technology Strategy (NHSME 1992b) containing the following aims:

* information will be person-based

* systems may be integrated

* information will be derived from operational systems

* information will be secure and confidential

* information will be shared across the NHS.

The strategy covers systems for information generation and management for purchasers, providers, GPs and community health. It presents a vision of an information-based NHS where computer systems within and between sites can exchange communications and share information (Bloomfield et al 1994).

NHS Trusts now have a set of options ranging from incremental developments of the NHS's most widely used PAS systems to replacement by integrated packages like HISS, to the NHS Information and Technology Strategy for such concepts as electronic medical records. However, a combination of new purchasing regulations brought in after revelations about the failure of IT projects in Wessex and the London Ambulance Service (Public Accounts Committee 1993), tight political scrutiny and shortage of financial resources has slowed progress towards the Management Executive's vision of an electronic NHS. The NHSME's goal was for every large acute hospital to have 'integrated systems' by the year 2000. While early contracts were partly paid for by the ME under the RMI or HISS Project, trusts should now expect to have to finance IT developments themselves. Central funding for HISS projects fell from £21.2m in 1992/93 to £6.7m in 1993/94. This year a further £1.7m is earmarked (Cross 1994).

Our findings support those of the Health Service Journal/Touche Ross survey *Fit for the Future* (1993). This survey showed that acute hospitals priorities for information systems were integration, the improvement of contract-management and electronic links with GPs. But for most, the first choice was whether to build piecemeal on existing systems or begin again with an integrated package like HISS (Cross 1994). The majority of our sites were addressing system integration issues; few had come to a decision.

Following the reforms, most purchasing authorities inherited IT-based systems developed around DHA activities. The data requirements for purchasing have evolved with the function and many sites have adopted IT solutions most appropriate to fit both local needs and the existing hardware. The NHS Management Executive DISP project team worked with HAs to define specifications for a purchasing system; however, full implementation of the purchasing system specification has been confined to project pilot sites.

In both the public and the private sector there have been problems with the implementation of IT systems. For example, confusion about the potential of IT, lack of awareness of new developments and an absence of IT know-how at senior management levels (Boddy and Buchanan 1986, Kearney 1990). The public sector has suffered from poorly focussed, technocratically-oriented efforts to bring in IT in the face of rapid and large-scale legislative change (Willcocks 1994) and lack of clear benefits. This has led to the open questioning of the value of existing investments in information systems (Audit Commission 1992, Willcocks 1993). Human resource, political and organisational contexts surrounding IT were often neglected, only to re-emerge as problems during the implementation stage of IT development (Willcocks 1994).

Our research suggests that purchasing and providing organisations in the NHS are still grappling with these thorny issues and that it will be some time yet before the vision of the NHS Information Management and Technology Strategy becomes reality. The lack of integrated and appropriate information does, as we have seen, have considerable implications for the nature of managerial work in both purchasers and providers.

7.5 Summary

- The pattern of internal contacts within purchasing and providing is broadly similar, except there is more emphasis on lateral contacts in purchasing and hierarchical contacts in providing. Clinically qualified managers have proportionately less contacts with other functions or departments and with those above them in the hierarchy, when compared to general or functional managers.

- The pattern of external contacts reflects the core areas of importance for purchasers and providers. They are each the others most frequently mentioned contacts. Whereas more respondents from providing maintained more frequent contact with their own external professional or functional group, respondents in purchasing identified a significantly higher level of contact with local authorities.

- Managers of all types and levels who participated in this study, felt that they could improve their managerial and organisational performance if they had access to more accurate, more timely and more relevant information. Paradoxically, on the one hand they felt there was "too much information" and "too much paper" and yet on the other, that what they needed was not easily accessible or in the right form to facilitate their management activities. It was acknowledged that considerable investment and attention had been made in information systems development and implementation but it was felt that there was significantly more work to be done in this area.

- In nine of the twenty-one sites in the study, four providers and five purchasers, there was a formal information function within the management structure. In seven of the nine sites there was an IT or Information Director at senior level.

- For purchasers good information systems are fundamental to their purpose. They need an information strategy that supports the healthcare objectives laid out in the purchasing plan. They require information exchange with providers for contract negotiation and contract management, and they require the IT systems and technology to produce appropriate data for their new tasks. Development work is required in all three areas; information strategy, information exchange and IT investment.

- In general, there was a view among purchasers that their access to and use of information was improving but as yet could not be described as a strong component of their organisation. Financial, activity and health outcome information from providers remain areas of concern. Purchasers also want to secure more robust information on health needs and population profiles. General concern was expressed about the paucity of qualitative information and about information support for strategic analysis.

- Historically, most provider sites have paid little attention to the development of a common information strategy. The demands of the internal market have highlighted this gap and prompted considerable developments which are not always integrated one with the other. Integration of financial, activity, payroll and personnel information is seen as critical.

- There was a general feeling that provider information systems suffer from inadequate investment, and a lack of investment appraisal. Expectations, among clinicians, for information are greater than the present computer systems are able to deliver. Most sites were dealing with dated computer hardware and some reported difficulties with introducing organisational innovations, such as service level agreements, because information systems are not good enough.

- Ironically one reason why information is poor, is that regardless of the hardware, clinicians are not careful to ensure accurate and comprehensive data input - often expressing a lack of awareness and understanding of the relationship between their actions in input and subsequent output.

- While information systems appropriate to the new provider units are emerging, information on outcomes is less good; clinical and medical audit has yet to make a strong impact in this area.

- For purchasers and providers alike there were concerns about the lack of shared information between purchaser and provider organisations. Providers and purchasers depend on each other and yet often, in the name of competition, are secretive. Information is sometimes now seen as "commercial" and a source of power in the marketplace. It is felt that each side seeks to hide aspects of their business from the other.

Chapter 8 Management Development

Introduction: The Context for Management Development in the NHS

Within the NHS a plethora of management development activities, programmes and policies exist at the national, regional, and local level.

Stewart (1994) has argued that management development is vital for the success of the restructured NHS, and suggests four criteria for assessing its effectiveness:

–   An organisation's future needs for managers are provided for within all the constraints of uncertainty;

–   Individuals are equipped with the knowledge, skills and experience that are currently needed and that are likely to be needed in future;

–   Individuals are helped to continue to develop themselves and remain open to learning;

–   Individual managers take seriously the development of their staff and are good coaches.

Despite many national and local initiatives, Stewart asserts that the NHS has never had fully planned management development because of its separate authorities, and strong professional and bureaucratic rigidities. She concludes:

"The NHS has a poor history of management development .... The danger is that the pressures from reorganisation may lead to even greater neglect."

This chapter presents a brief review of recent national initiatives and then proceeds to discuss findings on executives' experience and perceptions of management development. It focuses particularly on the **content** of management development required by managers and their views on the utility of different **types** and modes of delivery. There is some discussion of recommendations to prevent "its neglect" and to consolidate its importance to the restructured NHS. The issue of its link with performance management systems highlighted in the NHSME Management Development Strategy has already been discussed in Chapter 5, the roles and responsibilities of managers and their repercussions for management development in Chapter 4, and the role of management development in facilitating career progression in Chapter 3.

This chapter is divided into the following sections:

- National Initiatives: an overview

- Senior Executives' Learning Needs

- Experiences of Management Development Programmes

- The Value of Role Models, Mentors and Coaches

- Summary

8.1 National initiatives: an overview

At the national level the NHS Training Directorate was, at the time of the field work, overseeing programmes in management and organisational development such as MESOL (Management Education Scheme by Open Learning), MTS (Management Training Scheme), MAP (Management Development Action Planning), and Management Development for Clinicians. NHSTD was also co-ordinating management development activity in response to external initiatives, such as MCI (Management Charter Initiative) competences and standards, IIP (Investors in People) and NVQs (National Vocational Qualifications). It was also acting in respect to other Government initiatives which are more specifically in the NHS context and have ramifications for management development, such as "Community Care" and "Health of the Nation".

In October 1991 the NHSME launched 'A Management Development Strategy for the NHS' (NHSTD 1991) with the intention of providing a guiding framework in which management development activity would be formed. It was felt that management development required a national framework, as more than 250,000 staff exercised managerial functions; training and education had been fragmented, and many people who needed to develop managerial competence were "slipping through the net". Also it recognised that the training of clinical managers had been uncoordinated and separated from the mainstream of management development.

The action plan of the strategy set out eight key measures to be introduced nationally:

- The expectations of the NHS Management Executive will be made clear through publications and workshops.

- A national framework of competences for all levels of management will be developed.

- Measurement of management performance as it contributes to organisational objectives and personal development will be improved.

- Assessing managers' performance and potential will be improved.

- Access to management development programmes will be improved.

- Performance measures will be introduced to improve return on investment in management training.

- National and regional databases will be introduced.

- A national management centre will be established.

This was underpinned by key points for its implementation at the local level, based on assessment of best practice:

- All units must have a written strategy for management development. In time this might be part of the business plan.

- All jobs should be charted against the competence framework, which has been developed in support of the strategy.

- An assessment process should be established.

- Appraisals should be documented so that outcomes can be followed up.

- All staff should have a personal development plan, specifying action to be taken.

- Local databases with details of courses and other development opportunities should be established.

- Targets should be set for increasing the numbers of women in management.

- Units must develop succession plans.

The implementation of the strategy was also supported through a series of working papers and other products in the 'Managers Working for Patients' series, which included publication of a management standards competence pack (NHSTD 1992). Thus at the national level the NHS "pinned its colours to the mast" of a competence approach to management development, for both identifying the content of management development programmes, and to a lesser extent influencing the mode of delivery, where considerable variety is possible. Although the competences described are based on the MCI national management competences they are adapted and made more relevant to the NHS context. The flexibility given enables diversity in management development activity. Thus for example, where some regional authorities have favoured an approach to developing managerial competence which focuses on intended outcomes in the workplace, other authorities may concentrate on inputs in their training and development centre programmes. Whatever the chosen approach there is a concern to link management development with strategic business and organisational development needs to ensure some coherent process of career and succession planning. During 1994 the NHSE was reviewing its Management Development Strategy in the light of the changing context of the NHS.

There has been enduring concern that certain groups have not gained access to "the grapevine" for management development opportunities and subsequent career progression. Another national development in the 1990s has been the setting up of a women's unit and a unit relating to issues for ethnic communities, to give a clear lead in the promotion of equal opportunities in management development. One important example of activity in this area is the setting up of a senior management career development register and its associated assessment and development programmes for women. This acts as a vehicle to bring capable women to the attention of recruiters (supported by policies aimed to prevent all male short-lists), to by-pass and create alternatives to informal "male" networks, and to provide practical management development help for aspiring women managers, to "put them in the frame" for senior jobs.

At the regional level there has been considerable diversity in management development provision, with some regions developing links with local educational institutions to provide management development support, and others designing assessment centres for managerial assessment and development.

At the local level, managers have been provided with wide opportunities for management development ranging from enrolment on external management courses, secondments, and developmental projects. These have often resulted from individual initiative and have taken place in an unsystematic and unplanned way, without local policies and strategies, and without the underpinnings of a self development culture. Some national initiatives have been designed to help the individual organisation cope with management development (for example MAP), and research and consultancy has been conducted to identify more clearly the management development needs of particular types of organisation; for example Key and Dearden 1993 identify a framework for management development within the context of organisation development in purchasing.

The agenda for management development has widened with the recent restructuring. The purchaser provider split, reorganisation of regions, and the enabling of trusts to develop their own staffing policies and procedures, have emphasised the importance of management development and yet led to concern that management development activity could fragment further, and that new barriers may develop to prevent statements of intent set out in the NHSME strategy documents from being translated into practice. In particular, anxieties have focused on the difficulties for management development should managers find it harder to move freely between purchasers, providers, and regions; and the concern that financial stringency measures in trusts may reduce the likelihood of investment in planned management development, with little self development happening in a chaotic fashion, and without the support of a self development culture. Finally, the reforms have thrown up new areas of competence that need to be developed by managers within the NHS.

8.2   Senior Executives' Learning Needs

All respondents were given a list of 25 skills or knowledge which had been identified in pre pilot discussions as areas where various groups of our respondents might have significant learning needs.

Respondents were asked to tick one of the following boxes for each skill:

- Possess,
- Possess like to develop further,
- Like to develop,
- Not relevant to me.

Table 8.1 presents the results in terms of the total percentage of respondents who ticked 'possess but like to develop further' and 'like to develop'. Their responses are shown separately for each of the 'present job' group i.e. general, functional and clinical managers, as well as for the subsample of our total respondents who qualified as doctors. Almost every skill/knowledge was identified as representing a significant learning need by a majority of respondents.

Table 8.1 Skills & Knowledge to be developed: (Qu.K.1)

| | | (a) Analysis by Present Job | | | | | | (b) ALL | | (c) by Medical Background | |
| | GM (n=113) | | FM (n=43) | | CM (n=96) | | | | (n=252) | | (n=75) | |
	1	2	1	2	1	2			1	2	1	2
K1.1	Strategic planning	66	9	70	14	59	18		64	13	61	15
K1.2	Business planning*	68	15	74	5	49	24		62	17	42	25
K1.3	Evaluation of organisational performance*	60	24	55	41	46	30		54	29	37	37
K1.4	Negotiation of service contracts*	33	25	43	16	34	38		35	28	30	35
K1.5	Evaluating new services for development*	50	29	37	37	55	26		50	29	54	24
K1.6	Developing new services*	52	15	41	31	52	18		50	19	50	18
K1.7	Health needs assessment*	27	46	7	47	33	28		26	39	34	21
K1.8	Health economics – purchaser only	22	56	42	53	59	29		33	51		
K1.9	Evaluating service delivery*	50	17	55	19	54	19		52	18	46	23
K1.10	Evaluating contract performance*	42	14	46	7	36	25		41	17	31	23
K1.10a	Managing service delivery – provider only*	37	4	38	17	35	10		36	9	28	14
K1.11	Managing contract performance	39	15	44	5	39	17		40	14	37	15
K1.12	Marketing your services*	43	40	26	38	38	40		38	40	40	33
K1.13	Project management	42	18	51	26	36	31		41	24	39	25
K1.14	Financial planning / forward budgeting*	40	17	27	11	37	27		37	20	37	25
K1.15	Controlling financial resources*	35	8	27	5	37	20		34	12	37	23
K1.16	Managing across organisational boundaries	45	24	40	34	43	28		43	27	38	32
K1.17	Managing across professional boundaries	45	20	49	22	49	18		47	20	45	19
K1.18	Individual performance review & appraisal*	34	8	63	10	46	22		43	13	46	29
K1.19	Team building	50	5	64	9	42	19		49	11	39	25
K1.20	Time management	47	17	52	24	41	27		45	22	46	26
K1.21	Managing your colleagues	46	9	61	12	42	17		47	12	46	22
K1.22	Personnel management*	29	11	43	16	41	20		36	15	36	25
K1.23	Computing and IT	27	34	59	25	37	41		36	35	36	38
K1.24	Interpreting data	50	18	58	5	40	25		47	18	40	18
K1.25	Communication skills	55	3	75	2	52	6		58	4	54	7

Key:

*   differences between clinical, functional and general managers statistically significant at p <0.05.

GM   General Manager

FM   Functional Manager

CM   Clinical Manager

(c)   by Medical Background: indicates respondents from any job category who are qualified doctors

1   'possess but like to develop further'

The most popular skill areas, which over 70% of respondents would like to develop (ie falling in categories 1 and 2 as shown in Table 8.1), are as follows: (in decreasing order of popularity)

K1.3   The evaluation of organisational performance (83%) which was most popular with functional managers (96%)

K1.2   Business planning (79%), which was especially popular with general managers (83%)

K1.5   Evaluating new services for development (79%)

K1.12   Marketing your services (78%), which was least popular with functional managers

K1.1   Strategic planning (77%)

K1.23   Computing and IT (71%)

Within purchasing, a particular need for health economics (K1.8) was identified, with 84% of the purchaser respondents identifying it as a skill they wished to develop.

The only skill areas which were scored for development by less than 50% of the group as a whole were:

K1.10a   Managing service delivery (provider only), (45%)

K1.15   Controlling financial resources (46%).

Arguably these are skills in which people in the NHS have had long experience, but even they were scored by over 40% of respondents. Whilst relatively fewer managers wish to develop further their skills in financial control (K1.5), this was an item which was scored by 60% of those who were medically qualified. Proportionately more functional and clinical than general managers wanted to develop their skills in managing people (K1.22). Proportionately more of those with a background in nursing were concerned to be able to develop skills in negotiating service contracts (K1.4), compared to those with other backgrounds.

Looking particularly at the 75 respondents with a medical background (category C in Table 8.1), it can be seen that their priority learning needs are similar to those of the group as a whole, except that a few more skills enter the 'over 70%' category. In addition to strategic planning, evaluation of organisational performance, evaluating new services for delivery, marketing services and computing and IT, over 70% of the qualified doctors with senior managerial responsibility wanted to develop their skills in:

K1.18   Individual performance review and appraisal (75%)

K1.20   Time management (72%).

Table 8.1 presents a large agenda for management and self development, with the key areas identified being business and strategic planning, marketing and service evaluation, which arguably are the areas which typically were not much required in the NHS before the 1991 reforms.

8.3   Experiences of Management Development Programmes

In Britain we have been castigated for our poor performance in management development. It has been suggested that we do "too little, too late, for too few" and in an ad hoc unsystematic fashion (for example see Constable and McCormick 1987, Handy 1987, 1988, Mangham and Silver 1986, Storey 1989, 1990). This literature points particularly to the failings of many formal management development courses, their inappropriateness and irrelevance and the lack of consolidation of learning in the workplace. The MCI initiative was derived in part to address this problem. Our findings show that many NHS managers engage in formal management development activities, and although some do experience these failings, many of their comments show that there has been experience of courses as interactive and relevant, ensuring ongoing development on the job.

Table 8.2 shows experiences of management development courses and programmes for the sample as a whole. Most respondents had some experience of such programmes, demonstrating the high level of activity and investment in this area.

Twenty people (10%) had MBAs and 21% had attended senior management programmes at established business schools. As well as there being rich variety in the types of courses and programmes attended, as can be seen from the quotes below, there was great variety in respondents' perceptions of their benefits. Also although there were some "sceptics" it was refreshing to see so much enthusiasm and interest in formal management development activities.

Statistically significant differences among respondents were found in that proportionately more functional managers had an MBA qualification and more general managers than other groups had IHSM qualifications. Experience of NHS programmes was more likely to be found amongst managers with a nursing and

Other Health Professional background compared to other groups. This category includes the Managing Health Services or MESOL programme developed jointly by the Institute of Health Services Management (IHSM) and The Open University (OU) (IHSM 1992) which was more likely to be mentioned by managers at lower levels in the organisation, although some clinical directors also mentioned it as a component of their management training. More nursing and OHP respondents had experience of NHS programmes of one week or more duration than did other respondents.

Programmes/workshops described as interesting and useful by respondents were those offering one or more of the following elements:

- created an awareness of management and put own role in context

- an appropriate mix of personal development and relevant management skills

- participative

- opportunities for making contacts/networking

- opportunities for comparing practices in own and other organisations

- good ideas and methods

- well structured and presented

- allowing consideration of team building and working

- enabled learning across the purchaser provider divide

- available at an appropriate point in their career

- a good investment for career development.

Examples of the types and methods of management development interventions described as being particularly helpful were:

- learning sets,

- away days with management team, courses with own team,

- in house day courses drawing diverse groups of managers from within the organisation,

- networking through conferences (eg. BAMM) and professional associations (eg. IPM),

–   secondment – eg. to the NHS national level or to an outside organisation e.g. a bank or a hotel,

–   management exchanges – eg. to heath service organisations in Sweden.

Table 8.2 *Experience of Management Development (Qus A.11, K.2)*

Type of Experience		All Respondents %
a)	National Training Schemes	8
b)	GMTS 1	2
c)	GMTS 2 and 3	1
d)	MBA	10
e)	Senior Management Programmes	21
f)	General Management for Specialists	11
g)	IHSM qualification	17
h)	Dip. Management Studies (DMS)	9
i)	NHS Programmes (one week or more)	20
j)	NHS one day courses	11
k)	In-House Programmes	10

Notes:

1. Total number of respondents (n) = 271 for a,b,c; 201 for d-k.

2. Respondents could mention more than one experience

It must be emphasised however that there is no one best way for all managers, and the variety in responses do to some respect reflect individual's different preferences and learning styles (Kolb 1984, Honey and Mumford 1986). There continues to be a need for flexibility and choice in provision.

In general formal courses were seen to create a climate of awareness of management and the basis for better evaluation of learning needs and understanding of their role within their particular context. There were divergent opinions on the extent to which the courses should focus on the **NHS context**. Respondents commented:

"I have found two types of course invaluable. First, one year intensive general management and corporate management programme at x. Second, courses dealing with specific issues pertinent to the organisation eg. strategic management course. Generally I am an enthusiast but you need to ensure the course is related to the needs of the organisation". (general manager, provider, board level)

"I deliberately chose a non-NHS MBA. Now realise there are more similarities than differences between the NHS and other organisations. The MBA has given me a more strategic view and confidence in management knowledge and abilities, useful but not much direct practical use". (general manager, provider, board level)

"You have to make a careful choice geared specifically to your job - the best ones are tailored - although some just change the titles and apply the private course to the public sector - they don't really understand the NHS." (functional manager, provider, board level)

"I would like a course on marketing in the context of the NHS - those offered are usually costly one day seminars largely aimed at profit-making orientated companies with little relevance to the NHS - there is a big niche there. Also I would like one on negotiating and contracting - lessons to be learnt and how to relate them to the organisation." (marketing manager, provider, level below board)

Some managers also appreciated courses which allowed for greater **self awareness**:

"x course was very strong on the personal development side. One got to know potential failings and danger points ... I found it very helpful, I probably need to do something on a local basis but it is easier with total strangers. It is very interesting being with business people highlighting the differences between the real world and the NHS." (clinical manager, provider, level below board)

Respondents appreciated opportunities to stand back from their organisation, raise their sight above their everyday work, and to compare themselves and their own organisations with others, whether through **benchmarking** or structured opportunities for observation of other organisations.

"Scholarship gave me the opportunity to go and see other hospitals - I went to four in x. It started thought processes, widened horizons .." (clinical manager, provider, level below board)

Many appreciated the opportunity to work with people from other organisations with similar problems:

"I prefer practical courses where I can work on my own data with similar people from other hospitals and re-think what we have built up and share experiences." (functional manager, provider, level below board)

Much was said about the need for development of greater understanding of **team working,** whether or not this was through the content of a course, or through the way it was taught.

"I've twice been on personal interaction training – team exercises and analysed performance – they were very enlightening experiences – we had facilitators and a group of 5-6 people who tackle tasks, for example building something or setting priorities and we underwent the activity and learnt about how to perform in the group and learnt about interpersonal skills – and how important are influencing skills and managing people" (functional manager, provider, board level)

"I prefer a team-working focus over 3 or 4 days where you are concerned with problem solving and tackling issues." (clinical manager, provider, level below board)

"Developing skills – should in general be done with one's own team, for example do business planning as a team." (general manager, provider, board level)

Many formal programmes incorporate the **learning set approach**, and in general, this approach was described as helpful. Comments suggest that it is an important forum for confidence- building.

The learning set was also one good vehicle for team building:

"the learning set was superb."

"...the learning set is very powerful, it allows you to explore issues outside of the work environment, it is a safe house". (clinical manager, provider, level below board)

"I have learned and been influenced partly through educational experience, and self-managed learning through a management diploma. No set curriculum, identify own needs and go about meeting these, and I was helped in doing this. The learning set was a key element, it provided support, questioning and guidance. We are still meeting after 10 years and 3 – 4 times a year." (general manager, provider, board level)

"I'm on a learning set of six aspiring CEOs from our region. There is a good facilitator, and it is the opportunity to discuss common issues and be away from work." (general manager, provider, board level)

Away days were also another vehicle for team building, and many stressed their value:

"When I became a clinical director, we had away days and that was useful because it got the team together and working for the hospital." (clinical manager, provider, level below board)

"Away days with the team are valued highly – strategic thinking that is what we are here for." (clinical director, purchaser, board level)

Some managers emphasised the need for management development across **the purchaser provider divide:**

"A purchaser has to have worked in and have understanding of service delivery to have credibility with providers." (general manager, purchaser)

"It is sad to see public health expertise all at purchaser level and none at provider level. Public health is a good catalyst for change." (clinical manager, purchaser, board level)

Others felt that where courses purported to cater for both purchasers and providers, the role of purchasing would be under-represented:

"I have been disappointed by the courses available, there is a lack of awareness of the difference of commissioning from providing organisations, I find I have to spend time explaining that." (general manager, purchaser)

There were mixed views on the value of **conferences**:

"For information, a straight conference is as good as anything." (general manager, provider, board level)

"I'm impressed by big seminars - if you go with the right expectations then it is money well spent." (general manager, purchaser, board level)

"Conferences are a bit of a disappointment - no impartial critique of services." (general manager, provider, board level)

There were also mixed views and experiences of management development targeted at **women**:

"the performance improvement executive coaching run by x as part of opportunity 2000 was good" (general manager, provider, level below board)

"I enjoyed the opportunity 2000 women's accelerated development day." (general manager, provider, level below board)

"I went on the management development course for women at x. There was only women and this was a bit of a turn off. Also we had aggressive woman lecturers at first." (general manager, provider, level below board)

However some women experienced problems specifically because their needs weren't taken into account:

"x was devastatingly awful. I was the only woman out of 17, the course tutor wouldn't look at this as a problem - "honorary chaps" type stuff. At the course dinner they invited the navy, so I was the only woman out of 40. I was in a group where one member was very hostile to me. Basically it was all very sexist" (general manager, purchaser, level below board)

Programmes/workshops described as poor contained one or more of the following elements:

- too theoretical or abstract,

- did not connect with the real world,

- material not put in context,

- little opportunity for participation or interaction,

- little feedback or follow-up,

- poor content,

- poor delivery, boring,

- too expensive.

Although experiences varied according to institution and lecturer, on the whole, external formal courses were less well received than management development tailored to the management team and taking place either within the organisation (albeit facilitated from outside) or with relevant peers (eg. with other HR managers of trusts, or through learning sets). A strong preference was expressed for contextualised courses where knowledged was related to the NHS. The following remarks made by respondents illustrate the need for clear **objectives, relevance** and for learning to be used and developed in the work situation:

"Majority are disappointing because trying to sell to a market so too wide and watered down and poor speakers who do not contribute very much. Prefer interactive type of management development, there is a lot to be said for in-house courses and away-days with own colleagues. Chunks of work are needed, day courses do not do very much and you need to reinforce them when come back to work, back to square one otherwise". (general manager, provider, level below board)

"Lot are not effective because of the way they are organised, isolated occurrences without follow up or assessment and targeted to the wrong population, poor in content. It is better where you are involved in assignments and have to explore a number of different ideas back at work." (general manager, provider, level below board)

"They have been uniformly poor because of lack of objectives, preparation of course content, material and they have been unduly expensive" (general manager, provider, board level)

Many emphasised lack of opportunities for **participation** as a problem:

"The worst course was all talk on a programme basis and no opportunity for intervention and feedback." (functional manager, provider, level below board)

"The type of courses that fail tend to be those that do not involve a great deal of participation with individual managers - too much being talked at." (general manager, purchaser, board level)

Some managers just did not like management development courses *per se*. For example:

"I have the gut feeling that good management is common sense applied properly. I did not have a proper training before but have been successful in managing departmental matters." (clinical manager, provider, board level)

"I don't learn very well from courses. I've not been on any recently and I avoid them." (functional manager, purchaser, board level)

Finally, we did find some managers "shopped around" in order to maximise the benefit and avoid the poorer courses. In some cases, where there weren't any catering for their needs, they were willing to engage in self development and design their own:

"On quality I report direct to the CEO, and we are looking at how to take quality forward so I organised a programme for myself and went to look at non - NHS organisations in the country, eg. BUPA etc. to find out about customer satisfaction, internal education, organisation audit. Also I contacted the local universities. The CEO and I went on a 5 day course master class in quality to find out what BR are doing etc." (general manager, purchaser, board level)

Management Development Programmes for Doctors

All the provider sites had participated in some way in the national schemes for doctors in management.

At the national level, evaluation of the three year Department of Health programme of management education for clinical directors concluded that the second wave management for consultants programme was largely successful for both the individual and the organisation. However it suggested that in the longer term, the impact may be limited, for this largely self selected sample is too small to form a critical mass dispersed over specialties and hospitals (Newman and Cowling 1993: 34).

The comments below show ambivalence and a variety of responses from clinical directors in our study to these and other programmes. On the one hand they were disappointed where courses hadn't been of practical help and were thought to be expensive "timewasters":

"Don't like theory and abstract stuff. I like practical guidance - how to negotiate, how to influence, how to handle different people" (clinical director, provider)

"A lot of money has been spent on a few people going on prolonged management courses, the results of which I have yet to see. Need courses on good communication and doing the job properly. For management training need to bring people into the hospital, cannot afford to send them out" (clinical director, provider)

"the material is not relevant to what we do. Also management courses are very expensive compared to the medical." (clinical director, provider)

"The course was very long winded and could have been done in half the time. They hadn't focused what they wanted to get across. On the learning set the facilitation went completely wrong." (medical director, provider)

On the other hand, they enjoyed the opportunity to stand back and reflect on the issues:

"the ambience and surroundings were great. It was good quality content, pragmatic, they brought it together extremely well. I enjoyed meeting others from other organisations, and I stopped thinking that the NHS is unique." (clinical director, provider)

"3-week residential business school component brought about a big shift because I was with people from other organisations and looking at the concept of teams and people working together, how teams function - that brought about a big shift in seeing and have been able to build on that, I realise management skills are about the team and how to cope with change, be adaptable and operate in an environment with others. Different to the professional approach, hearing about self and new roles, self and other people so getting the snobbishness knocked out. Wife and colleagues report that I am now easier to live with". (clinical director, provider)

An executive director now in a purchasing authority, commented on what he saw as a major cultural difficulty in securing productive management development for doctors:

"If management is a frame of mind then textbooks are not so useful unless you have this frame of mind. So lots of doctors don't see the relevance of management, It seems to them a mixture of commonsense and Eastern mysticism....Doctors want to know why management text books are not like anatomy text books." (executive director, purchaser).

Smith (1992) emphasised the importance of contextualising management training for consultants in their work experience, this was a point made in our study by managers from all backgrounds. He found that the effectiveness of the training depended upon the extent to which there was sound preparation before the programme and integration after the programme, and we reiterate this finding.

If we focus more specifically on what doctors in management want to learn we need to build on the learning needs highlighted in the section above. Disken et al (1990) reviewed alternative models concluding even if a doctor was not a clinical director or clinical manager *"the normal clinical role (of a consultant) demands more sophistication in managing people, using financial and clinical information, managing time and communicating well. The context ... also needs to be understood."* In a study of competences displayed by doctors in management, Turrill et al (1991) found that facing conflict, learning and being aware of others were critically associated with doctors judged to be excellent in managing. *"Perhaps the most important prerequisite for effective clinical management is for doctors and managers to know more about and better understand each others roles and responsibilities"*. Our study found that as well as doctors needing better understanding of managers, managers also benefit from better understanding of clinicians and their standpoint:

"I went on a management in medicine course. It was useful to see the problems in terms of clinicians and understand the terminology they use, how they view the hospital and how we can respond better to their aspirations and demands." (functional manager, provider, board level)

Another reason for providing management development for clinicians is that some respondents suggested that it was the only way one was to achieve organisational change:

"I believe strongly in management training for consultants. The mechanisms of contracts won't get the changes in medical practice and effectiveness that is needed. You need to win hearts and minds. All this is to do with personal development with consultants and senior nurses. The medical profession is very subtle - they can avoid doing things." (executive director, purchaser)

As well as identifying what clinicians in management need to know, we need to examine when it is appropriate for this learning to take place. As well as it needing to fit in with their busy schedules, there is another issue of early exposure, and some doctors and nurses in our study commented on the need for management development to take place throughout their training. For example:

"Management training should begin very early in a person's career - with student nurse training." (nursing director, purchaser, board level)

Taken together then, the existing literature on management development for clinicians, our findings on key roles and responsibilities (in Chapter 5), and on managers learning needs above, all point to specific types of programme:

- management development for consultants should be placed in the organisational context;

- management development for doctors and nurses should be a theme throughout their undergraduate and post graduate training;

- public health physicians need particular programmes of management development;

- whilst there should be programmes of management development focused on each of the groups of main players, there is great merit in mounting some programmes which are specifically constructed to bring people from different disciplines, backgrounds and parts of the health care sector together, in order better to facilitate learning across functions and across departments.

8.4   The Value of Informal Role Models, Mentors and Coaches

When asked about who or what have been particularly influential in their development as managers, interestingly only 10% mentioned the influence of training or development courses, whereas, as Table 8.3 shows, most managers mentioned the influence of **role models** and **mentors**.

Literature has already asserted the value of mentor, (Clutterbuck 1985, Cunningham and Eberle 1993, Hunt and Michael 1988); it has already been researched from many different aspects (for example see Bates 1993, Noe 1988, Meggison 1988, Newton and Wilkinson 1993,) including within the context of the health care sector (for example see Fagenson 1988, Kazemek 1988, Newton and Wilkinson 1993, Vance 1982) and for clinicians (Raelin 1987). Mentoring is traditionally defined as where an experienced manager offers guidance, stimulus, encouragement and support to a younger or less experienced employee. We are able to refine this concept through the observations of our respondents, and are able to relate it to the concepts of coaching and protégé relationships on the one hand, and role models on the other. Role models are less well explored in the literature, being usually mentioned within the context of mentoring (for example see Willbur 1987). However our study emphasises their importance as a concept in management development in the NHS, and delineates it more clearly from other aspects of mentoring.

The outstanding influence on the development of the sample as a whole was that of positive **role models**, which were mentioned as influential by 70% of respondents. Some (13%) also said they had learnt from negative as well as positive role models. These categories included previous bosses, current bosses, colleagues and other people with whom the interviewee had worked, many citing the chief executive. Role models were a particularly popular response from nurses, 80% of whom mentioned it, and from younger respondents (75% of respondents under 45).

Where role models were mentioned by older respondents they said they had been particularly useful earlier in their career. Significantly more older than younger respondents claimed no one in particular had been influential in their career.

TABLE 8.3   *Influential people or events in management development (Qu.H2)*

		Background			
	GM n=66	FM n=47	Dr n=70	Nr n=36	Total n=237
(a) Positive role models	77	75	51	83	70
(b) Negative role models	15	13	6	17	13
(c) Mentors	5	0	9	0	5
(d) Training and development programmes	9	9	13	6	10
(e) no-one/nothing in particular	8	6	20	8	11
(f) Circumstances opportunities chances	15	28	19	14	19

Key: GM = General Manager, FM = Functional Manager, Dr = Doctor, Nr = Nurse.

The influence of the role model was largely perceived to be through the observation of a more senior manager within a person's organisation. It was someone for whom they had respect, and whose qualities and behaviour they wished to emulate (or in the case of negative role models, through avoidance of their mistakes). Thus it is largely a passive process whereby the role model may not even be aware of their influence. The most commonly cited qualities which had been observed in role models were:

- political skills: politically aware

- integrity

- people skills: cares about people
  "keeps people on board"
  inspires and motivates people
  good team management skills
  listens

- develops others: delegates
  insures people have opportunities to develop

- persuasive, influential and diplomatic

- toughness, resilience, assertive, brave

- drive, energy

- enthusiasm, thinks positively
  aims high, sets high standards, aims for excellence

- good technical skills and financial and business acumen
  good problem solving and analytical skills

- clear thinking, clarity of expression

The qualities of **negative** role models included:

- poor interpersonal and lobbying skills
  dictatorial style, tells people what will happen

- adversarial, destructive
  refuse to accept when in wrong

- management by default - lack of interest

- speak in jargon
  won't give out information, tell people what is going on
  won't answer people's questions

- racist, sexist

- lack of NHS experience

For example, the following comments were typical on positive role models, their style and qualities:

"He had a great deal of understanding of what the organisation was there for – good technically and could also persuade people without getting aggressive." (functional manager, provider, board level)

"... Diplomacy in the jungle, he hacked his way through a demanding set of organisational challenges in a way that kept people on board. He had a very informal approach to people, and dismissal of problems in a way that disarmed potential opposition." (executive director, provider)

"(A former) CEO – to see him in action in most areas – He had the ability to make people do things that they didn't think they could do. He showed the power of a set of values and clarity of what he wanted to achieve, and put effort into getting people to achieve. ... (He believed) all have ability ... (he had) determination and a pain barrier, (he would) do simple things well and consistently – simplicity. Also ... the balance between intensity and fun. So focus, fun and flexibility sum it up" (chief executive, purchaser)

"Ability to depersonalise issues and create calm and confidence." (functional manager, provider, board level)

"Previous boss influenced me – she was highly gifted intellectually and could inspire people, had motivational ability and helped me to think positively about opportunity and work rather than complaining. Also she had good team management skills." (general manager, purchaser, level below board)

"The present boss has been influential in exposing me to the idea of team work, showing how an organisation can work corporately and through the support of individual directors." (general manager, purchaser, level below board)

"The CEO – had political understanding and knew the way to get things done, especially with consultants." (general manager, provider, board level)

"The last DGM – her open style and she was well respected by everyone at every level of the organisation – politicians to porters, and she allowed you to develop the role, she encouraged self development and was very supportive." (general manager, purchaser, board level)

"The DGM – He is very good in terms of being a politician, tactician and strategic thinker, for acquiring board skills he has been very good to watch. Certain skills are acquired by doing and observing a good role model." (general manager, purchaser, board level)

"I went to x because it had a reputation for excellence in the area. The director was very much a leader in that field. His comments helped but I have learnt more from the style of organisation he

ran. It was a style I warm to – looking to achieve excellence, as an organisation or as a person – always looks to personal development, didn't pigeonhole people, get them to contribute in all areas." (functional manager, purchaser, board level)

And one woman manager said:

"the Chief Executive has been a big influence as a mentor, and many others of the top management team, but I miss a female role model" (female functional manager, provider, level below board)

Comments about negative role models included the following examples:

"Negative role models – they had the total inability to get on with people – autocratic." (general manager, provider, level below board)

"I got negative lessons from my former general manager: no NHS experience, not a good people manager, he bypassed people." (general manager, purchaser, level below board)

"I am allergic to particular types of managers, anyone who will not admit that they are wrong. In medicine I find it difficult to discuss with people who are adamant about what is going to happen, and I am bored with the 'not answering the question' techniques. Also management who speak in jargon that no-one can understand and have to ask them what does that mean in English – these are all negative qualities I've observed and try to avoid" (clinical director, provider)

A more active developmental role is that of **mentor** where a manager actively shows interest in the respondents career and provides support, encouragement and exudes confidence in their ability.

Very few respondents cited a formal arrangement with a mentor – 5% in Table 8.3, but informal mentoring (not identified in the table but widely mentioned in qualitative data) is critically important. Informal mentors came from a variety of sources, but the most commonly mentioned sources of successful mentoring came from immediate bosses, chief executives, other senior managers, and even tutors on formal courses. Some also mentioned regional managers, consultants, husbands, wives, and friends.

The main beneficial qualities noted into practice in informal mentoring were:

–   supportive, encouraging

–   confidence, belief and trust in person being mentored

- showing interest in person being mentored

- approachable

- helpful

Typical comments here are:

"She pulled me into management" (general manager, purchaser, two levels below board)

"I had a manager who nurtured and encouraged me to go further and move into management quite early on in my career, she gave me professional support." (general manager, provider, two levels below board)

"Being given opportunities by different senior managers. I've also been looking for opportunities. Senior managers opened a few doors." (general manager, provider, level below board)

"My boss in x had a huge impact on my development because he just said 'here it is, get on with it'. He was supportive when necessary, otherwise he trusted me enough to delegate completely." (general manager, purchaser, level below board)

"The CEO ... boosted my confidence, I've much respect for him, got organisational tips from observation. I'm given increasing amount of things to do – key developmental things." (functional manager, provider, board level)

"The challenge is to overcome the destructive influence of some of my colleagues, the ex general manager was very helpful in the early stages at showing me how." (clinical manager, provider, level below board)

"The CEO exposed me to certain situations, opportunities, developed me but never formalised. The key thing is development is often about exposure to things, he makes a decision on when it is right to expose people." (functional manager, purchaser, board level)

"A manager in x a few years ago was influential – he played a mentoring role and pushed you as far as you could go, he was enabling and supportive when necessary, and acted as a catalyst and kept pushing me in terms of my career and I will always be grateful to him for that. He was a natural developer of people." (functional manager, provider, board level)

"Colleagues in x ... had habit of demanding of me more than I felt able to deliver – this is very important." (general manager, purchaser, board level)

"I had a manager who believed in me and knew I could do things and made me do them, stretched me and I did stuff I did not think I could do. He set me up to succeed." (general manager, provider, level below board)

"She gives you space to think where you are going and then supports you in it" (general manager, provider, two levels below board)

And one woman manager said:

"X is particularly keen on developing women managers, is very committed to giving them opportunities." (functional manager, provider, level below board)

Thus informal mentoring is very much about a manager's awareness of their responsibility for developing others, and taking an active interest in them, their career and problems. Where the manager is the direct line manager for an individual, this role may develop into that of **coach**. As a coach a manager provides advice and guidance, "shows them the ropes" and discusses their activities with them providing feedback on their performance.

Alternatively, the informal mentoring relationship may develop into that of a **sponsor** and **protégé**. In these cases managers may have had an active involvement in creating career opportunities for an individual, and may have vocalised their positive assessment of the protégé's qualities throughout the organisation and elsewhere.

Nineteen per cent of respondents found **circumstances or chance** to be influential in their development. This group of respondents was significantly older (over 45) than other groups. They were referring to change itself, crisis, as well as, previous and current jobs where they had been given opportunities to make decisions and excel. For example:

"It was a baptism of fire, I was thrown in at the deep end" (clinical director, provider)

"experience in the commercial sector, and development of the computer system – focus mind on a problem and try and solve it." (clinical manager, provider, level below board)

Comparatively few respondents mentioned that they had been proactive in shaping their own development. Respondents in this minority generally cited their own ability to "survive" and "be thrown into the deep end and swim". They said they had contributed to their own development by reading, planning their own education, and steering their own experience. Indicative comments here are:

"I relied on my own experience and wide reading" (general manager, provider, board level)

"literature – Belbin, Handy, 'Gods of Management', they were my guide'" (general manager, purchaser, level below board)

11% of respondents identified **'no one'** and 'nothing in particular' as being influential in their development. The older the respondent the more likely they were to say their development was not influenced by any one in particular.

Finally although many managers felt they had benefitted from the support of a positive role model or mentor, there was very little said about self-development or the development of others, which are perhaps the other "sides of the coin" in successful mentor relationships. We saw in Chapter 5 that there was considerable complaint that seniors at every level, gave less effort than was thought desirable to formal appraisal and support of juniors, and many paid scant regard to informal support of others. Comments from three respondents underline this problem:

"There's no obvious career path, much flatter structures. Not many places at the top. NHS is particularly bad at helping you. For example, what about seconding, career planning and guidance ... giving opportunities for wider experience. This is as important to me as a pay rise. But its difficult to get any advice or find anyone to discuss this with." (clinical services manager, provider)

"I'm unsure of the future, previously there was a logical progression.... I know you have to make opportunities for yourself, there's no succession planning. I know its my responsibility, but our organisations could do more. For example, I'm very interested in a secondment to a purchaser or outside the NHS and I think it would be good for the Trust too – but I can't get any one interested." (clinical manager, provider, two below board level)

"I've stopped thinking about career. Reorganisation and restructuring in the NHS means we need to be adaptable, to be creative, to be mobile. But the culture doesn't support that. the NHS expects a lot from its managers but it's not supportive." (general manager, provider, below board)

We know that some managers do acknowledge the importance both of self development and developing others but more could be done to recognise, reward and develop these processes, need more encouragement if they are to flourish.

Investment to encourage self-development and the development of others is likely to have wide ranging benefits. In return for modest sums, such programmes will become self-supporting if they become part of the culture 'of the way things are done around here'. They will thereby touch many more individuals than can the 'lumpy' blocks of investment which inevitably have to be made to the comparatively few individuals who at any one time are sponsored to participate in major formal development programmes. This is not an argument against investment in formal programmes, their value and place has already been established. Rather it is an argument to ensure additional support to encourage and sustain informal processes of self-development.

8.5 Summary

- The restructured context of the NHS has made a difference to the learning needs of managers, in that it is unlikely that the key areas highlighted now would have been highlighted before the reforms. There is an increased requirement for management development in the evaluation of organisational performance, business planning, evaluating new services for development, marketing services, strategic planning, and computing and IT. Within purchasing, a particular need for health economics was identified.

- Clinical managers have particular learning needs which should be addressed in the areas of strategic planning, evaluation of organisational performance, evaluating new services for delivery, marketing, computing and IT, individual performance review and appraisal, and time management. However, the dual nature of many of their jobs may require courses to be designed which fit in with, and allow for, their clinical schedules, for example through short immersion courses tailored to their context, and supplemented with work which can be done at times to suit individuals.

- Management development still continues to exhibit enormous diversity in terms of content and mode of delivery, and to be conducted largely in an ad hoc way at the instigation of individual managers, often without consolidation in the organisational context.

- Although the opportunity to reflect on objectives and priorities in IPR is welcomed, IPR is not widely perceived as a main vehicle for management development.

- When asked about who or what have been influential in their development as managers, only a minority mentioned the influence of training or development courses. Formal programmes are, however, thought to be important in creating a climate for greater understanding of managerial roles, awareness of the issues and the processes of management.

- Where formal management development programmes and courses were said to be successful, this usually resulted from their being "contextualised" so that skills were related to the NHS, from structured opportunities to reflect on the managers own context and careers with help for self development, or from opportunities to network and learn from other participants.

- Informal mentoring, coaching, protégé relationships and role models are seen to be central to the development of managers, and these were believed by our respondents to have been highly influential in their own development and progression. Observation in action and to a lesser extent, emulation were the main modes of learning from role models, whereas learning from informal mentors was more through advice, support, encouragement, and being given opportunities.

- Self development, where managers believe they engage in it, is perceived as "learning by experience" and reading around an area rather than anything broader. It is not on the whole supported by mechanisms to provide managers with the skills to develop themselves in a more pro-active way, such as with personal development plans and access to information about opportunities which are available.

Chapter 9 Concluding Comments

This report has presented the results of a study, begun in January 1992, on senior executives in local purchasing and providing organisations in the NHS. Each chapter has concluded with a summary of the main points. These are reiterated in the Executive Summary which also includes recommendations which can be drawn from the discussion of the results. This final section is therefore concerned only to draw out some of the important themes to emerge from the study as a whole, rather than to provide an additional summary.

9.1 Differences and Similarities Between Purchasing and Providing

The agendas for purchasing and providing are different. Effective health care within the present structure requires this. However with difference must go effective collaboration. The NHS is no longer one organisation, but its various parts are dominant players in one sector. In three respects at least, it is important to maintain a strong federation of NHS organisations.

The first is the strength which derives from adherence to common values which emphasises a public service ethos, and leads to a commitment to provide excellent services which meet agreed standards of:

– equity
– acceptability
– choice
– appropriateness
– effectiveness.

At a time when commercial organisations are spending a lot of time trying to create a core of shared values as a basis for securing co-ordination, control and communication in contexts where organisations are flatter, leaner, less hierarchical and composed of a variety of semiautonomous business units, the NHS should be careful not to throw away the common values base which it has nurtured over the past 50 years.

The second reason to emphasise the strength of the NHS federation is that as participants in one sector, it is important to secure cross fertilisation of ideas and skills between the parts and organisational means for collaboration.

The third reason derives from the second: a clear commitment to seeking to maintain communication and understanding between the parts may also help to increase morale and allay fears about the creation of major career barriers within the service.

9.2 Responsibilities for Management Development and Career Planning

At the local level it is vitally important that organisations have a management development strategy. This needs to be underpinned by resources and support for self development, and the appointment of a local champion to oversee the dissemination of information and options for management development and career progression. Whilst the appointment of a local champion is important, nothing can replace commitment from the top of each organisation in establishing management development as a priority and self development as part of the culture.

Effective management development requires partnership between individuals, their superiors and peers and their employing organisation. None of these parties can achieve the desired benefits from personal and corporate investment in management development unless they each take responsibility for part of the process.

In Chapter Three we outlined a "climbing frame" as a vehicle to explore various managerial career routes in the NHS. At the local level, this should be discussed and developed internally for each organisation. A "champion" of career progression and management development could help identify routes for people from different professional backgrounds who wish to pursue a predominantly managerial career. Where people are finding their desired managerial career paths blocked due to lack of skills or experience in the desired area, or lack of stepping stones to cross from one area to another, or even historical or cultural barriers, discussions should take place and plans developed to facilitate appropriate movement. A local champion could help to ensure that the necessary mechanisms were put in place to overcome such obstacles, for example a purchaser and provider could engage in joint proJects, or secondments to help managers get the necessary exposure to work in the other organisation.

Although some barriers are planned and reasonable, others may just be the unplanned consequences of the restructuring, and can be altered. People fear being unnecessarily pigeonholed and management development activity needs to be targeted to prevent this. Action centred learning packs which outline alternative next steps for people in various roles could be developed, perhaps drawing on national templates which could be adapted for the local level.

At the national level there continues to be a role for the dissemination of good practice in management development, the operation of career registers and support for programmes to ensure equality of access to managerial positions. There is also a national and regional role in evaluation of performance to national targets. With regard to national management development programmes, their existence must depend on the extent to which local organisations and managers find them useful.

Economies of scale and effort can be achieved in national initiatives, but they should be made within a context which ensures that management development is always seen to relate both to the particular needs of the employing organisations and to the individual needs of participants. With the development of different types of organisation at a local level within the internal market and the current restructuring at regional and national level, work needs to be done to consider the implications of the f1ndings of this and other work on the new NHS, for identifying organisational requirements for management development, for each of the participating professional groups.

9.3 Self-Development, Management Development and Organisational Development

Our study found many examples of managers having gained awareness and confidence from formal programmes of management development. It has also shown that there is another equally important aspect of management development: that which occurs informally and on the job through the use of role models, informal mentors and sponsors. There are also many examples of successful learning sets, away days, secondments, project working and so on. These examples could be drawn together in one short practical document giving advice on how to improve management development at the local level.

In terms of the content of management development, two themes perhaps emerge above all others as the key areas for interventions:

–   support for team working, with the priority for providers being cross functional working and for purchasers being management across organisational boundaries,

–   support for the setting of organisational priorities and their cascading down to the identification of priorities and objectives at individual and team levels.

Management development will continue to take place in an ad hoc and fragmented way without capturing its full benefits in practice unless steps are taken to ensure it becomes a more vital part of the culture of the NHS. Steps need to include:

–   strong leadership from the top of organisations emphasising its value,

–   a champion of management development at the organisation level,

–   a commitment to evaluate management development initiatives from an organisational and individual perspective,

–   a commitment to determine the priorities for management development within the context set by careful consideration of the strategy and objectives of organlsations,

–   a commitment to identify "the development of others" as an aspect of managerial performance which will be evaluated when individual performance is reviewed.

If local agendas for management development are to be effectively constructed, two organisational characteristics need to be developed. First, commitment and action to encourage and support individuals to recognise the importance of self-development and their own responsibility for their careers. Secondly, commitment to management development as a major responsibility not least because it is a key vehicle to facilitate effective change management and thereby organisation development.

9.4   Change

The organisation of the NHS has been the subject of considerable and frequent change in the last 20 years. Even in the period between the fieldwork being conducted for this project and the production of the report, there will have been changes in the organisations which are its subject. Every change implies some difference in emphasis in managerial roles, and creates new opportunities and closes off others for the diverse occupational groups which are represented in the NHS. It is a debatable point whether the present period of restructuring and change is different in kind. The majority of our respondents felt they were witnessing a step change in health management and that the reforms of the 1990s have set a significant agenda for management and organisational development which will not evaporate with the next set of changes and which still leave much work to be done.

As a snapshot of reality, the report has shown that many aspects of the working lives of senior executives in the NHS have recently changed, that others need further development and still others are subjects of complaint, anxiety and frustration. But on the other side, through their own voices, these senior executives who were responsible for purchasing and providing health care show how they are thriving on change, how they are thinking about new opportunities and are seeking, with energy, to develop themselves, others and their organlsatlons.

Bibliography

Arthur, M.B., Hall, D.T. and Lawrence, B.S. (eds) (1989) *Handbook of Career Theory* Cambridge: Cambridge University Press.

Arthur, M.B. (Ed.) (1994), 'The Boundaryless Career', a special issue, *Journal of Organizational Behaviour*, July.

Audit Commission (1992) *Caring Systems* London: HMSO

Audit Commission (1993), *Their Health, Your Business: the new role of the DHA*, London, HMSO.

Audit Commission (1994), *Trusting in the Future: Towards an Audit Agenda for NHS Providers*, London, HMSO.

Ashburner, L., Ferlie, E, Fitzgerald, L (1993), *Leadership by boards in health care.* Paper 12, Authorities in the NHS, NHSTD.

BAMM, BMA, IHSM, RCN (1993) *Managing Clinical Services* A Consensus Statement of Principles for Effective Clinical Management, London, IHSM

Barton Cunningham, J. and Eberle, T (1993) 'Characteristics of the Mentoring experience: a qualitative study' *Personnel Review* Vol. 22 No. 4 pp 54-66

Bell, N.E. and Shaw, B.M. (1989) 'People as sculptors versus sculpture: the roles of personality and personnel control in organisations' in Arthur et al (op cit.)

Bellamy, C. and Henderson, S. (1992) 'The UK Social Security Benefits Agency: a case-study of the information polity' *Information and the Public Sector* Vol.2 (1) pp. 1-26

Bevan S. and M. Thompson (1992) 'An Overview of Policy and Practice' '*Performance Management in the UK: An Analysis of the Issues*' IPM

Bloomfield, B.P., Coombs, R.W. and Owen, J. (1994) 'The NHS Information Strategy: A Triumph of Optimism over Practicality? Paper to Conference: *Implementing Health Care Reforms*, Oxford: Templeton College, 11-12 April.

Boddy, D and Buchanan, D. A. (1986) *Managing New Technology* Oxford: Blackwell.

Bolton, R and Gold, J (1994) 'Career Management: Matching the Needs of Individuals with the Needs of Organisations' *Personnel Review* Vol. 23 (1) pp. 6-24.

Boyatzis, R.E., (1982) *The Competent Manager: A model for effective performance,* John Wiley & Sons.

Brown, H. and Goss, S (1993) 'Can you hear the sound of breaking glass' *Health Service Journal* 23rd September pp26-27

Burgoyne, J., (1988) 'Management Development for the Individual and the Organisation', *Personnel Management* June p.40-44.

Burgoyne, J and Lorbiecki, A (1993) 'Clinicians in Management: The Experience in Context', *Health Services Management Research* Vol.6 (4) November pp. 248-259

Bywater, M (1994) 'Bread and Jam' *British Journal of Healthcare Computing and Information Management* Vol.11 (2) March pp. 22-23

Canning, R., (1990) The Quest for Competence, *Industrial and Commercial Training Journal,* November, vol.22,No.5.

Charlwood, P (1994) 'From Ladders to Climbing Frames' *MESOL Update 5,* Spring

Clutterbuck D. (1985) *Everyone Needs a Mentor: How to Foster Talent Within the Organisation* London: IPM

Cockerill, T., (1989) The Kind of Competence for Rapid Change, *Personnel Management,* August.

Collin, A. (1986) Career Development: The Significance of the Subjective Career *Personnel Review* Vol.15 No.2 pp. 22-28

Colling, T and Ferner, A (1992) 'The Limits of Autonomy: Devolution, line managers and industrial relations in privatised companies' *Journal of Management Studies* Vol.29 (2) pp. 209-227

Collins, A., (1989) 'A Critique of Managerial Competence?', *Personnel Review.*

Constable, J. and R. McCormick (1987) *The Making of British Managers* BIM / CBI April

Coombs, R. and Cooper, D. (1990) Accounting for Patients?: Information technology and the implementation of the NHS White Paper *PICT Policy Research Paper No.10* Swindon:ESRC

CNAA, (1992) *Review of Management Education,* London:CNAA

Cross, M. (1994) 'From genesis to revelations' *Health Service Journal* IT Update 26th May

Cunningham J.B. and T. Eberle (1993) 'Characteristics of the Mentoring Experience: A Qualitative Study' *Personnel Review* 22, 4, pp. 54-66.

Dawson, SJN, Sherval, J, Mole, V, (1993) In or Out of Management? Dilemmas & Developments in Public Health Medicine in England, Conference paper *'Professions and Management in Britain'* University of Stirling August 1993.

Dawson, SJN, Mole, V, Winstanley, D, Sherval, J (1992) Management, Competition & Professional Practice: Medicine & The market Place, Conference Paper *'Knowledge Workers in Contemporary Organisations',* Lancaster University, September 2-4. (A subsequent version of this paper will be published in *British Journal of Management,* 1995.)

Dawson, S.J.N., (1993) 'Changes in the Distance: Professionals Re-appraise the Meaning of Management', (Management School Working Paper, subsequently published in the *Journal of General Management*, Vol.20 No.1 Autumn 1994).

Day, M., (1988) 'Managerial Competence and the Charter Initiative', *Personnel Management* 20 (8), August p.30-34.

Devine, M. (ed.) (1990), *The Photofit Manager: building a picture of management in the 1990s.* London: Hyman.

Disken S., Dixon M., Halpern S., Shocket G. (1990) *Models of Clinical Management* London: IHSM

DOE, (1981) *'A New Training Initiative: A Programme for Action*, Cmnd 8455, London: HMSO.

DOE and DES, (1984) *Training for Jobs*, Cmnd.9135, London:HMSO.

DOE and DES, (1988) *Employment for the 1990s*, Cmnd. 540, London: HMSO.

Department of Health (1990) *Framework for Information Systems: the Next Steps* London: HMSO.

Dockery, E. (1992) 'Management and the usefulness of information' in Willcocks & Harrow (eds) (1992) *op cit.*

Dopson, S. and Stewart, R. (1990) What is Happening to Middle Management?, *British Journal of Management*, Vol.1 (1) pp.3-16.

Driver, M.J. (1982) 'Career Concepts: a new approach to career research' in R.Katz (ed), *Career Issues in Human Resource Management*, New Jersey Prentice Hall.

Drucker, P (1991) 'The coming of the new organisation' in W. McGowan (ed) *Revolution in Real Time* Boston: Harvard Business School Press.

Evetts, J (1992) 'Dimensions of Career: Avoiding Reification in the Analysis of Change', *Sociology* Vol. 26 No. 1 pp. 1-21.

Fagenson, E. 'The Power of a Mentor: Protégés and Non Protégés' *Group and Organisation Studies 13, 2* June 1988 pp. 182-4.

Ferlie, E., Ashburner, L, Fitzgerald, L. (1993), *Board Teams: Roles and Relationships*, Paper 10, Authorities in the NHS, NHSTD.

Fitzgerald L. and Sturt, J. (1992), Clinicians into Management: on the Change Agenda or Not?, *Health Services Management Research*, Vol.5 (2), July.

Fletcher, C. and R. Williams (1992) 'Organisational Experience' in *'Performance Management in the UK: An Analysis of the Issues'* London IPM

Fletcher, C. (1993) *Appraisal: Routes to Improved Performance* London IPM

Fonda, N., (1989) 'Management Development: The Missing Link in Sustained Business Performance' *Personnel Management*, December p.50-53.

Fonda, N. and Stewart, R. (1992) 'Understanding Differences in General Management Jobs', *Journal of General Management* Vol.17 (4) Summer pp. 1-12.

Fulop, L (1991) 'Middle managers: Victims or vanguards of the entrepreneurial movement? *Journal of Management Studies* Vol. 28 (1) January.

Gibson, A. (1994) 'The Wizards of OZ' *Health Service Journal* 5th May pp.22-24

Goffee, R. & Scase, R. (1992), 'Organisational Change and the Corporate Career', *Human Relations*, 45 (4), 363-385.

Goss, S. and Brown, H. (1991) *Equal Opportunities for Women in the National Health Service.* London: Office for Public Management and National Health Service Management Executive.

Greatrex, J. and Phillips, P., (1989) 'Oiling the Wheels of Competence', *Personnel Management* 21,(8) p.36-39.

Griffiths, R (1983), *Report of the NHS Management Enquiry,* Department of Health & Social Security, London.

Guest D. and R. Peccei (1992) *The Effectiveness of Personnel Management in the NHS* Report of Research Project, Department of Occupational Psychology, Birkbeck College, London, October

Gunz,H (1989) 'The Dual Meaning of Managerial Careers: Organisational and Individual levels of Analysis' *Journal of Management Studies* Vol.26 No.3 pp.225-250

Gunz, H (1989b), 'Career and Corporate Cultures: Managerial Mobility in Large Corporations', London, Blackwell.

Hales, C.P. (1986) 'What do manager's do: A critical review of the evidence', *Journal of Management Studies,* Vol.23:1.

Handy, C. (1984) *The Future of Work.* Oxford: Blackwell.

Handy, C. (1989), *The Age of Unreason,* London Penguin.

Handy, C (1991) 'Management training: perk or prerequisite?' *Personnel Management* May pp 28 - 31.

Handy, C (1987) *The Making of Managers* MSC/NEDC/BIM April

Handy, C (1988) *Making Managers* Pitman

Harris, George T (1993) 'The post-capitalist executive: an interview with Peter Drucker' *Harvard Business Review* May/June pp 114-22

Harrison, J. and Thompson, D. (1992), 'A Flat Earth Syndrome' *Health Service Journal,* Vol.102 No.5320 17th September p.29

Hay, J. (1990) 'Managerial Competencies or Managerial Characteristics?' *Management Education and Development*, Vol.21,5, pp 305-315.

Heginbotham, C. et. al (1992), 'Jam tomorrow: purchasing dilemmas' *Health Service* Journal, Vol.102 No. 5292 5th March pp.24-25

Hendry, C. and Pettigrew, A. (1990) 'Human Resource Management: an Agenda for the 1990s' *International Journal of Human Resource Management*, Vol. 1 (1) pp. 17-45.

Herriot, P., Gibson, G., Pemberton, C. and Pinder, R. (1993) 'Dashed hopes: organisational determinants and personal perceptions of managerial careers' *Journal of Occupational and Organisational Psychology* 66, pp. 115-123

Holland J. L. (1985), *Making Vocational Choices: A theory of causes* Prentice Hall.

Honey, P and Mumford A (1986) *The Manual of Learning Styles* Maidenhead: Honey

Hopfl, H. and Dawes, F (eds) (1993) 'Management Competence: The debate in Management Learning' *Personnel Review* Special Issue Vol. 22 (6)

Hunt, D. M. and C. Michael (1988) 'Mentorship: A Career Training and Development Tool' *Academy of Management Review* 8, 3, pp 475-485

IHSM (1990), *Models of Clinical Management* London: Institute of Health Service Management

IHSM, (1991) *'Report on IPR'*, Institute of Health Service Management.

IHSM (1992) *NHS Management Development: The Emergent Culture*, Conference Proceedings.

IHSM Consultants (1994), *Creative Career Paths in the NHS: Report No. 1 Top Managers* London, Department of Health: NHS Women's Unit. Subsequent reports appeared in 1994 and 1995.

Iles, P. and Mabey, C (1993) 'Managerial Career Development Programmes: Effectiveness, Availability and Acceptability' *British Journal of Management* Vol. 4 pp 103-118.

Jacobs, R. (1989) 'Getting the Measure of Management Competence', *Personnel Management*, June.

Kanter, R.M. (1983) *The Change Masters* London: Allen & Unwin.

Kanter, R. (1989a) 'Careers and the Wealth of Nations: A Macro-Perspective on the Structure and Implications of Career Forms', in Arthur et al *(op.cit)*

Kanter, R (1989b), *When Giants Learn to Dance*, New York, Unwin.

Kazemek, M. (1988) 'Four Basic Techniques Can Improve Managerial Skills' *Healthcare Financial Management*, 42, 6 June 1988, P 150

Kearney, A.T. (1990) *Barriers 2 - Barriers to the Successful Implementation of Information Technology* London: DTI/CIMA

Key, P, Dearden, B (1993) *Fanning The Flames of Purchasing*, a report for the NHSME, Dearden Associates.

Keen J. (1994) Should the National Health Service Have An Information Strategy? *Public Administration* Vol.72 (1) Spring pp. 33-53.

Kolb, D. (1984) *Experimental Learning* New York Prentice Hall

Kolb, D, Lublin, S., Spoth, J., & Baker, R, (1991). Strategic Management Development: Experimental Learning and Managerial Competencies, in Henry, I (Ed.) *Creative Management*, Milton Keynes, Open University.

Kotter, J.P. (1982) *The General Managers*, New York, Collier Macmillan.

Leaning, M.S. (1993) 'The new information management and technology strategy of the NHS' *British Medical Journal* Vol.307 24th July p.217

Lemieux-Charles (1992), Hospital-Physician Integration. Case Studies of Community Hospitals, *Health Service Management Research*, 5:2 82-98.

Luthans F.R., Hodgetts M. and Rosenkrantz S.A., (1988) *Real Managers*, Cambridge MA: Ballinger.

Mahmood, R and Chisnell, C (1993) 'Do doctors want to become involved in management? *The Clinician in Management* Vol. 2 (4) p. 12-13.

Management Charter Initiative, (1990) *Management Development in Practice*, MCI.

Mangham, I and Pye, A. (1991) *The Doing of Managing*, Oxford: Basil Blackwell Ltd.

Mangham, I. and M. Silver (1986) *Management training - Context and Practice*, School of Management, univ. of Bath.

Mansfield, B (1989) 'Competence and Standards' in Burke, J. (ed) *Competency Based Education and Training* Lewes: The Falmer Press.

Margetts, H. and Willcocks, L. (1993) 'Information systems in public services: disaster faster?' *Public Money and Management* Vol.6 (2) April/June

Mark, A. (1991a) 'Clinical Directorates: Will the glass ceiling be double-glazed" *Health Manpower Management*, Vol.17 (4) pp.14-17

Mark, A (1991b), "Where are the medical managers?", *Journal of Management in Medicine*, Vol.5 No.4 p.6-12.

Mark, A. and H. Scott (1992) 'Management of the National Health Service', in L.Willcocks & J.Harrow, (eds.) *Rediscovering Public Service Management*, London, McGraw Hill.

May, A. (1992), 'Perfect Purchasing', *Health Service Journal*, Vol 102 No. 5311, 16th July, pp.22-24

Mayo, A. (1992), 'A Framework for Career Management' *Personnel Management*, February pp. 36-39.

Mayo, (1994), *"Managing Careers: Strategies for Organisations"*, Institute of Personnel Management.

Meggison D. (1988) 'Instructor, Coach, Mentor: Three Ways of Helping Managers' *Management Education and Development* 19, 1 pp. 33-46

Mintzberg, H. (1975), 'The manager's job: folklore and fact', *Harvard Business Review*, 53.

Mintzberg, H, (1979), *The Nature of Managerial Work*, New Jersey Prentice Hall.

Mole, V. and Dawson, S. (1993) 'Clinical management: Pole to Pole' *Health Service Journal* Vol. 103 No. 5343 11th March

Morgan, G. (1986) *Images of Organisation* London: Sage.

Morgan, G. (1989) *Riding the Waves of Change:* Developing managerial competences for a turbulent world, Oxford: Jossey-Bass

Muid, C (1994) Information Systems and New Public Management -A View from the Centre *Public Administration* Vol. 72 (1) Spring pp.113-125.

Mumford, P. (1989) 'Doctors in the Driving Seat' *Health Service Journal*, 99 (5151) 18th May.

Nalgo Survey of IPR, (1992) London: Nalgo

National Audit Office (1987) *Inland Revenue: control of major developments in the use of Information Technology* London: HMSO

National Audit Office (1990) *Managing computer projects in the National Health Service* London: HMSO

National Health Service Management Executive (1992a) *Women Managers in the NHS: a celebration of success*, London: Department of Health.

National Health Service Management Executive (1992b) *Women in the NHS: an implementation guide to Opportunity 2000* London: Department of Health.

National Health Service Management Executive: Information Management Group (1992c) *Getting better with information: Information Management and Technology Strategy overview* London, Department of Health.

National Health Service Management Executive (1992d), *The Nurse Executive Director Post*, London, Department of Health.

National Health Service Management Executive (1993) *Women in the NHS: an employee's guide to Opportunity 2000* London: Department of Health.

National Health Service Executive (1994a), *Building a Stronger Team: the nursing contribution to purchasing*, London, Department of Health.

National Health Service Management Executive (1994b) *Opportunity 2000: the challenge in General Practice*, London: Department of Health.

Neal F. (ed) (1991) *A Handbook of Performance Management* IPM

Newman, K & Cowling A (1993), "Management Education for Clinical Directors: an evaluation", *Journal of Management in Medicine*, Vol.7, No.5 pp.27-35.

Nicholson, N. and West, M (1988) *Managerial Job Change: Men and Women in Transition*, Cambridge: Cambridge University Press.

Nicholson, N. and West, M (1989), 'Transitions, Work Histories and Careers' in Arthur et al. *(op cit.)*

Nicholson, N.C. (1993), "Purgatory or place of safety? The managerial plateau and organisational age grading", *Human Relations*, 46(12), 1369-1389.

Noe R. (1988) 'Women and Mentoring: A Review and Research Agenda' *Academy of Management Review* 13, 1, January pp. 65-78

Osborne, D and Gaebler T (1992) *'Reinventing Government: how the entrepreneurial spirit is transforming the public sector'*, Reading, MA: Addison-Wesley.

Pettigrew, A.M., Ferlie, E., Fitzgerald, L., Wensley, R. (1991) *The Leadership role of the New Health Authorities : An Agenda for Research and Development*, CCSC, University of Warwick, February.

Pettigrew, A & Whipp, R (1991), *Managing Change for Competitive Success*, Oxford, Blackwell.

Pollitt,C., Harrison, S., Hunter, D. and Marnoch, G. (1990) 'The reluctant managers: clinicians and budgets in the NHS,. *Financial Accountability and Management* 4 pp.213-33.

Prahalad, C.K and Hamel, G (1990) 'The Core Competence of the Corporation' *Harvard Business Review* May/June pp. 79-91.

Quinn, J. (1992) *Intelligent Enterprise: a knowledge and service based paradigm for industry* New York: Free Press.

Raelin J. (1987)'Understanding Can Help Physician-Manager Relations' *Modern Healthcare* 17, 21 p78

Rea, C. (1992), Clinical Management: Gang Mentality, *Health Service Journal*, 25 March 1992.

Redman T. and E. Snape (1992) 'Upward and Onward: Can Staff Appraise their Managers?' *Personnel Review* 21, 7, pp. 32-46

Rosenbaum, J.E. (1979) 'Tournament mobility: career patterns in a corporation' *Administrative Science Quarterly* 24, pp 220-241.

Raftery, J and Stevens, A. (1994) 'Information for Purchasing' in J.Keen (ed) *Information Management in Health Services* Buckingham: Open University Press.

Scase, R and Goffee R (1989) *Reluctant Managers: their work and lifestyles*, London: Unwin Hyman.

Schein, E. (1978) *Career Dynamics: Matching Individual and Organisational Needs*, London: Addison-Wesley

Senge, P. (1990), The Leaders' New Work: Building learning organisations, *Sloan Management Review*, Fall, 7-23.

Sheaff, R. (1991) Marketing in the NHS: Prospects and Variants *Public Money & Management*, Summer.

Barbara Shelborn Developments Ltd (1990), *Components of Occupational Competence*, R&D Series No.3.

Sheldon T. (1992) 'Caines Proposes IPR Overhaul' *Health Service Journal* 26th March

Shortell, Morrison & Friedman (1990), *Strategic Choices for America's Hospitals*, San Franciso, Jossey Bass.

Simpson, J (1993) BAMM clinical directorates survey *The Clinician in Management* Vol. 2 (4) p.13 - 14.

Smith, P (1992), "Consultants in management training: learning and doing", *Journal of Management in Medicine*, Vol.6, No.2, pp.11-26.

Sofer, C (1970) *Men in Mid-Career* Cambridge: Cambridge University Press.

Sonnenfeld, J.A. (1989), 'Career Systems Profiles and Strategic Staffing, in Arthur et al. *(op.cit)*

Stamp, G. (1989) 'The Individual, the Organisation and the Path to Mutual Appreciation', *Personnel Management* July pp. 28-31.

Stewart, R. (1982) *Choices for the Manager*, Maidenhead: McGraw-Hill Book Publ. Co. Ltd. 1982.

Stewart, R. (1994) 'The Right Stuff' *Health Service Journal* 10th February

Stinchcombe, A.L. (1983) *Economic Sociology*, London: Academic Press

Stock, J, Seccombe, I and Kettley, P (1994) 'Personnel Services' *Health Service Journal* 20th January.

Storey, J, (1989) 'Management Development: A Literature Review and Implications for Future Research part 1: Conceptualisations and Practices' *Personnel Review*, 18, 6.

Storey, J, (1990) 'Management Development' *Personnel Review* 19, 1, 3-11.

Taylor, J. and Williams, H. (1990) 'Themes and issues in an information polity' *Journal of Information Technology* Vol.5 (3) September pp.151-60

Turrill, T, Wilson, D, Young, K. (1991). *The Characteristics of Excellent Doctors in Management*, a report produced for the NHS Management Executive, Resource Management Unit.

Tyson S. (1985) 'Is This The Very Model of A Modern Personnel Manager?' *Personnel Management* May, pp. 22-25

Tyson, S. and Jackson, T. (1992) *The Essence of Organisational Behaviour*, Prentice-Hall International (UK) Ltd.

Vance, C.N. (1982) 'The mentor connection' *Journal of Nursing Administration*

Veiga, J.F. (1983) 'Mobility influences during managerial career stages', *Academy of Management Journal*, Vol. 26 (1) pp. 64 - 85

Willbur J. (1987) 'Does Mentoring Breed Success?' *Training and Development Journal*, 44, 11, November pp. 38-41

Willcocks, L (ed) (1993) *Information Management: evaluation of information systems* London: Chapman and Hall.

Willcocks, L (1994) 'Managing Information Systems in UK Public Administration: Issues and Prospects', *Public Administration* Vol. 72 (1) Spring pp.13-32.

Willcocks, L and Harrow, J (eds) (1992) *Rediscovering Public Services Management*, London: Mc Graw-Hill Book Company.

Winstanley, D. (1992) 'Performance Review in the NHS: Routes out of the Chasm' *Imperial College Management School Working Paper*

Winstanley, D. (1994) 'The Golden Thread' *Imperial College Management School Working Paper*.

Wood, S J (1989) 'New Wave Management' *Work, Employment & Society* Vol.3 (3) pp.379- 402

Woodruffe, C. (1991) 'Competent By Any Other Name', *Personnel Review*, September.

Interview Schedule in Condensed Form

The Schedule below shows the Questions asked and some of the Precoded Response Codes

CONFIDENTIAL

Project on Senior Executives in the NHS and their Organisations

The Management School
Imperial College of Science, Technology and Medicine

Introduction

Please ensure the following points are made:
>   Purpose of research
>   Personal confidentiality
>   Feedback
>   Procedure

A.   Personal Biography: Education, Qualifications, Career

Fill out as many details as possible before the interview begins.

A.1   *Name / Organisation address*

A.2   *Organisation*   *Region* _____ ☐

DHA   ☐ 1   FHSA   ☐ 2   Joint Commission   ☐ 3
Trust   ☐ 4   DMU   ☐ 5

For Providers Only

A.2.1

Acute	☐ 1
Community	☐ 2
Both	☐ 3

A.2.2 *Provider: Trust status*

not yet applied	☐ 1
applied, no answer	☐ 2
applied, approved, not started	☐ 3
applied, approved, started	☐ 4
not applicable	☐ 5

if 3 or 4 date applied _____

date started _____

For All

A.4 *Job Title - Nature of responsibilities* **(write notes here and code after interview)**

A.5 *Membership of executive board*

Executive member	☐ 1
Non executive member	☐ 2
Non member	☐ 3

A.6 *Do you have any other formal / official responsibility on the Trust Board*

no ☐ 1   yes ☐ 2   N/A ☐ 3

If Yes

A.6.1 *Give details of this responsibility*

A.7 *Can you please give me a brief resume of your career and qualifications* **(Write notes here and code after interview)**

Ask if not already indicated

A.8 *Why did you decide to become a Doctor / Nurse / NHS Manager / other * (* delete where applicable)*

A.10 *Year joined NHS* _____

A.11 *NHS schemes*

national trainee ☐ 1   GMTS1   ☐ 2
GMTS2   ☐ 3   GMTS3   ☐ 4

A.12 *Length of time in NHS* _____

Experience Outside the NHS: Coding for Interviewer

A.13 *Work experience outside the NHS*

     no   ☐ 1   yes   ☐ 2

If No, Then A.14 to A.20 are n/a

A.14 *Prior to joining NHS*

     no   ☐ 1   yes   ☐ 2   n/a   ☐ 3

A.15 *Between jobs in the NHS*

     no   ☐ 1   yes   ☐ 2   n/a   ☐ 3

A.16 *Whilst working in the NHS*

     no   ☐ 1   yes   ☐ 2   n/a   ☐ 3

A.17 *Manufacturing*

     no   ☐ *1*   *yes*   ☐ *2*   *n/a*   ☐ *3*

A.18 *Service*

     no   ☐ *1*   *yes*   ☐ *2*   *n/a*   ☐ *3*

A.19 *Other public sector*

     no   ☐ *1*   *yes*   ☐ *2*   *n/a*   ☐ *3*

which _____

A.20 *For each period of non-NHS work state whether:*

     full time salaried   ☐ 1
     part time salaried   ☐ 2
     freelance   ☐ 3
     N/A   ☐ 4

Work Experience within the NHS: coding for interviewer

Substantial working experience in the following

A.21 *Provider units*   no   ☐ 1   yes   ☐ 2

A.22 *Region*   no   ☐ 1   yes   ☐ 2

A.23 *DoH/ME*   no   ☐ 1   yes   ☐ 2

For All: Hours and Places

A.24 *On average how many hours a week do you work* _____

For Clinicians Only (A.25-A.29)

A.25 *What proportion of your time do you now spend on management* **(give approximate hours of total per week)** _____

A.26 *Would you like to spend more, less or about the same amount of time on management*

more   ☐ 1   less   ☐ 2   same   ☐ 3

A.27 *Are you fulltime in the NHS*

fulltime   ☐ 1
max part time   ☐ 2
part time   ☐ 3

A.28 *Is all your NHS work in this hospital*

no   ☐ 1   yes   ☐ 2

If Yes, Go to B.1

A.29 *Where else do you practice*

B. Job Definition and Present Managerial Responsibilities

For Those with Health Professional Background

B.1 *When did you first formally take on managerial responsibility?*

B.2 *Why did you take on this managerial responsibility*

For All

B.3 *Could you describe the responsibilities of your managerial position.*

B.4 *By what criteria do you set priorities in your job?*

B.5 *What support do you receive to do your job*

–internally from specialist professional support, business managers, colleagues, the Board etc.

–externally - from region, ME etc.

B.6 *What do you identify as the **main barriers,** if any, that prevent you from doing your job in the way that you would like to do it.*

Interviewer Introduces Self Completion Sheet

B.7 *Please pick from this list the managerial duties and activities that your job involves and indicate their **degree of importance**.*

If your job does not include one of the activities, tick the N/A (not applicable) box.

Degree of Importance

N/A	very little	some	moderate	highly	extremely
[0]	[1]	[2]	[3]	[4]	[5]

List of Activities

- ☐ strategic planning
- ☐ business planning
- ☐ evaluation of overall organisational performance
- ☐ negotiation of service contracts
- ☐ developing new services
- ☐ health needs assessment
- ☐ evaluating service delivery
- ☐ evaluating contract performance
- ☐ managing service delivery
- ☐ managing contract performance
- ☐ marketing your services
- ☐ allocating financial resources
- ☐ controlling financial resources (meeting budgets)

- [ ] recruitment and selection
- [ ] promotion
- [ ] succession planning
- [ ] allocating performance related pay
- [ ] individual performance review and appraisal
- [ ] training and development
- [ ] grievance, discipline and dismissal
- [ ] job design
- [ ] organisation of your team
- [ ] motivation of your team
- [ ] External liaison and networking
- [ ] Internal liaison and networking

B.8   *Time*

On this card are descriptions of several aspects of managing.

Interviewer Shows Card

Given this range of managerial activities which are the two areas that take up most of your time as a manager?

B8.1   *Managing Strategy:* This includes involvement in strategic planning, business planning, evaluation of overall business performance, negotiation of service contracts, developing new services, and health needs assessment

B8.2   *Managing Services:* This includes involvement in managing and evaluating the delivery of services and contract performance, monitoring contract performance, and marketing your services.

B8.3   *Managing Financial Resources:* This includes allocating financial resources and controlling financial resources (meeting budgets)

B8.4   *Managing People:* This includes involvement in recruitment and selection, promotion, job design, succession planning, appraisal, training and development, grievance, discipline and dismissal, the organisation of your team and the motivation of your team.

B8.5   *Managing: Liaison and Networks:* This includes involvement in external liaison and networking, and internal liaison and networking.

B8.6   *Other*, please specify

C Performance Management

C.1 *Is anyone formally accountable for evaluating your individual performance*

Chief Exec. □ 1   Chairman / Board □ 2

Other _____ □ 3   No one □ 4

If someone, go to C.5

C.2 **If no one,** *is your preformance evaluated informally*

    no □ 1   yes □ 2

    If yes, go to C.4

C.3 **If no one,** *would you like to be evaluated*

    no □ 1   yes □ 2

    If no, go to D.1

C.4 *By whom*

If Evaluation Takes Place

C.5 *How is this done. What criteria do you think they use* **(Check on frequency and formality)**

C.6 *Would you like to change any aspect of the way your performance is evaluated*

    no □ 1   yes □ 2

C.7 *How would you like to change the way your performance is evaluated* **(check method / people / criteria)**

D Organisation / Unit Management Team Process

D.1 *Who do you see as part of the top management team here*

D.2 *Can you highlight any particular **strengths or weaknesses** in the way the top management team works*

If not in top team

D.4 *Do you see yourself as part of any team (who? what?)*

D5–D10 For Top Team (If Member) or other Team (If Specified)

D.5   *What part do you feel you play in the (specify) team?*

D.6   *Have you ever done a personal evaluation exercise on the part you play in teams*

   no   ☐ 1   yes   ☐ 2

If No, Go to D.6

D.7   *Which one* ___

D.8   *What did it show your preferred role to be* _____

D.9   *Do you detect recurring sources of disagreement and conflict between members of any groups in the (specify) team*

   no   ☐ 1   yes   ☐ 2   don't know ☐ 3

If No, Go To D.11

D.10   *How does this show itself*

D.11   *Do you think that people with a clinical/professional background make a different contribution to the management team than those with a managerial background.*

   no   ☐ 1   yes   ☐ 2   don't know ☐ 3

If no, go to section E

D.12   *In what way do they make different contributions*

E   Information

Show Card

E.1   We are interested in the sort of information you use to do your job. Can you please look at these headings and tell me briefly what information (in any) you get under each, how you get it, and how often (frequency).

Finance
Quality
Activity
Staffing
'Other' information

E.2 *Are there any areas in which you feel you need more / better information*

no ☐ 1 yes ☐ 2 don't know ☐ 3

If No, go to F.1

E.3 *If yes, which*

F Contact with Others

F.1 *Please give the names of the three people **within** your organisation whom you regard as your **most important** internal contacts (most important to do the job) and why*

F.3 *Please give the names of the three most important **outside** organisations with whom you come into contact in the course of your work.* **(Check why are they important. With what matters do you deal with them).** An outside organisation refers to any offices, departments, divisions, groups or levels OUTSIDE your organisation.

G Critical Incident

G.1 *Describe one incident in which you feel you have been particularly effective in your job, for whatever reason* **(request specificity, clarification and further examples whenever possible).**

H Personal Evaluation

H.1 *In your opinion what are the three most important attributes you personally possess which lead you to being an effective executive*

Please explain why you chose those three

H.2 *What or who has been particularly influential in your development as a manager.*

I Personal Attributes

Interviewer Introduces Self Completion Sheet

I.1 *Please indicate the degree of importance you attach to the possession of the following personal attributes for an effective executive in your position*

Degree of Importance

little	moderate	highly
1	2	3

List of Personal Attributes

- ☐ efficiency
- ☐ ability to get things done
- ☐ self confidence
- ☐ skill in logical thought
- ☐ skill in the use of alliances and networks
- ☐ ability to develop others
- ☐ adaptability
- ☐ ability to work in a team
- ☐ ability to provide leadership
- ☐ willingness to take risks
- ☐ creativity
- ☐ communication skills
- ☐ personal integrity
- ☐ other, please specify

J Career Aspirations

J.1 *Has the recent restructuring the NHS affected the way you think about your career*

no   ☐ 1   yes   ☐ 2   don't know ☐ 3

J.2 *How would you like your career to develop in the future?*

J.3 *Can you do anything to seek to achieve these aspirations What can you do* **(check what needs to be done by others)**

K Learning Needs

Interviewer Introduces Self Completion Sheet

K.1 *Here is a list of skills and knowledge which people in the NHS may require.*

Please indicate those you already possess, those you feel need further developing, those you would like to develop from scratch, and those you regard as not relevant to you now or in the future.

Degree of Possession

possess	possess but like to develop further	like to develop	not relevant to me
[1]	[2]	[3]	[4]

List of Skills and Knowledge

- [ ] strategic planning
- [ ] business planning
- [ ] evaluation of organisational performance
- [ ] negotiation of service contracts
- [ ] evaluating new services for development
- [ ] developing new services
- [ ] health needs assessment
- [ ] evaluating service delivery
- [ ] evaluating contract performance
- [ ] managing service delivery
- [ ] managing contract performance
- [ ] marketing your services
- [ ] project management
- [ ] financial planning / forward budgeting
- [ ] controlling financial resources
- [ ] managing across organisational boundaries
- [ ] individual performance review and appraisal
- [ ] team building
- [ ] time management
- [ ] managing your colleagues
- [ ] personnel management
- [ ] computing and IT
- [ ] interpreting data
- [ ] communication skills

K.2 *What has been your experience of training courses, conferences and seminars with a managerial content or purpose* **(identify courses etc)**

L   Other Details

L.1   *Age - How old are you?* _____

        25-34   ☐ 1
        35-44   ☐ 2
        45-54   ☐ 3
        55-64   ☐ 4
        over 65   ☐ 5

L.2   *Gender*

        male   ☐ 1   female   ☐ 2

Thank you for completing the interview

Appendix 2 Description of Senior Executive Respondents

This appendix gives information on the frequencies of and relationships between, the demographic variables (type of organisation, background, present job, present level, age and gender) which are used to describe the sample of senior executives who participated in this study. The appendix takes the form of a series of tables in which each demographic variable is shown as a cross-tabulation of all the others.

In each Table row and column percentages are shown. The first figure in each cell is the row percentage, the figure beneath it is the column percentage.

Statistically Significant Relationships between Variables

Any table heading which is accompanied by an * indicates that the frequency differences between the cells are statistically significant at $p < 0.05$. Hence we know that there was a statistically significant relationship between the following variables:

Type of organisation (Purchaser/Provider) and background (Table A.1)
Type of organisation (Purchaser/Provider) and present job (Table A.2)
Type of organisation (Purchaser/Provider) and present level (Table A.3)
Background by present job (Table A.6)
Background by present level (Table A.7)
Background by age (Table A.8)
Background by gender (Table A.9)
Present job by present level (Table A.10)
Present job by age (Table A.11)
Present job by gender (Table A.12)
Present level by gender (Table A.13)

These interdependencies indicate that it is more appropriate to call these demographic variables, interdependent rather than independent variables. Account needs to be taken of these interdependencies in interpreting the results.

Table A1 *Purchaser/Provider by background**

	Pur (n=104)	Pro (n=167)	Total n	Col %
General manager	61.4	38.6	70	
	41.3	16.2		25.8
Functional	41.2	58.8	51	
	20.2	18.0		18.8
Doctor	26.2	73.8	84	
	21.2	37.1		31.0
Nurse	24.4	75.6	45	
	10.6	20.4		16.6
Other health provider	33.3	66.7	21	
	6.7	8.4		7.7
Total Row %	**38.4**	**61.6**	271	**100.0**

Table A2 *Purchaser/Provider by present job**

	Pur (n=104)	Pro (n=167)	Total n	Col %
General manager	54.2	45.8	118	
	61.5	32.3		43.5
Functional manager	44.4	55.6	45	
	19.2	15.0		16.6
Clinical manager	18.5	81.5	108	
	19.2	52.7		39.9
Total Row %	**38.4**	**61.6**	271	**100.0**

Table A3 *Purchaser/Provider by present level**

	Pur (n=104)	Pro (n=167)	Total n	Col %
Executive board	47.3	52.7	93	
	42.3	29.3		34.3
Non board direct	42.9	57.1	35	
	14.4	12.0		12.9
Reporting to board	38.1	61.9	118	
	43.3	43.7		43.5
Reporting to level 3		100.0	25	
		15.0		9.2
			271	
Total Row %	38.4	61.6		100.0

Table A4 *Purchaser/Provider by age*

	Pur (n=104)	Pro (n=167)	Total n	Col %
25–34	40.5	59.5	37	
	14.4	13.2		13.7
35–44	44.6	55.4	112	
	48.1	37.1		41.3
45–54	34.1	65.9	91	
	29.8	35.9		33.6
55–64	25.8	74.2	31	
	7.7	13.8		11.4
			271	
Total Row %	38.4	61.6		100.0

Table A5 *Purchaser/Provider by gender*

	Pur (n=104)	Pro (n=167)	Total n	Col %
Male	36.7	63.3	169	
	59.6	64.1		62.4
Female	41.2	58.8	102	
	40.4	35.9		37.6
Total Row %	**38.4**	**61.6**	271	**100.0**

Table A6 *Background by present job**

	GM (n=70)	FM (n=51)	Dr (n=84)	Nr (n=45)	Ohp (n=21)	Total n	Col %
General manager	57.6	6.8	4.2	24.6	6.8	118	
	97.1	15.7	6.0	64.4	38.1		43.5
Functional manager		93.3		4.4	2.2	45	
		82.4		4.4	4.8		16.6
Clinical manager	1.9	.9	73.1	13.0	11.1	108	
	2.9	2.0	94.0	31.1	57.1		39.9
Total Row %	**25.8**	**18.8**	**31.0**	**16.6**	**7.7**	271	**100.0**

Table A7 *Background by present level**

	GM (n=70)	FM (n=51)	Dr (n=84)	Nr (n=45)	Ohp (n=21)	Total n	Col %
Executive board	34.4	28.0	23.7	12.9	1.1	93	
	45.7	51.0	26.2	26.7	4.8		34.3
Non board direct	45.7	34.3	11.4	2.9	5.7	35	
	22.9	23.5	4.8	2.2	9.5		12.9
Reporting to board	16.1	9.3	49.2	14.4	11.0	118	
	27.1	21.6	69.0	37.8	61.9		43.5
Reporting to level 3	12.0	8.0		60.0	20.0	25	
	4.3	3.9		33.3	23.8		9.2
Total Row %	**25.8**	**18.8**	**31.0**	**16.6**	**7.7**	271	**100.0**

Table A8 *Background by age**

	GM (n=70)	FM (n=51)	Dr (n=84)	Nr (n=45)	Ohp (n=21)	Total n	Col %
25–34	45.9	32.4	5.4	8.1	8.1	37	
	24.3	23.5	2.4	6.7	14.3		13.7
35–44	25.9	23.2	27.7	16.1	7.1	112	
	41.4	51.0	36.9	40.0	38.1		41.3
45–54	22.0	14.3	38.5	18.7	6.6	91	
	28.6	25.5	41.7	37.8	28.6		33.6
55–64	12.9		51.6	22.6	12.9	31	
	5.7		19.0	15.6	19.0		11.4
Total Row %	**25.8**	**18.8**	**31.0**	**16.6**	**7.7**	271	**100.0**

Table A9 *Background by gender**

	GM (n=70)	FM (n=51)	Dr (n=84)	Nr (n=45)	Ohp (n=21)	Total n	Col %
Male	26.6	23.1	39.1	7.1	4.1	169	
	64.3	76.5	78.6	26.7	33.3		62.4
Female	24.5	11.8	17.6	32.4	13.7	102	
	35.7	23.5	21.4	73.3	66.7		37.6
						271	
Total Row %	**25.8**	**18.8**	**31.0**	**16.6**	**7.7**		**100.0**

Table A10 *Present Job by present level**

	General manager (n=118)	Functional manager (n=45)	Clinical manager (n=108)	Total n	Col %
Executive board	54.8	24.7	20.4	93	
	43.2	51.1	17.6		34.3
Non board direct	62.9	28.6	8.6	35	
	18.6	22.2	2.8		12.9
Reporting to board	33.1	10.2	56.8	118	
	33.1	26.7	62.0		43.5
Reporting to level 3	24.0		76.0	25	
	5.1		17.6		9.2
				271	
Total Row %	**43.5**	**16.6**	**39.9**		**100.0**

Table A11 *Present Job by age**

	General manager (n=118)	Functional manager (n=45)	Clinical manager (n=108)	Total	
				n	Col %
25–34	51.4	29.7	10.9	37	
	16.1	24.4	6.5		13.7
35–44	45.5	20.5	33.9	112	
	43.2	51.1	35.2		41.3
45–54	42.9	12.1	45.1	91	
	33.1	24.4	38.0		33.6
55–64	29.0		71.0	31	
	7.6		20.4		11.4
				271	
Total Row %	**43.5**	**16.6**	**39.9**		**100.0**

Table A12 *Present Job by gender**

	General manager (n=118)	Functional manager (n=45)	Clinical manager (n=108)	Total	
				n	Col %
Male	36.1	20.7	43.2	169	
	51.7	77.8	67.6		62.4
Female	55.9	9.8	34.3	102	
	48.3	22.2	32.4		37.6
				271	
Total Row %	**43.5**	**16.6**	**39.9**		**100.0**

Table A13 *Present level by age*

	Executive board (n=93)	Non board director (n=35)	Reporting to board (n=118)	Reporting to 3 (n=25)	Total	
					n	Col %
	27.0	29.7	29.7	13.5	37	
25–34	10.8	31.4	9.3	20.0		13.7
	36.6	11.6	42.9	8.9	112	
35–44	44.1	37.1	40.7	40.0		41.3
	37.4	9.9	45.1	7.7	91	
45–54	36.6	25.7	34.7	28.0		33.6
	25.8	6.5	58.1	9.7	31	
55–64	8.6	5.7	15.3	12.0		11.4
					271	
Total	34.3	12.9	43.5	9.2		100.0

Table A14 *Present level by gender**

	Executive board (n=93)	Non board director (n=35)	Reporting to board (n=118)	Reporting to 3 (n=25)	Total	
					n	Col %
	40.8	12.4	43.8	3.0	169	
Male	74.2	60.0	62.7	20.0		62.4
	23.5	13.7	43.1	19.6	102	
Female	25.8	40.0	37.3	80.0		37.6
					271	
Total Row %	34.3	12.9	43.5	9.2		100.0

Table A15 *Age by gender*

	25–34 (n=37)	35–44 (n=112)	45–54 (n=91)	55–64 (n=31)	Total n	Col %
Male	11.2 51.4	42.0 63.4	36.7 68.1	10.1 54.8	169	62.4
Female	17.6 48.6	40.2 36.6	28.4 31.9	13.7 45.2	102	37.6
Total Row %	13.7	41.3	33.6	11.4	271	100.0